Naomi Arnold is an award-winning journalist and natural history writer. She has contributed to most national publications including *RNZ*, *North & South*, and *New Zealand Geographic*, as well as international outlets including *The Washington Post* and *The Guardian*. Her acclaimed story of New Zealand astronomy, *Southern Nights*, was published by HarperCollins in 2019. She lives in Nelson.

Visit her online at naomiarnold.net

NORTH BOUND

NAOMI ARNOLD

HarperCollins*Publishers*

AUTHOR'S NOTE: This is a work of non-fiction. Some names, places, and personal details have been changed to preserve individuals' privacy.

HarperCollins*Publishers*
Australia • Brazil • Canada • France • Germany • Holland • India
Italy • Japan • Mexico • New Zealand • Poland • Spain • Sweden
Switzerland • United Kingdom • United States of America

First published in 2025
by HarperCollins*Publishers* (New Zealand) Limited
Unit D1, 63 Apollo Drive, Rosedale, Auckland 0632, New Zealand
harpercollins.co.nz

HarperCollins Publishers
Macken House
39/40 Mayor Street Upper
Dublin 1, D01 C9W8, Ireland

A catalogue record for this book is available from the National Library of New Zealand

ISBN 978 1 7755 4244 5 (paperback)
ISBN 978 1 7754 9275 7 (ebook)
ISBN 978 1 4607 3006 5 (audiobook)

Cover design by Louisa Maggio, HarperCollins Design Studio
Cover illustration by Sophie Watson
Author photograph by Lottie Hedley
Printed and bound in Australia by McPherson's Printing Group

MIX
Paper from
responsible sources
FSC® C001695
www.fsc.org

For Douglas, who walked with me

Cape Reinga
Te Rerenga Wairua
Ninety Mile Beach
Russell
Raetea Forest
Whangārei Heads
Pākiri
Auckland
Te Kūiti
Whanganui River
Meretoto
Ship Cove
Tararua Ranges
Nelson
Wellington
St Arnaud
Otira
Ōhau
Takapō
Queenstown
Telford Burn
Merrivale
Longwood Range
Riverton
Bluff

CONTENTS

Chapter 1   Bluff to Riverton   1

Chapter 2   Riverton to Merrivale   27

Chapter 3   Merrivale to Telford Burn   54

Chapter 4   Telford Burn to Ōhau   72

Chapter 5   Ōhau to Otira   95

Chapter 6   Otira to St Arnaud   115

Chapter 7   St Arnaud to Meretoto Ship Cove   133

Chapter 8   Meretoto Ship Cove to Te Kūiti   151

Chapter 9   Auckland to Pākiri   175

Chapter 10   Pākiri to Whangārei Heads   197

Chapter 11   Te Kūiti, again, to Auckland   210

Chapter 12   Whangārei Heads to Russell   225

Chapter 13   Russell to Ninety Mile Beach   245

Chapter 14   Ninety Mile Beach to Cape Reinga
             Te Rerenga Wairua   268

Chapter 15   Nelson   288

Epilogue   298

Acknowledgements   305

CHAPTER 1

BLUFF TO RIVERTON

On the drive from Invercargill to Bluff that summer day, I saw my first Te Araroa walker. She was around 60 and struggling north, laden with a huge blue backpack. She would have already walked 20km from the trail's start at Stirling Point that day and had another 12km to go until she reached Invercargill. In the moment I glimpsed her from the passenger seat she looked desperately sore, walking with a rolling, painful gait. It was like she carried an invisible piano on her back. I flashed past in the car, saw her shambling along the footpath in a private world of pain, and then she was gone.

That'll be me soon, I thought. I looked out the window at the Tiwai Point aluminium smelter smoking on the horizon, at the large pylons marching along the skyline. A sign hoisted into some trees read 'When the truth comes out, you can't just unvax

1

your children'. A grey ute overtook us, sporting a bumper sticker: SEND NUDES. Another ute followed it, a brand-new orange Ford Ranger with the licence plate DMIN8R, roaring towards the bottom of the country. Next to me, in the driver's seat, Doug pointed out the Longwood Range to the west, 85km along the trail – its 764m summit would be my first decent hill.

'Huh,' I said, twisting in my seat to look. 'I'm going that way?'

'Haven't you thought this through?'

'I'm not that good with directions.'

'Jesus, Naomi. You're not filling me with confidence.'

Otherwise we were mostly silent on the drive south, the weight of the entire country looming above us.

We'd flown from Nelson that morning. Doug was staying in Invercargill for a couple of days to see me off, but once we'd arrived in the city I was too excited to wait and wanted to start walking right away. We got the last carpark at Stirling Point. It was the final days of 2023 and the famous yellow-and-white signpost marking the end of the country was crowded with sightseers, but I was the only hiker, and this signpost was my beginning. I smiled at an extended family of about twenty, the adults struggling to get all the kids looking at the camera at the same time as one of the dads fiddled with the tripod and self-timer, calling directions and rushing back and forth to capture himself in the shutter's click.

Doug and I watched the procession at the signpost for a bit and then took our turn at photos before walking along a path to the small, rocky beach. I crouched to run my hand through the water and tossed a few pebbles into the sea, then picked up another handful and pocketed them.

'You're carrying rocks up the country?' Doug said. He held out his hand and took them from me. 'To keep until you get home safe.'

If I do, I thought, but I didn't voice it. Fear had been stabbing my gut for the last few weeks: *I am not coming home. I cannot walk the length of the country alone for six months. I will die out there. I am in my last year of life on Earth.* The thoughts felt real to the point of certainty. They felt like prophecies. I knew he had fears, too. But neither of us bothered to mention them anymore.

'Well, I guess I should go do this,' I said, hoisting my pack. Doug walked me back to the signpost and offered a last warning. 'If the Alpine Fault goes while you're on this walk, stay out of the waterways,' he said. 'Watch out for rivers drying up.'

'What? Why?'

'If a river's dried up, then you'll know there's a slip further up and it's dammed. It could go at any moment.'

Of all the very specific worries I had – abduction; murder; snapping my femur and the bone tearing through my skin; falling and striking my head; falling and striking my head in a river and then drowning, unconscious – this particular set of circumstances seemed a fairly remote possibility, but I nodded. I gripped the cold, white metal pole of the signpost, and then Doug walked me to the start of the steps that wound up onto the Bluff Motupōhue. I stood there, gazing up the steps curving through a green arch of vegetation, then looked back at him. He gave a little wave, his face collapsing in grief and dread.

'Bye,' I squeaked.

'Bye,' he managed.

What am I doing?

I turned around, feeling a bit sick, and started up the steps. I had 3028km to go. From here, I'd walk alone.

* * *

The blackberries were just beginning to ripen. I began with a steady climb through bush to the summit. It was a 265m-tall hummock of ancient volcanic rock older than New Zealand itself, formed before our split from Gondwana. The pathway was quiet, but I could imagine, on another day, southbound Te Araroa walkers running down the steps, laughing, their hearts thudding, tears filling their eyes, eager to grab the signpost and be done with the trail at last. But today there was no one but a solitary runner, a pair of ngirungiru, or tomtits, and a kererū landing heavily on a tree bough before whomping off into the forest as I passed.

At the top of the hill, I looked out at Stewart Island Rakiura, a long, dark hump on the horizon across silvery Foveaux Strait, which was dappled with smaller islands and shot with beams of cool sunlight breaking through the cloud. I took a few steps closer to the cliff and then stopped, startled; there was another hiker curled in a patch of tall summer grass at the base of some bushes, napping against his massive, brand-new blue Osprey pack. I crept away, down the path back to the sea, brushing past knee-high ferns, pushing aside flax heads nodding heavy with seed. The path down the hill was enclosed by a narrow, head-height tunnel of kānuka, the wind having forced every twig into smooth bolsters, as neat as a suburban hedge.

At the base of the hill, overlooking the strait, was a plaque remembering the passengers who had died in those waters in August 1998, when both engines on a Southern Air flight from Rakiura to Invercargill cut out just six minutes after take-off. The plane sank into the icy waters just 2.8km from the Bluff coast. Some of the passengers were still looking for their lifejackets when the plane ditched. Five hypothermic survivors were rescued after spending 75 minutes clinging together in the wintry sea, but the other five, including the pilot, drowned. One of the dead was seven-year-old Russell Chisholm, who died of hypothermia in his father's arms before rescuers arrived. 'He was so brave,' the plaque said.

Pale golden light spilled onto the memorial stone. Someone had placed white hebe flowers on the plaque. I looked out at the grey sea and thought of the passengers – including Russell's brother, sister and 78-year-old grandfather – huddling together in the southern cold, so close to the big, blocky boulders of the mainland. The plane had ditched at 4.43p.m.; sunset would have fallen on that winter evening as they waited for rescue. They never found Russell's body, despite scouring the ocean and the shoreline here at my feet. I plucked another hebe flower and placed it on the stone, and turned north again to Invercargill.

* * *

The rusted corten steel Bluff sign suited the town: practical, big, solid and square. I stopped there to chat to Peter and Barbara, who were taking pictures of each other and their e-bikes. Peter had grown up here; now they'd sold their home up north and were travelling around the country, cycle-touring while living in their motorhome.

'We're some of Jacinda's homeless!' Peter said in a way that suggested this was a regular quip.

'Houses are so expensive now,' Barbara said.

'You don't get much for $1.2 million these days,' Peter agreed. He pointed at the windmills scything on the hills beyond. 'They're a bloody eyesore,' he said. 'They weren't there when I was growing up.' He had dark eyes set deep in a narrow, grey-whiskered face. Work had taken him up north but he'd never felt comfortable there; when he came back to Bluff he knew he was home.

'As soon as you see the lay of the land and smell the air, you feel like you belong,' he said.

I wished them well and set off along Te Ara Taurapa, a new walking and cycling path that snakes along State Highway 1 to

Invercargill. I was grateful for it; the cars ripped past like they were tearing paper, and I was soon feeling deaf in one ear. The wind rattled the blue RAPID numbers on the letterboxes, the sun blazed from the blue dome of sky, and to keep myself from going mad from the wind and car noise I counted the pieces of rubbish strewn every few steps: balled-up foil, dozens of empty V and Red Bull cans, McDonald's cups, baling twine, half a hubcap, a shred of wallpaper, a dead magpie, a single electric blanket. I watched my striding feet, I watched the blank sky. The world shrunk to highway, footpath, grasses, weeds, flax, and the railway to my right. Beyond its stretching iron arms, yachts and rusty fishing boats bobbed upon the sea.

Cyclists zipped past me, the wind blowing out their jackets. A figure came into view on the path ahead, slowly growing larger as he strode towards me. As he got nearer, I recognised that his total dishevelment meant he was a thru-hiker, the first Te Araroa southbounder I'd encountered. He had a bushy black beard and carried a polished walking stick, and wore round sunglasses on a battered leather thong. His nut-brown arms were like twigs sticking out of his ragged white T-shirt, and his loose shorts were belted tightly above bandy legs. I stopped him to chat, overexcited.

'Are you nearly finished the trail?'

'Just about,' he said, and gave a quick outline of his circuitous path down the country, beset by bad weather and bursting summer campgrounds. He was American, and clearly wanted to be on his way, not inclined to chat much, but I turned to watch him as he strode on, as dazzled as if I'd just met a celebrity. I'd not yet walked 25km; he'd walked nearly 3000. Would I look as hard-bitten and bedraggled as him, at the end of all this?

A dozen tōrea were huddled on the railway tracks next to me, hunched into the wind. A stoat scampered across the road. Two women led a white goat along the walkway, letting him nip at a clump of bright-pink wild roses. I stopped to chat; the goat's name was Newton. Ahead and to the west I could see the Longwood Range Doug had pointed out, dark blue on the horizon, the same age as Bluff Hill and the Takitimu Mountains, 180km ahead and the first decent mountain obstacle on the trail.

I passed the huge former freezing works that stretched across the neck of the headland. It had closed in 1991 after nearly a century of operation, with the loss of the jobs of 1500 workers, many of whom were Māori from up north, a sign told me. It looked derelict and still bore the name The Ocean Beach Freezing Company Limited, a fire escape installed right through the word Ocean. A bit further along was a handsome red-brick church, with cabbage trees splintering up through the garden and tall wooden crosses arrayed out front. I crossed the highway to have a look, but once I got there I realised it wasn't a church but someone's home; and that someone was chatting to a mate in the driveway, both standing with their arms crossed, legs astride.

'Sorry,' I said, and started to walk away, but one of the men said, 'Nah nah, you're right. You're quite welcome to come in and have a wee look.'

'I'll catch ya later, Ken,' his mate said, and got back in his car.

'You're about the third one today that's come in off the walking track,' Ken said to me. 'This is what it's for, for people.'

He was a wiry fellow in black jeans and a hi-vis vest, with a nest of grey and white hair. A solid, purebred white Staffy wiggled at my feet, her face split with a huge smile.

'What's your name?' I asked her.

'Have a guess,' Ken laughed.

'Uhhhh … Snow!' I said, and he laughed again, delighted.

'Yep, Snow White,' he said. 'Everybody loves her. She loves everybody, that's the trouble.'

Snow White jumped up on me and Ken shut her in his car, where she wagged and grinned from the passenger seat.

Ken had been a truck driver for 25 years and had farmed sheep in Southland, but he was a semi-retired gardener now, busy planting natives on his property and along the road reserve.

'It's what I do at nighttime when I get finished with work. People think it's a hard job but I find it quite relaxing.'

'It's really cool, Ken,' I said, when I'd toured his garden and returned to the driveway. 'You've done so much.'

'Imagine – when I bought it, this was all gorse right through here,' he said. 'I just put gardens everywhere. People say "How far are you gonna go?" And I say "I might keep going until Bluff."'

* * *

9

Like many of the world's other long trails, Te Araroa is designed to channel thru-hikers through wilderness areas to urban or village resupply locations, depositing them each night at backcountry huts, tenting or accommodation spots. The official trail notes offer recommended daily mileage, mostly between 15 and 40km, but everyone walks it differently.

The first section, from Invercargill to Colac Bay, is some 80km, mostly on concrete and hard-packed sand. The trail notes suggested it would take three days, but I'd decided to break up the first 300km of the trail over a few weeks because of work, but also to give my body a chance to adjust to the new demands I was placing on it, and make sure my feet and gear were sorted before I entered more remote areas.

Most people walk Te Araroa (TA) southbound, starting in Te Rerenga Wairua, Cape Reinga, in mid-September to early December, but as I was starting in late December, I'd chosen to go north. The usual spring start date for southbounders is sensible; it gets them through lambing closures and prepares their bodies with long days on the flat, slowly building elevation and complexity, ready for the demands of the remote South Island high country and alpine passes, which they'd reach in midsummer.

But a January start required a different approach. I had a bit of long-term work to do in the first few months of 2024, which would mean taking a few days or weeks off-trail here and there. I didn't want to begin walking at Cape Reinga at this time of year and then spend five to six months on the trail rushing south, worrying about snow and ice on the southern alpine passes in winter. Going north meant I could take more time and be out of the last alpine areas at the top of the South Island – the Waiau Pass and Travers Saddle, and the Richmond Ranges behind Nelson – in autumn, and through the North Island's Tararua Ranges and the alpine Tongariro Crossing by early winter.

Northbounders also tackle the South Island high country soon after beginning their thru-hike, rather than spending months easing into it. I'd tramped for years but I definitely hadn't been spending the last few months regularly walking 15–40km every day with a fully loaded pack across rough terrain in all kinds of weather. In fact, the most time away from my desk I'd managed in the last six months was a couple of overnight tramps, some weightlifting in the shed, and finishing *Wilderness* magazine's annual Walk1200km challenge, which averaged out to a 3.3km walk every day for a year. I'd added a 10kg pack to my daily walks for the past six weeks, aware that I'd be reaching that 1200km milestone in a couple of months on Te Araroa.

This wasn't necessarily the recommended way to prepare for a thru-hike, but I thought the trek was doable if I gave myself a longer build-up, to develop my muscles and tendons to help avoid the most common trail injuries: blisters, tendinitis, stress fractures, sprains, iliotibial band syndrome, and hip and knee pain, often caused by walkers rushing excitedly through the first few weeks in a body new to thru-hiking. Any one of them could end my trail dreams early.

11

Anyway, I was tired of pushing hard. I was mostly interested in enjoying the trail, finishing it, and not destroying myself in the process. All the reading about thru-hiking that I'd been immersing myself in for years was skewed heavily towards American locations, and had a competitive aspect that seemed to be all about ticking off the miles – the fastest hikers with the lightest packs going the hardest over the longest days. Like everyone else who embarks on Te Araroa, I was curious about just how fit I could get and how far I could go, but I also craved a chance to slow down and admire the scenery.

* * *

Outside the backpackers' in Invercargill, I fell into conversation with a Japanese man with enormous calves who had landed in New Zealand a few days before. He was about to ride south to Bluff to catch the ferry to Rakiura.

'I am going to circumnavigate Stewart Island by bike,' he said. 'What maps do you use?' I showed him my topo map app.

'Thank you,' he said. 'Be safe on your walk.' He clacked over to his bike and clipped in, and I couldn't help but smile; it was tiny, a clown bike, a foldable contraption the size of a suitcase. He cycled away, and it was only then that something occurred to me. I'd never been to Rakiura; how much road does it have? I checked Google; the roads on Rakiura total about 30km. It was going to be a short trip.

Another Te Araroa thru-hiker, a woman in her 50s named

Julie, was waiting outside the backpackers' too. She had developed such crippling blisters in her first days on trail that she'd hitchhiked back to Invercargill from Colac Bay so she could bus to Queenstown, where she could stay in relative luxury until her blisters healed.

She'd just spent Christmas at a holiday park, and warned me, with the dark authority of someone a couple of days ahead on the trail, to avoid it.

'Absolute shitshow,' she said. 'It was packed. Awful.'

On New Year's Eve, I walked a few kilometres out of town to the Beach Road Holiday Park at Otatara, and stood in a line of holidaymakers waiting to check in.

'If you're a TA walker, we give you a cabin for the same price as a tent,' the owner said. 'But we're full right now, so take your pick of tent sites.'

It was beginning to rain as I crossed the grounds and found a spot between a couple of trees that I thought might be sheltered in at least two directions. I put up my new tent for only the second time in my life. The wind snatched the fly and peppered me with cold rain, and my walking poles, which doubled as tent poles, kept slipping. I couldn't figure out the guy rope system or where the poles were meant to go, and was soon so exasperated that I was swearing in little, savage bursts.

I crouched in the rain and watched the tent company's instructional YouTube video on my phone, then finally managed to secure the guy ropes and poles. I stood back; the tent stayed up, its bright green sides snapping in the wind. I crawled in and lay down, exhausted, to recover for a few minutes. But when I went to get out, I realised I wasn't used to manoeuvring in such a tiny space on my knees, or hunching over, and it was difficult, uncomfortable and quite hurt, actually. So did sitting cross-legged, and so did unfolding myself and trying to get in and out of the low door in one movement. That was a little shameful; I didn't recall getting in and out of a tent being difficult when I was ten, or even twenty, but supposed I'd limber up in time.

The gusts sucked at the sides of the tent and the rain hardened. I dragged my pack in and tipped it out, inflated my sleeping mat and crawled into my sleeping bag. I heard a few faint *braaarps* on the wind and realised I'd camped next to a speedway. Burt Munro's famous world-record attempt on his Indian motorcycle had happened just down the road at Oreti Beach. I fell asleep. It was 1p.m.

When I woke a couple of hours later, I hitched back to the city to grab a couple of things I'd forgotten. A woman who'd been walking her dog on Oreti Beach picked me up and told me to sit in the back seat. Her dog was in the boot and he was lovely, but he also very much wanted to smear his tongue and drool all over my neck. When we got to Dee Street and I went to open the door, I found it was kiddie-locked. I flicked at the lever helplessly.

'That's because I'm going to murder you,' she said, swinging her upper body around from the front seat to stare at me, stone-faced.

I chittered a laugh, my hand still on the door. She waited a beat.

'Don't panic. I'm just joking,' she said, and got out of the car to open the door and let me go.

* * *

The first time I saw a Te Araroa trail marker, a white metal rectangle featuring a black path winding through silhouetted cabbage trees, was on a clifftop track that wound past mansions near Murrays Bay beach on Auckland's North Shore. It was June 2015 and I was out for a walk. The marker was embedded in a post, its four screws rusted by salt. The trail had officially opened three and a half years earlier.

So this was Te Araroa. I was on the trail. Kilometres of path suddenly unspooled in my head, behind me and in front, and I stood for a minute, poleaxed by the thought that I could simply follow these markers and end up in Bluff. That was the beginning of it seriously haunting me for the next eight years.

I'd first encountered the trail in my friend's parents' spare room in Taupō when I was in my early 20s. It was summer, and Geoff Chapple had recently released his book, *Te Araroa: One Man Walks His Dream*, about connecting a string of the nation's walkways to form a trail that wound the length of New Zealand, supported by inns and volunteers and businesses and walkers from all over the world. Sat on the edge of the bed, I had picked it out of the ladder bookcase and started reading, feeling a thud of determination lodging in my gut, where it stayed.

What would it be like, I thought, *to walk it? All at once? Could I do it?*

I borrowed the book, but must have neglected to return it, because one day nearly two decades later I was moving a dryer downstairs for Mum and found it in a cardboard box of my old things. The box had collapsed at one end, but I opened it and lifted out old clothes, novels and Chapple's book.

I inspected it. It was the 2003 reprint and was in good nick. For years – while I went back to uni; then overseas, living in Australia and South Korea; then in Christchurch and Nelson – it had sat in the dark with this box of university detritus in my mother's basement storage cupboard in Tauranga. It had ended up under her house when she moved to Nelson, and found its way back into my hands. It had been nearly twenty years since I'd borrowed it – not the longest time I've taken to return a book, but pretty close.

When, it asked, *are you going to return me? And when are you going to walk this trail?*

Since this book was first published, after years of dogged work, Chapple had realised his dream. Te Araroa had officially opened on the south coast of Wellington on 3 December 2011. Ever since, I'd been seeing it in the wild as I criss-crossed its path, darting back and forth across the country for work, friends, family.

I saw a bronze trail plaque embedded in the footpath outside the New World on Willis Street in Wellington. I went for a run in its wake on the Queen Charlotte Track. I sat on it at Linkwater in the Marlborough Sounds, eating an ice block outside the petrol station, and followed it for a bit in Arrowtown. When we visited Doug's whānau at Koroniti marae I was aware of it sliding past on the Whanganui River. When I mountain-biked the Timber Trail in Pureora Forest Park I spent 80km in its company as Te Araroa followed the old logging railways, cool and damp under the rimu, tōtara, matai and kahikatea trees that had escaped the saw. My derailleur broke for the last 5km of the ride, so I pushed my bike on the road and followed Te Araroa on the highway before I was rescued by car. I farewelled it as it left me and snaked towards Tongariro National Park.

I followed it to the Travers Saddle in Nelson Lakes National Park on an assignment for *Wilderness* magazine, chasing the last steps of Christian Prehn, a young German tramper who had disappeared there in February 2014. On another trip into the same park, I followed it to Blue Lake, and gazed wistfully as it disappeared into the bush to travel past Lake Constance, Waiau Pass and south, while we turned back for home.

In summer, whenever I spotted the black-and-white cabbage tree logo nailed to a post or stuck on a DOC sign or glued to urban concrete, I would feel a little dizzy with the thought of all the thru-hikers following it right then. They would put one step in front of another for 3000km until they reached the other end of the country. And as the years passed and word of the trail spread, I began to see these walkers all over the place. I picked up TA hitchhikers in Omarama: a pair of scabbed, tanned, dreadlocked Germans, conferring over logistics and replete from a few hours' contentedly feasting in town. I saw a young blonde American in St Arnaud smile grimly and endure our older male tramping companions mansplaining her massive pack, as though she hadn't already carried it 1970km. I saw them browsing the aisles of the most scenic Four Square in New Zealand on the lakeshore of Takapō. I watched curiously as they sat in the laundry at a Queenstown hostel wearing only raincoats and rain pants; every other stitch of clothing they had was revolving in the washing machine.

In hut books, I noted their strange American tradition of taking on trail names, shedding their home identities and finding a new one more to their liking. I read their messages: the lunches taken, the belongings found, notes for each other, bad biro art, the New Zealanders scolding them about hut etiquette. In 2015 my *Nelson Mail* colleagues wrote about the first person to die on the trail, 41-year-old British radiographer Andrew Wyatt, who fell from Lake Constance Bluff in Nelson Lakes National Park.

The trail was haunting me. Things reached a head one weekend in February 2023 when my friend Haidi, her daughter Maisey and I were staying with our friend Nicole on Buckley Road in southern Wellington. At 6.45 one morning, I eased out of bed, crept upstairs and clicked the front door shut, heading out for my usual morning walk. I strode off down the road, but before I'd been gone a minute I was stricken by a short post on a corner bearing the black-and-white cabbage tree logo. I'd walked straight onto Te Araroa again.

I stopped to stare at the logo, once more paralysed by the images unspooling in my head: the trail winding back downhill to the city; past 50 Willis Street, where my great-grandfather Guy Morris once had his jeweller's shop; up the Tararua Ranges and flying along the Whanganui River; past Koroniti and the volcanoes and through the regenerating forests of the Timber Trail; up to the beaches of the north, to the leaping-off place of Te Rerenga Wairua, where an ocean and a sea collided. I thought of the walkers strung out along it, like beads on a necklace, struggling up hills and knee-deep in mud and drinking lime milkshakes outside dairies and taping their heels and batting away mice in some sun-striped southern hut.

I gazed down from Buckley Road to the coast. This must be near the North Island terminus, I thought, and took out my phone to zoom in on the map. Yes, I was on the City to Sea Walkway, and the end of Te Araroa's North Island leg was just a few kilometres downhill.

Compelled, I turned off the road and followed a grassy path down to the sea. I walked past a pony club and dog parks and then for a couple of kilometres along the rocky coasts of Houghton Bay and Island Bay, the sand strewn with seaweed. Past the salt-battered wooden houses squatting beneath the cliffs; past the damp, triple-storey stone castle Airbnb Doug and I had once stayed in a few years earlier, where we'd stargazed from the trapdoor roof and watched a pink sunrise and the ferries ploughing out to Cook Strait.

The streets were quiet this early on a Saturday morning, no one about but runners and dog-walkers. It had started to rain. I crossed the Esplanade and went through a small gate into the Shorland Park playground. I spied a large stone in the southern corner and strode across the grass towards the North Island terminus of Te Araroa, possessed.

The trail ended here with a map encased in steel, and a pyramidal stone inset with a plaque commemorating its opening by the Governor-General, and a blessing:

Kia tupato kia pai to hikoi *Walk the path in safety*
Me te titiro whanui, kia koa *Look deeply and learn*
Ki nga taonga kei mua i a koe *From your surroundings*

It was all very New Zealand. Our national trail's beginning and end points did not need to be on lofty mountaintops, like those of the storied Appalachian Trail. A playground would do. A war memorial, a band rotunda, a grassy mound, and a view south to the sea. I looked out across the Esplanade at Island Bay, towards the South Island and my home. I felt the echoes of everyone who had come before. From here, the northbound walkers, known as NOBOs, would touch this stone and follow the path I'd just traversed, through the city and out to the Kāpiti Coast. The southbound walkers, or SOBOs, would touch the stone and go to the ferry terminal in the city to cross to Picton, before taking a water taxi deep into the Marlborough Sounds to pick up the trail again at Meretoto Ship Cove.

I could not imagine doing it. I had to do it.

I was getting cold, wet and hungry. I had no raincoat. When I got back to Nicole's, I bounded up her steps, heeled off my shoes and opened the door. Everyone was up, sitting at the table having breakfast. I walked into the kitchen and flicked on the jug, leaving damp sockprints on the polished concrete floor.

'How was your walk?' Haidi said.

'Good,' I said. The jug began to simmer. 'I need to walk that fucking trail.'

* * *

New Year's Eve at Otatara was shaping up to be a New Zealand summer holiday classic: lashing wind and icy rain. When I got back to my tent from town, I discovered I'd angled its pegs poorly; the wind had pulled a couple of guy ropes loose and it thrummed the tent fly as I tried to re-secure them. I couldn't believe I'd even considered bringing my summer sleeping bag.

In the evening I went to the TV room to charge my phone and battery packs for the next day's section along Oreti Beach to Riverton. I walked between rows of silent campervans, many with large screens flickering blue-white through Venetian blinds. Most had tinsel and Christmas decorations arranged around them: sparse statuaries of illuminated plastic Santas and candy canes flashing bright red and white in the fading light.

Ocean's Eleven, *Twelve* and *Thirteen* were on TV that night, so I settled in to wait for my electronics to charge. Soon a troop of five children filed in, led by a tween girl vigorously pedalling a trike too small for her.

'Excuse me,' said a boy of about nine. 'I'm not allowed to watch this. Can we watch something else?' He grabbed the remote and started flicking through the channels. Another ran to the toybox, said 'WHERE'S BATMAN?' and started flinging toys behind him.

'I've got some popcorn,' a girl of about six said, standing in front of me and gazing deep into my eyes, holding the bag in both hands like a precious urn. The other girl was pedalling around the lounge, ramming the cracked vinyl couches, but this one sat down next to me and methodically worked her way through the bag, eating a single piece at a time. A third boy vaulted onto the couch opposite and stared at me too, wordless and unblinking, holding the muzzle of a Nerf gun under his chin and clicking the trigger over and over.

Their mums came in shortly after, carrying a brace of Barrel 51 bourbon and colas. 'Are you kids bothering this lady?' one of them asked; they chorused '*Nooo!*' and commenced couch acrobatics.

'They're fine,' I said.

'Jesus, we've been in the tent with them all day,' she said, and they sat down and each cracked open a can.

'Great place for families,' I offered.

'Yep,' she said. 'Oh, mean – *Ocean's Twelve*. It's a Sandra Bullock marathon.'

The other one said to me, 'I was in the line behind you at reception. I heard you're a TA walker. What's that?' I realised she'd heard the owner offering me the walker discount, and explained the trail.

'All by yourself?' she asked.

'So far.'

'Mean.'

* * *

I woke at 6a.m., packed up, and left to walk the 29km to Riverton along Oreti Beach. This was the longest distance I'd walked so far in a day; in fact, I could recall only ever having walked farther once before; a 36km 15-hour alpine epic in Nelson Lakes National Park with Doug, an ordeal which had rendered me so obnoxious and belligerent that Doug had punched a ponga in frustration.

The wind was already swirling sand down the road, and when I got to the beach I saw I'd be in for a serious blasting. I turned my face into the wind and started plodding west along the hard-packed sand. I hadn't weighed my pack but whatever it was, it was far too heavy, and each time I stopped and thoughtlessly put something down – a pole, my hat – it skittered off down the sand and I had to run to stomp on it and catch it. The wind shrieked and drove black flecks into my teeth, nose and pores. It was exhausting.

10.30a.m. Twenty-one kilometres left; a half marathon. *Jesus. How do people do this?* I might make Riverton Holiday Park by 5p.m. at this rate. *Jesus Christ. A whole day of just walking?*

I tried walking backwards, drawing mountain ranges in the sand with my poles. At midday I headed into the dunes and managed to find a spot out of the wind for the first time. I'd walked 12km and felt absolutely wrecked. I looked up at the white coin of the sun, glowing intermittently behind scudding grey clouds. I flopped back on the soft, dry sand and groaned and ate a protein bar. My feet were aching. I got up and struggled on.

A woman approached. She had brown braids and blue eyes rimmed with dark eyelashes, bright under a beige cap. She was Dutch and her name was Else. She was northbound, but was walking backwards today to 'fill in the gap', having hitched to Riverton the day before.

I was already learning how differently people tackled the same trail: you had to go off trail and hitch to town to get food supplies in some places, but some people wanted to hitchhike all the roads that Te Araroa traversed as well. Some walked sections backwards, or 'flip-flopped', if they struck bad weather or were injured but couldn't wait it out. Some people were purists who wanted to walk every inch. Others didn't care and just went for the highlights. Some were walking only the South Island. Some had limited time or visas. No one cared what anyone else did. The international thru-hiker mantra is 'hike your own hike'.

Everyone made their own little rules to keep themselves going. Unfortunately, I am congenitally suited to the purist approach and was already indelibly wedded to the principle of EFI, or Every Fucking Inch. I was entranced by the simplicity of following the line, which I already conceptualised as The Line: sacred, inviolable. No skipping, no rides. And I knew myself. If I cheated even once, the whole thing would fall apart and I'd see no reason not to skip further chunks. I wanted to say I'd done the whole thing, with no caveats, though I'd conceded to Doug that if it came to a health or safety matter I'd reconsider it.

'I already have tendonitis after walking so many kilometres on this hard flat ground,' Else said, and asked how I was going. I said I was extremely unprepared and was taking the first few weeks easy.

'Well, good luck,' she said. 'It's going to be hard for you. You have the wind in your face and your pack is heavy.' With that, she set off in the opposite direction.

They say you pack according to your fears. My big problem today was two large and heavy bags of food. I barely knew how much I ate during the day normally, let alone on a 27km walk, and I deeply feared going the slightest bit hungry. As the afternoon waned I slowed to a shuffle and ate jet-plane lollies and protein bars and sunblocked my face. The wind blew up my hat brim, then blew it off and down the beach. I ran after it.

I dropped my pole and the wind rolled it away, too fast for me to grab. I ran after it. I checked everything on my pack was tucked in, and the laundry I'd attached to my pack with carabiners was still there.

I walked and catalogued my pains so far. Left calf: a hot pinprick lodged deep. Right heel: pain on the outside, kind of the Achilles and underfoot? *Oh God, I've got plantar fasciitis already.* My pack was rubbing my lower back and it ached. *I need to sit down.*

I stopped trying to find a good, sheltered rest stop. I just sat on the sand, my legs stretched out, back to the wind, sand grains filling the greasy sunblocked creases on the back of my neck. I held onto my hat and lodged my poles under my calves to stop the wind from snatching them away.

CHAPTER 2

RIVERTON TO MERRIVALE

The next morning my eyes were so puffy that my phone's facial recognition didn't recognise me and it took several attempts to unlock it. The corners of my eyes were piled with black beach grit and I had a red rash under them. The tent's greenish light made me look even sicker. My right hip ached. A headache was already pounding, so I swallowed two ibuprofen and stayed in my tent.

The TA tent sites at Riverton Holiday Park are on a grassed flat next to a small play tower and slide. I lay like a sack of feed on my sleeping mat, overheating, listening to the campground kids jumping and hooting on the slide, then whispering and giggling as they ran past my tent, daring each other to run up and touch it. I hauled myself out and sat on the grass sorting gear, squinting in the bright sun. Eventually the kids' dad strode over to tell them off for abusing the slide, so they came over to me instead.

'Can we get in your tent?' Their dad looked aghast.

'Sure,' I croaked, and they flung themselves inside and began bouncing on my sleeping mat. The dad dragged them out and hissed at them and marched them away, and I levered myself off the ground to fetch water and stand under the shower for as long as I could keep myself upright.

I spent the day trying to get rid of my headache, which eased in the early evening after doses of ibuprofen and paracetamol, three litres of water, ice and enforced darkness. I still felt electrocuted, but slept well. The next morning, as I slowly came to, I became aware of a string of tiny digital *bocks* ringing out, the sound an iPhone makes when you dictate text. A German man was nearby, reciting a message into his phone, sighing in frustration, then starting again. Then I heard my phone vibrate. I read the message and recognised the dictation; the man had sent his text to the Te Araroa NOBO WhatsApp group. Another hiker.

I poked my head out of my tent, curious. He must have arrived at night and pitched in the dark, next to me and the pair of Australian cyclists who'd arrived yesterday afternoon. He had the unmistakable tiny, lightweight, almost transparent tent of a TA walker, and was sitting in the entrance playing a slow, sad piece on his harmonica. I greeted him and the Australian woman, and she and I shared our itineraries and the local food options, exchanging brief exclamations of horror at the cost of fish'n'chips these days. The German man kept playing.

'What is that tune?' I asked. He had wild grey-black hair and a nose the colour and shape of a root vegetable.

'Some part of Johann Sebastian Bach.'

'It sounds almost Irish, doesn't it?' said the Australian appreciatively.

'I play a little bit every morning to get started,' he said. 'It lets the soul get wings.'

* * *

I decided to take another rest day. I was still too stuffed, and I needed to post some gear home; my pack was ridiculously heavy. Later that afternoon, the German man abruptly unzipped my tent fly and stuck his head in. I was wearing only my bra, and hastily grabbed my T-shirt.

'Hello?' he said.

'Uh, hi?'

'I'm going to the supermarket. Are you going?'

As we walked to the township, along the harbour edge, I asked what made him want to walk the trail.

'It's pouring rain in Germany,' he said. 'I think, where can I go where it's not winter? All the rivers get flooded. My wife gave me three months off. New Zealand has friendly people. Nice landscape. It was feeling like summer in Auckland, but this is not feeling like summer yet.'

He had a nervous, declamatory sort of way of speaking, and entirely reminded me of Sam Hunt. We stopped to chat to two more northbounders who were returning from the supermarket, but he seemed anxious. After we farewelled them, he extricated a small bag from his pack and said: 'I need a second in the woods – I'll see you in the supermarket, ya?'

He dashed across Bay Road into a small copse of flax, and I couldn't think what he was up to until I realised what he'd been clutching in his hand was a plastic bag of toilet paper. We'd been gone from the holiday park about five minutes. I kept walking, down to the combined supermarket and post office. I supposed Kiwi food didn't yet agree with him.

In the evening, I walked to Riverton Beach, where I sat in the blustery wind, eating a Cornetto and looking back at the massive curve of coastline, and where I'd travelled so far. I could see Bluff Hill across the bay, faint and blue now. A man on a stand-up paddleboard was teaching three kids on surfboards how to ride the rolling, perfect little waves. I had walked just 60km and the beach walk had completely wrecked me. At least I didn't have blisters yet.

Again, the weight of the entire country loomed above. I felt a stab of disbelief at the mammoth task I'd set myself, and the dawning realisation of how much I was going to suffer each day to get the kilometres done. I hadn't even hit any proper hills.

Bluff Hill on the horizon would soon shrink until it was invisible. And so would every other peak I'd traverse. I'd struggle up each one until it receded behind me, and keep going north. *You'll just have to do it*, I thought. *People get fitter. Why wouldn't you get fitter?*

The next morning, I packed up my tent in a campground of still-sleeping souls, but as I left the holiday park my fellow campers had begun to emerge. Men batted rain off their awnings and turned on gas bottles and did things to caravan hitches. Women schlepped to the ablutions block in their dressing gowns, trailing small children.

It was only 15km to Colac Bay, so I spent the morning working at a café in town, but that meant I missed a fine-weather window. It was beginning to rain heavily when I started on the trail around lunchtime. In a public toilet at Mores Scenic Reserve, a lovely patch of restored native bush, I put on my wet-weather gear and made sure my internal pack liner was secured, then set off for Colac Bay through paddocks of long, whipping grass, heavy with water and seedheads. Southland was having its windiest summer in 70 years and the gusts blew ice-cold needles into my face. The rain began to slam down and I got so cold I actually started to feel a bit concerned, but when I descended onto a string of small, rocky coves in Colac Bay I was too entranced to worry.

The beaches were a mosaic of stones and shells, scraps of broken-up pink and white sea creatures I had never seen before. There were giant kina skeletons, huge slabs of kelp slumped on the shore like elephant trunks, scatterings of mauve and fuchsia seaweed. The waves were crashing eggshell blue, dragging the pebbles back to themselves, sorting them according to size. A bird crouched in front of me as I walked across the shells, then dropped its wing, feigning injury and leading me, the threat, away from its nest. Three black oystercatchers, their eyes ringed in deep red, shrieked at me and waddled away like little hunched professors in black robes, then wheeled up, landed in front of me and flew off again, landing a little way away and screeching again.

The world in the rain was reduced to gold-bronze sand and the stones, jewels in the wet; the delicate, twirly shells; the heavy grey skies, the deep blue sea, the green dune grasses, the pale eggshell sky tinged with yellow, the afternoon drawing to a close. I thought I had never seen anything so wild and beautiful.

On the shore at Colac Bay surfers were towelling off. One said: 'Where the hell did you come from?' as I trudged along the heavy, stony beach, my feet sliding down with every step. I walked along a beachfront road of broken, glistening black tarmac the council had obviously given up on fixing, covered in sea-thrown rocks. The gulls hung motionless in the breeze.

Colac Bay had its back to the wind, the trees bent over, the bus shelters built facing away from the prevailing gusts. I was headed to a friend's brother's home to stay the night, and when I left the beach to find his house, I took a long look at the sea. It would be the last time I would see it until Havelock at the top of the South Island, 1250km away.

I was soaked through and freezing by now, so I turned my back on the ocean and went off to find Colin's. When I got there,

I saw he had dozens of scrunched-up teabags arrayed outside his door, set to dry in the sun like wrinkled walnuts. I puzzled over these as I heaved my pack down, levered off my sopping shoes and peeled my socks away. I was wet to the skin; even waterproof jackets never seemed to keep the rain out for long.

'Gidday,' Colin said as he opened the door. 'Bit damp out there, is it?'

He fed me steak and vegetables, explained the vagaries of the hot water in his shower, hung up my wet merinos and socks by the fire, and showed me to my room. He was recovering from cancer, and over a slow half-hour told me about what he'd suffered, while he gripped the sink with both hands and leaned on it, staring out the window at his paddocks and his sheep and the ruffling pink sky.

'I'll run you up the road to the start of the Longwoods in the morning,' he said while I washed the dishes, but I had to say no.

'I have to walk it,' I said.

'Why? It's just five k of road.'

'I don't know,' I said. 'It's The Line. I have to walk the whole thing.'

'All right. Suit yourself.'

I hung the dishcloth over the tap and looked at all the teabags squeezed out in the other sink, presumably about to join their kin outside when the sun came back. I couldn't think what he was using them for, and finally had to ask.

'Firestarters.'

Genius.

* * *

My socks and shoes had dried out next to the fire overnight. I thanked Colin for the food, shower and bed, and hoisted my pack again. I walked up the road a few hundred metres and passed the Colac Bay Tavern and Holiday Park. Despite Julie's dire warning a few days before, it looked pleasant, and nearly empty. The rain was coming again and I made a snap decision to stay two nights there and get some work done before disappearing into the Longwood Range. I turned back down the road and they gave me a five-bed cabin for $25 a night.

A caravan was parked near the kitchen, and when I was hanging out my wet clothes I noticed a little sign on it: *Kiwi Pie Radio. Radio for Nomads.* As I spent the rest of the day on the couches in the central lounge area, typing and editing on my iPad, I learned the caravan belonged to a man who emerged several times a day to sit and smoke outside one of the units with a cup of tea, his elbows on his knees and his head occasionally hanging low. He had his own chair and a pāua shell ashtray filled with cigarette butts. A campground mate joined him sometimes, and the pair of them yarned and watched the Te Araroa walkers stumble in and out, at first muddy and exhausted, then fresh and revitalised the next day. Most of them were southbounders on their last few days of the trail, and I eavesdropped, awed, by the distances they'd covered. Forty kilometres in a day? Every day?

'You walking the trail?' the man said to me the next afternoon, as I parked myself on the couch again.

'Yes,' I said. 'Northbound. Oh, you're the man with the radio ... the, uh ... the ham radio ... caravan thing,' I said, fumbling for the right term. This was a mistake.

'It's not a ham radio,' he growled, and they were the tones of a veteran broadcaster, deep and precise. I noticed he was wearing a beautiful, classic watch and a square, gold, diamond-studded ring on his finger. 'It's a broadcasting caravan.'

He was Lindsay Abbott, the television and radio personality and an Invercargill City Councillor for nearly 20 years; when he was first elected in 1974 at the age of 22, he was the youngest elected councillor in the history of New Zealand. Now he'd retired from council, sold his Invercargill home and lived on the road, running his radio station, where he offered motorhome and caravanning information and interviewed guests in between taking music requests and playing country music from a huge base of songs built up over 40 years.

'Familiar country. Nice country,' he said. 'Not this new hip-hop country and not that old country. And I play a bit of Irish as well.' He ran the whole thing himself through a small satellite dish.

'Technology, huh?' he said. 'In the old days you used to have to have a tech person and I was just a voice. But now I do everything.' He sat back on his chair, pulled on his cigarette and crossed his bare legs, feet stuck into a pair of Crocs. He was waiting for surgery in Dunedin, he said; he'd recently fallen from the caravan and broken his ribs and punctured his lung, which had delayed his operation, so he was here at the holiday park to recuperate, broadcast, and wait.

'It's a bugger. But you know. That's life.'

* * *

There were more utes than cars in the carpark at the tavern that evening, and as the locals came in for a drink I ate a BLT and drank a beer. I smiled as a woman dropped off a chuckling pink-cheeked man in Stubbies. I admired his joie de vivre as he leaped nimbly down from the ute cab, wearing a brand-new Southland Stags hat and clutching his phone and a pack of cigarettes. As the bar got louder I slipped back to the cabins and met Sean, an Irish hiker who'd walked 46km the day before.

'I'm ruined,' he said. 'Are you headed north?'

'Yup.'

He indicated my hiking pants and said, 'You don't want to wear those in the Longwoods.'

'Why not?'

'They'll be wrecked,' he said. 'Wear shorts. You'll be two days in mud up to your knees and there's no avoiding it. You try to edge around the outside and realise it's just wall-to-wall mud. You just have to go straight through. But it's good craic. When else are you going to be doing that?'

I left the campground around nine the next day, wearing shorts as instructed. I walked along State Highway 99 towards the ranges, which were covered halfway in a band of heavy white cloud. The village was silent. A dog was rummaging through a bin on the corner, pulling out fish'n'chip wrappers and snuffling into them. He looked up as I approached and skulked off across the road to a dilapidated shed.

A Fonterra truck changed lanes to avoid rushing me and, grateful, I waved and he tooted. Cattle gathered at the fence to watch me. Little socks of spiderwebs covered stems of kānuka. I felt good; I could move quickly on the tarmac. In fact, it was lovely. So many hikers complained about all the road-walking on the TA; was it really so bad? I turned into Round Hill Road and admired a massive spreading macrocarpa, then greeted a man working in front of his tidy black cottage.

'I hope you like the mud!' he called with real glee. He had Radio New Zealand going and looked like he'd been in the garden. 'I don't bloody go up there anymore.'

'Probably because you've got too much to do around here, eh?' I said, not without a note of hope.

'No, no, no – it's too bloody muddy,' he said. 'Mud! Up to here!' His hand chopped his abdomen. 'Up to my waist! I'm retired now, anyway. Government pays me.'

He had a smiley face; laugh lines radiated out from his eyes and he still had a lot of very black hair. He was the sort of man you'd call twinkly, and he reminded me of my grandfather, who always had a glint in his brown eyes, always on the edge of a joke. He handed me two large, freshly dug radishes as big as peaches, and I was touched; I thanked him as though they were bars of gold.

'They're about to burst anyway, so you might as well have them.' He'd cut out the bad bits already.

His black Lab came panting up and licked my hand and then licked the radishes. I stowed them in my pack's side pocket.

'Orright, then. You best get on. And where are you from?'

'Nelson,' I said.

'Walking home, are you?'

'The whole thing.'

'Welp. You got two days in mud coming. Enjoy!'

* * *

At the entrance to the Longwood Range track, I sat down on an old water pipe that had once served goldminers and ate some fruit leather. In December I'd made piles of it out of cooked-down apples from our tree, blended with kilos of passionfruit pulp and frozen peaches I'd scored for $20 on a food-rescue app. But I'd put in too much passionfruit and it was tart as hell. I'd be eating it for months.

Three women with running children and a panting golden Lab were just emerging from the bush. *Well, they don't look too muddy*, I thought. In fact, the grandmother was snappily dressed in leopard-print Birkenstocks and black-and-white striped harem pants, and her pink-painted toenails were perfectly clean. I chatted with them a bit, and they asked where I was going.

I had started to hesitate answering this question. 'Cape Reinga' sounded too grand.

'Through the Longwoods,' I said. 'I'm walking Te Araroa.'

This got them talking among themselves as I sat there reluctantly chewing my fruit leather.

'What's Te Araroa?' one of the women muttered to the other.

'It's that trail the length of New Zealand,' she replied.

'Where does it start?'

'Bluff, then goes to Riverton.'

'Bit of a roundabout way.'

'Yeah, she hasn't come very far,' the first one said, then addressed me. 'When did you start?'

'Boxing Day,' I said, adding defensively, 'I'm having a gentle start. I'm working along the way.'

The grandmother said kindly: 'It doesn't matter what speed you do it at,' and asked me how I, going north, would tackle the south-flowing Whanganui River, where she was from. She gave me a few suggestions, then they all climbed into two utes. 'May blisters not bless your house!' she called as they drove off.

I soon learned why their feet were so clean. The Longwoods has a beautiful network of maintained bush trails through the old mining grounds, mostly worked by Chinese miners in the 19th century. I'd looked it up and read some *Southland Times* articles from the 1860s covering the discovery of gold there and the completion of the Gold Fields Track, on which I was now walking. 'This track is reported to be well defined, and such as a foot-traveller carrying the "indispensable swag" may readily pass along,' one said. I smiled when I read this, feeling a connection across the centuries. Later came a water race for alluvial mining, and by 1878 Southland was full of rumours of gold being struck. Miners rushed in.

'It is to be hoped that a good reef has been discovered,' one correspondent wrote that year. 'Goodness knows we want something of the sort to make things a little more lively.' He got his wish, because four years later there were around five hundred Chinese miners living there in a township near Round Hill nicknamed Canton, the largest Chinese settlement in New Zealand at the time. Where I was walking there was once a full town of shopkeepers, hoteliers, opium dens, gambling parlours, boarding houses and gardens. The water races were still here, as were deep pits; a sign warned walkers to stay on the tracks. But everything else was gone or buried. Instead there were tall trees, flitting tītipounamu and korimako calling alarm at my approach, my footfalls crunching quietly on the humus below.

My indispensable swag and I soon left the manicured day-walker tracks and almost immediately I saw the first pool of ankle-deep mud, oiled on its surface from microbes breaking down vegetation. I paused for a second before plunging in, taking a moment to honour the death of my new socks. Your choice of sock could make or break your trip. Mine, which I was pleased had been a success so far, were aqua, calf-length, skin-tight compression toe socks from Injinji, which I'd chosen for blister prevention. They were about to be defiled forever.

I noticed all the boot prints heading north edged around the outside of the mud, while the ones headed south went straight into the middle; the SOBOs had clearly given up trying to stay clean. 'Well, here goes,' I said, and stepped straight into the pool as instructed, giggling with delight as mud filled my shoes.

But I was not ready. I could never have been ready for what was to come that day, and the next, and the next. The delight soon faded to astonishment, then betrayal, then rage, then despair. For the rest of the Longwood Range I could think only of the thick, grey, exhausting, 19th-century New Zealand mud from *The Piano*, so biblical in scale that it was essentially a supporting cast member; so much a part of that film that I thought of it even though I'd been eleven when the movie was released and had never actually seen it.

This patch of the Longwoods was the last remnant of a huge beech forest that had been heavily logged, though protests had stopped the last of it from disappearing in the 1980s. I had admired it as I stepped along the woodland pathways with a jaunty air, shoes as clean as a whistle, sanded fresh by the salt water of Colac Bay. But that was before the mud consumed me, because I was soon fervently wishing they'd cut the whole thing down and paved it instead.

* * *

I would say I waded through the mud, but that would imply forward movement. You wade through liquid, and this mud was more like hardening cement. It immediately filled my gaiters and dragged them down; they pooled around my ankles like stockings on a toddler, so that each time I pulled my shoe out of the mud an extra kilo in weight was added. I should have taken the gaiters off, but the sight of the muck and filth was so demoralising I couldn't face putting my hands into it. I soon got over that, however, because my hands and arms were quickly coated anyway.

There was no way to wash it off. There was no running water. I could only wipe my hands on moss, and despair.

I sank up to my knees, then tried to step over a mossed-green fallen trunk. Long minutes went by as I tried to extricate myself. I couldn't move my front or back leg, and had to try to wrench up each thigh with my hands. I leaned forward slowly and levered up my back foot; it came loose with a pop, and water seeped into the thick hole left behind. My shoe had come off and was now buried. I tried to turn around to find it, but I fell over, the muck coating my leg, shoulder, side and half my pack. I raised my head to the trees and screamed so violently I hurt my throat, and I grabbed at it, worried I'd split the flesh. Now there was mud on my neck, too. I had been going for two hours.

The mud stunk like rot. It stunk like shit. I levered myself out of the mud pool and dug into it for my shoe. For the rest of the day, I stepped into pool after pool of deep, sucking mud, pulling out one leg, then another, and I did that for 8km. In the worst of it, when each foot and knee got stuck and twisted so much that I worried I'd fall sideways and tear ligaments, each step took about 20 seconds. Drops of sweat rolled down my brow and off my nose and into the mud. I crawled over logs and under logs, and for balance grabbed on to the same trees as all the other hikers – I could see where their grasping hands had worn off the moss and bark. I floundered and cried, and hung over my hiking poles in exhaustion. Eventually I travelled through hysteria to mute acceptance. I didn't think it would be as bad as this. How was it so bad? How was this even *allowed*?

I got to the decrepit Turnbull's Hut at 3p.m. I looked down at my legs; I had transformed into a swamp thing. I wrote my name in a DOC hut book for the first time on trail. Many of the comments simply said 'Mud', though Guillame, a northbounder from France, had taken the opportunity to scrawl 'Legalise raw milk!' He must have recently arrived in the country and would have been missing his proper European cheese.

In the late afternoon I came across a decent stream and washed off the worst of the muck, then reached the first DOC hut I'd be staying in on trail, the four-bunk Martin's Hut, just 16km from my starting point that day. It was 6p.m. Martin's was a rickety slab hut built in 1905, and was one of the more characterful huts on Te Araroa. That meant damp, cold, and rats. As I approached, I met two Australian sisters setting up their tent on the sloping ground outside.

'Is there no room in the hut?' I asked.

'We prefer the tent,' one said.

I peeled off my wet socks, shoes and shorts, then went into the gloom and met two women, a slight German SOBO and a Dutch NOBO with beautiful dark eyebrows, chatting in the dark on their bottom bunks. They had placed their shoes neatly under their bunks and hung their gear from the rafters: clothes drying and food bags strung up away from vermin. A plank of wood was missing from the floor; in fact, a third of the hut did not even have a floor, but was simply bare dirt. TA hikers had left behind rubbish crammed into the fire bucket; food packets and a broken pole and empty tuna tins. There was a top bunk left, so I commandeered it; it meant my face would be close to the rafters and their rats, but today, I did not care.

'Be careful,' the German woman said. 'There's not much tank water left. So you shouldn't use it for washing.'

* * *

I had another late start the next morning. I was still struggling with how to organise everything in my pack; I seemed to need to take everything out and look at it, then repack it, every day, while others appeared to obtain items from their packs by osmosis and take a mere 20 minutes from waking to leaving. I had 26km to walk today to a farm called Merrivale, which had a private hut called Merriview. It sounded agreeably Tolkien.

I was surprised to feel energetic, and walked up to the ridge through glistening cities of spiderwebs nestled into ancient, twisted, moss-covered beech trees. The ground was soggy but it was less mucky than yesterday, and as I ascended to the tops, the vegetation thinned to spindly, sharp alpine plants, with tidy white cups of gentians and snowberries. The dark brown tarns were full of wriggling tadpoles. I passed my first 100km mark and reached the Longwood summit of 764m. I congratulated myself. Just 2900km to go.

I sat on a sunny set of rocks and ate plump dried apricots, some more of my fruit leather, cashews damp from dried fruit, carrots, a protein bar, and almond butter on crackers with cheese. Soon a spry woman in a pink top arrived. Her name was Judy, and she was a local tramper and pest-trapper. I noticed she'd been picking up rubbish along the way, and she said she'd already found someone's knickers with a safety pin through them, lost from their pack.

She ate her tidy cut lunch with me. She was section-hiking Te Araroa, and we griped over the TA hikers despoiling our huts with their rubbish.

I told her how much I'd liked the tomtits on Bluff Hill, and she said: 'I do a pest line on Bluff Hill. One of the long ones. It takes me a full day.' When they started five years ago, they had to regularly empty their traps of possums and rats. Now they were getting hardly any. We shared our outrage over feral cats.

'If we can educate humans to put dogs on leashes – I met someone just the other day whose dogs were running everywhere – then by 2028 we should be able to put kiwi on there,' she said. 'No reason why we can't.'

I farewelled her and set off for Merrivale. But I was soon fading. The ground was treacherous; every footstep came down unevenly on the twisted clumps of tussock. Finally, I stepped badly and rolled my ankle, falling heavily to the ground. My pack slammed on my back like a sack of wet sand, and I groaned. I lay there, thinking how nice it was to lie down. In fact, it was very nice. My face was resting in cool mud. I kicked out my twisted legs and feet and relaxed. The pack felt nice and heavy now, a comforting weight, and I turned my head and moved it a little to a patch of grass, silky under my cheek. I lay there watching grasshoppers hop around me, clicking. Then I remembered spiders that might bite, so I got onto my knees and levered myself up. I looked down; I was caked in wet dirt again.

That afternoon I came off the tops and back into the mud. Underfoot, the beech roots twisted into an uneven lattice with water pooling in each gnarled wooden triangle, an oily sheen glistening on top. I stepped into one and sunk up to my knee. With every footfall I broke small dams, and a torrent of muddy water dashed down behind me. I saw the traces of other hikers ahead of me; alternate routes around the worst sludge pits, deep holes where they'd sunk too, and what looked like knee holes where they'd fallen. Holes from their hiking poles scattered the firmer ground at the edges of the mud pools. I pushed my sweating, red face into a mossy ball covering a dead trunk and rolled it back and forth, groaning with relief at the cool, moist, enveloping pillow.

I came to a small drop, beyond which looked like a long swimming pool of mud, and carefully stepped down. I immediately sunk to the tops of my thighs and felt my last shred of control fray. This was a sensory nightmare, to be honest. What was on the bottom? What was clinging to my legs? I staggered through the slimy soup, dragging each leg forward, went through another pool, then edged downhill through more puddles.

'This. Is. A. *SLOPE*!' I hissed. 'Why. Doesn't. It. *DRAIN*?!' A slug, or a leech, or something, attached itself to my hand and I flicked it off, disgusted. It was driving me insane to move so slowly, and as the afternoon waned my mood began to plummet, then explode. I started to swear viciously, tried to run through the mud, tried to edge around it. I bent a pole I needed for my tent, so stowed them and tried to swing along the edges of the mud, hanging off the trees. When that didn't work I began to race through the forest wildly, throwing myself over soaking, rotting logs, my pack pulling me off-balance. I raked my shins. My body contorted itself against the mud, screaming at the limits of my ligaments, my tendons. I twisted my knee, nearly ripped my shoulder out of its socket. Branches gouged my face. My shoes threatened to pop off my feet, but if I tied the laces any tighter an ache started in my arches. Each puddle could be up to my calf, or my crotch; you couldn't tell. Some pools were cold, and some were warm, which was unnerving. It felt like wading through molten shit.

I knew I was in danger of getting injured, but I was too angry to stop. I was stuck in here, this close, dense, green hell, and there was no way out but through this bullshit for hours, and I'd put myself here. I attacked the forest, tried to bend it to my energy, my will, and raged at it when it wouldn't. A hidden, jagged branch in the mud stabbed into my shin, and I threw my head back and roared, then stood still in the pit of sludge, tears threatening again.

Then a clear little voice dropped into my head.

Stop fighting it.

And it was so loud and calm, so separate from the raging torrent of the rest of my thoughts, that I stopped to listen, panting, sweating, thunderstruck.

Stop fighting it, the voice repeated. *Stop resisting. You're only making this harder.*

Resisting was the story of my life; so much so that my mother had joked about it in her speech at my 21st. 'Baths. Dresses. Hugs. Haircuts. Sleep. Homework. You never walked into anything easily,' she'd said. 'Life was hard for you. The dental clinic aged two. Didn't want to be seen by a doctor. Didn't want to go to Brownies. The first day of kindy. The first day of school. The first day of intermediate. The first day of high school. You hated the sight of certain people. Jenny next door. The witchy-looking woman at the Historic Village when you were fourteen months old. I knew everything was going to be a drama and it always was.'

It was funny at the time; the punchline was that I'd been so eager to escape home as a teen that I'd sailed off to university and not looked back. But poor Mum – that was the 1980s, when kids like me were simply labelled attention-seeking, oversensitive, and dramatic. These days I would have been diagnosed with something when I was young, and probably been helped. But I resisted. And I continued to today. I resisted anything new or that I thought I couldn't do. Or anything I *had* to do, or was *told* to do, and then I got pissed off about it.

Now here I was, the only one making myself do this stuff. There was no one else to take it out on. I was taking it out on the forest, but it was indifferent. I would probably end up hurting myself, making me cut the trip short at 100km. Was being venomous to myself doing any good? I looked about me at the interminable trees and the impossible path, and down at my mud-caked body, my feet entirely hidden in muck. *You are wasting energy*, the voice said. *Calm the fuck down and walk on.*

Was it my mother? Was it God? Did God swear? My God probably did. But it worked.

I was stunned by this visitation; I hadn't had one like that before. But I listened, and I did calm down. I accepted the bullshit, and sunk each foot steadily through the mud. It was slow, but I was moving forward without snapping an ankle or puncturing my femoral artery on a broken branch. When the forest petered out into an old quarry with a burned-out car rusting away in the middle it was 6.20p.m. and I still had 15km through the bush to go.

It had taken me all day, from 9.30a.m. to 4p.m., to walk 11km. How was I going to make Merriview Hut tonight? At this rate I would be getting there at 10p.m., just as the last of the light was fading from the Southland sky. I wasn't going to make it, I realised. I was too tired. I felt as rusted out as that old car. I began to cry.

I washed my face and body and filled my bottles at a waterfall pool on the side of the quarry road, then drank a litre of water and filled the bottle again. The forest had been largely dry, despite the mud, and the three litres I'd carried were long gone. This was the first chance to refill all day.

I ate peanuts and a protein bar as I walked up the road and over Bald Hill, which at 805m had an expansive sweep of views across the paddocks of Southland and out to the coast. To the south, Rakiura and Whenua Hou were rising out of the sea, and there was the wide white curve of Oreti Beach, too, and Bluff Hill, far behind me now. I'd walked that. I was a little stunned. While I was raging over every step in the forest, I had actually been making progress.

It was now 8p.m. and there were still at least a couple hours of usable light remaining. I began to look for somewhere to camp, but panic was swelling in my throat. I'd tramped a reasonable amount over the past decade in Nelson, but I had never failed to reach my destination and been forced to camp. My friends and I went to huts and I'd never camped alone. And – was I, like, allowed? Did I have to ask someone? Would someone find me and be angry that I'd camped?

I wasn't in the bush; I was on top of a bare, windy mountain next to a massive communications mast that was humming like an alien spacecraft. Cars could get up here. I was scared of being attacked, of someone seeing me and bundling me into their boot. I rang Doug, and blurted: 'It's late and I have to camp and I don't know where and I'm scared.' I was crying again.

'I can see you,' he said. I knew he would have been following my GPS tracker, which updated my location every 10 minutes in case I fell and knocked myself out or couldn't activate my personal locator beacon. I'd written several 'missing tramper' stories for magazines. If I did die out here, I wanted to be found.

I waited for him to direct me, trying to slow my breathing and stop crying. I always asked Doug every question I had about nature and tramping: cloud names, plant names, directions, weather, what bird was making that noise and why. He always knew. He had lived in the bush for weeks at a time working for DOC, and was a science teacher and remembered everything he'd ever learned. But now he was uncharacteristically silent. And then he said, sounding a little stilted: 'Can you see somewhere you think would be sheltered?' I realised he was trying to let me figure it out for myself.

Fucking teachers.

I looked around. 'There are some flat gravelly spots here,' I said. 'But the wind is really rushing up. I'll go behind the hill. And into the bush? It'll be more protected from the coastal wind.'

'I'll stay on the phone if you like.'

I squelched through more tussocky bog, following a gentle slope back to the bushline. The views really were spectacular.

I could see the Takitimu Mountains now, a dark blue, rugged mane of mountains rising from patchy green paddocks. I stopped to gaze at them in awe. I had to walk through those.

'I can see the Takitimus!' I said. 'They look steep.'

'They are,' he said, and I could hear a smile in his voice. When I reached the beech trees again I saw a flat, empty patch of rough grass surrounded by forest on three sides. It felt enclosed, safe.

'OK,' I said, as I felt the wind drop. 'I think I've found somewhere to camp. It's sheltered as.'

'I think I can see about where you are on the GPS. That looks good. Nice work.'

* * *

I pitched my tent, fumbling with the guy ropes, fussing and straightening the fly and re-pegging it to get it perfect. I remembered you could camp anywhere on DOC land but couldn't recall the rules about how far you had to be from tracks, and I didn't know what classification of land this was or any local council bylaws. Well, it was too late tonight. I'd have to remember to figure that stuff out ahead of time in the future.

I was at least reasonably clean after my wash at the waterfall. I boiled water and soaked a dehydrated meal of cottage pie, then crawled into my sleeping bag at 9.30p.m. It was very light, and I was still wired, unsettled by the hard day and ending up somewhere I hadn't planned. Pain in my hip assailed me, and my legs twitched in shock. *Magnesium*, I thought miserably. *I need magnesium.*

Although I felt safer enveloped by three arms of bush, I was too scared to sleep. This was the first time I had ever pitched my tent somewhere random and camped alone. I'd expected to do so on trail but hadn't realised it would be such a psychological hurdle. Had a man been tracking me, seen me set up my tent, and was out there waiting to strike?

I lay awake for most of the night, alert to noises outside and rustlings in the bush – the sounds of both the creatures I expected to be out there, and the ones that existed only in my head.

CHAPTER 3

MERRIVALE TO TELFORD BURN

I reached the five-bunk Merriview Hut at 1p.m. the next day, desperately thirsty. My bottles were empty. I'd drunk six litres the day before and my last two that morning, then found a ditch with a tiny, clean trickle running into it. I'd plunged in my bottle and sucked that greedily through my filter, too.

I staggered into the little hut feeling drunk. I unpacked my gear, spreading out my wet tent to dry on the grass, then claimed a lower bed. The farmer had eggs for sale for $1 each and I boiled up two and ate them, then boiled my home-dehydrated pumpkin soup with dried peas and sat at the slab picnic table on the deck. I laid my head down on it while the dehy simmered.

I was done in. My face hurt. It actually hurt. I looked at my skin with my phone camera. It was scratched and bitten, sunburned, mud caked in my pores and even in my ear. The underside of my upper arm, elbow and forearm was speckled with prickles, scratches and red pinpricks, from where I'd fallen into a dead gorse bush that morning. I'd switched from my stiff mud-caked toe socks to regular socks, which had been a mistake; the skin between my toes was now red and raw. I ate my soup and swallowed two paracetamol and a Voltaren 75 and went to bed.

Other hikers arrived: five other NOBOs, including the pair of Australian sisters, all of us in varying states of grim shock about the mud. Near dark, Bruce, a Kiwi, floundered in, sat on the bottom of my bunk, and commenced a 20-minute bitch to the hut in general about the audacity of the trail coming south. He'd gotten lost in pine forest and stuck in mountains of slash, his GPS leading him astray in the fading light. He boiled up noodles and then vaulted onto the top bunk, accidentally using my feet as a step-stool. I gritted my teeth and worked hard to forgive him.

That night I lay awake again, my body aching, my limbs jerking from the electric shocks of muscle spasms. In the morning, one of the Australian sisters read aloud from the trail notes about the track ahead.

'The trail heads into Island Bush ... the track here isn't very clear, as in it's non-existent ... It goes through pine forest, with no clear ground trail and markers ...'

'Too bloody right,' Bruce muttered.

* * *

I had some writing work to do, so I hitched to Tuatapere and stayed there for a couple of days, then hitched back to Invercargill to find a cheaper backpackers' and better wifi. The work took longer than expected, so it was more than a week before I was back at Merriview Hut to tackle the next section, to Birchwood Station, a day's walk away. From there it would take about four or five days to cross the Takitimu Mountains to Te Anau, where I was keen to see some old friends, Vaughn and Joanna.

I found a ride out of Invercargill early one morning with a man named Greg. I have always liked the way a long car-journey sparks conversation. Two people, alone in a car, often without phone reception, are twinned in the front seats, yet respectfully separated. They're occupied by the unravelling journey, but their minds are free to roam. A bond forms. They might talk about things they'd never mention if they were meeting face to face. That was how, with my eyes pinned firmly to the road in front, I learned about the depths and vagaries of Greg's prostate.

'They thought they'd go up the urethra and bore it out, but they ended up not liking the look of it, and took it out entirely,' he said.

'Goodness me,' I said.

'This is a bit delicate, and excuse me,' he continued, haltingly, 'but you know, you ejaculate, but it just doesn't feel the same. You don't get that feeling.'

'That's tough,' I said, and after he was quiet for a minute I glanced over and saw both his extreme embarrassment and extreme need to talk about it, fighting on his scowling face. His wife had died years ago and he had cared for her in the last years. He was dating now, as an older man in an older body. I wondered if he had ever actually talked about this with anyone else. It occurred to me that if a long car-ride could spark deep conversation among friends and family, a hitchhiker was an even safer person to unload on. Hitchhikers were a temporary vessel. You could tell them things you couldn't say to anyone else.

We discussed the rest of his life and health and family as we wound west across rolling green fields. The paddocks were dotted with Reality Check Radio billboards, each with Peter Williams's familiar, kindly, authoritative, conspiratorial face smiling out at the nation.

'So, what do you think about this whole climate-change hysteria?' Greg said as we neared the hut. 'They don't let us dredge the rivers anymore, these greenies. That's what's causing the flooding.' He slid his eyes at me. 'You're not a greenie, are you?'

'I guess I try to follow the science.'

'Hmmmm,' he said, then started in on scientists, Jacinda, the council, Three Waters and DOC.

When we got to Merriview Hut, I saw a herd of ragged TA walkers strung out along the side of the road, trying to catch a ride into town. Greg pulled over with a scrape of gravel and looked directly at me for the first time. I grinned at him and shook his hand and thanked him for the ride.

'Nice meeting you,' he said. 'You be safe now.' I got my pack out of the back and shut the car door. It was 9a.m., and the sun was hot and bright. I waved at the other walkers. They had either just come off a long stretch on the Takitimu Mountains to the north or had faced the heavy, dispiriting mud of the Longwoods to the south. They needed coffee, breakfast, groceries and a shower.

Greg wound down his window. 'Where are you wanting to go?' he called over, but they wanted to hitch east to Otautau, and he was headed in the other direction.

* * *

At Merriview Hut I met Elle, a midwife from Hamilton also walking north. She had set up her tent and was 'taking a zero', a day when no kilometres were walked, and planned only to relax in the sun. We chatted while I paced about the grassy tent site, taking a last couple of work calls and repacking my bag, which was too heavy again. I was still scared about running out of food.

I set off down the road at 10a.m. and was soon joined, then swiftly overtaken, by a Belgian hiker. Walking pace wasn't something I'd considered previously; my earlier tramping was on preordained stretches between huts, and you simply got there when you got there. But now, with the help of my watch, I was getting a handle on my pace, which was 12–14 minutes a kilometre on a flat road, lengthened to 17–25 minutes in the bush and uphill, and had stretched, depressingly, to 30 minutes or more a kilometre in the Longwood Range. Knowing this would help me figure out how long sections were going to take. I was learning how to thru-hike.

From Merrivale it was 30km to Birchwood Station, a sheep station at the base of the Takitimu Mountains, which charged walkers $20 a night for a bunk and a hot shower. But I was soon as hopelessly lost in the Island Bush forestry as Bruce had been, led astray by a thick carpet of bronze pine needles that didn't hold a trail. I wasted an hour bashing through trees and slash. Like Bruce, I discovered following the GPS was useless; you could be two metres off trail but not see it through the forestry debris. I looked at the topo map and saw I was just a couple of contour lines west of the trail, so I tried to return to it by following them.

I clambered down valleys and up hills and through old streams choked with wineberry, blackberry and broken pine. I eventually popped out, covered in scratches, back on the trail, a forestry road that soon emerged into a field of stumps of recently felled radiata. Along with the mud now soaked into my socks, I had blood pouring down my legs in several thin streams, and the backs of my socks were shredded. I closed my eyes and thought of the mattress and hot shower waiting at Birchwood.

I walked down the forestry road, feeling once again shellshocked by the effort required to go a mere few kilometres, and looked at my watch. I still had 24km to walk – on roads downhill, then up through ancient beech to the 513m summit of Woodlaw Forest, down the other side, then across farmland and forestry to Birchwood. There was only one water source today, a small stream halfway up Woodlaw. There was no camping allowed in the forest. There were nine more hours of daylight. These were becoming familiar, dispiriting calculations.

I staggered up to the old shearer's shed at Birchwood at 10p.m. I could see the Belgian hiker in the gloom, the one who'd passed me at 10.30 that morning, brushing his teeth on the verandah. He greeted me cheerfully. I didn't want to know what time he'd arrived.

'Everyone's gone to bed,' he said. 'But I think there's one more mattress left.'

'Hiker midnight' was 8p.m., and I felt guilty about coming in late and disturbing the others. In the foyer, I walked past a towering pile of postal boxes that hikers had sent ahead to themselves, and into the kitchen, where I boiled water for a Real Meals Sri Lankan chicken curry. Finally, it was time for the steaming hot shower I'd been lusting after since approximately 11a.m. I undressed in the bathroom and turned on the shower. But the hot water must have run out, because it was cold.

* * *

I took a zero the next day. I was exhausted from the day before, tired and headachy. Thirty kilometres was the longest I'd gone so far on trail, and I was still trying to be cautious about overuse injuries, both old and new, and to listen to my exhaustion as much as possible.

A few others had the same idea; Birchwood was a bit of a hub, a beautiful, comfortable place to stay. The old shearer's quarters had rustic corrugated iron sides and a wide deck, with comfortable couches and armchairs, shady trees to lounge under, and farm animals to talk to. You could even hitch 16km to the pub and Four Square at Nightcaps.

As the day warmed up, people began to emerge from their bunks and tents. I was unusual in taking so much time off trail while I was getting through my summer freelancing work; everyone else was tackling it in one hit. The strain was showing on a few. I met Rachel, a New Zealander who'd hurt her ankle and was trying to rest it so she could continue. A cheerful Irishman had developed tendinitis and was going to Te Anau to rest. A Czech woman, Zuzana, was staying today for a rest day as well. Others limped around with blisters, strains or burns from their cooking stoves.

Elle arrived in the afternoon from Merriview Hut. She sat on the grass in front of the verandah and stretched out her legs. She showed me the tattoo on her arm, a white line illustration of a woman holding a baby. She was 36, and she and her partner had tried IVF but hadn't been able to conceive, so they had put aside their plans for a baby. She was walking the trail as part of her way of coming to terms with it. I wondered how she coped with being a midwife.

With the bigger group of hikers here, I saw how different our approaches were to the same trail. I had planned my schedule, meals and gear, but often abandoned them to whim, fatigue or serendipity. Elle had both planned more carefully than I had, and actually stuck to it. Her meals included plastic baggies of a green powder she'd made up that contained her essential fats, vitamins and minerals. It was much more sensible than my haphazard approach to nutrition.

In the afternoon there was a small commotion as a group of young, good-looking northbound Americans turned up, including a petite woman and a man with the most incredibly muscled set of thighs I had ever seen.

'That's Marvel. And that's Quadzilla. He's a hiking influencer on YouTube,' Rachel told me, as the group greeted friends and pitched their tents. Enormous, itchy-looking red hives covered Quadzilla's legs, from the paddock grasses they'd just hiked through. I looked at him curiously. His trail name was perfect. He looked like an anatomy lesson: his thigh muscles had muscles. They rippled under his tanned skin as he walked, his tiny shorts displaying them beautifully.

'He walked the Triple Crown in one year,' Rachel added, and I was even more impressed; only a handful of people had completed a Calendar Year Triple Crown, walking the United States' Appalachian Trail, the Continental Divide Trail and the Pacific Crest Trail in 12 straight months: a total distance of 12,674km, or more than four lengths of Te Araroa, with a total vertical gain of about 300,000m. It required precision organisation and timing – and luck – to capture the right weather for each trail. Quadzilla was just the fourteenth person to do it. The first woman to complete it, Heather 'Anish' Anderson, had done so only a few years ago, in 2018. I was witnessing thru-hiker royalty here.

Quadzilla, whose name was actually Jack Jones, made his living from hiking and documenting it on YouTube, to his 90,000 subscribers, and Instagram, where he had 50,000 followers. Now he set up his camera in front of the verandah to give his Argentinian trail friend Gonzalo a pack shakedown.

By now I had learned that most new thru-hikers went through this humbling experience. After suffering for the first few days or weeks on trail with a pack that weighed too much, a more experienced hiker would offer to go through their stuff and tell them what to toss or replace with a lighter version. Although the general recommendation for pack weight is no more than 20 per cent of your body weight, experienced thru-hikers try to get that down to as little as possible, so they can move fast and freely and reduce the risk of injury. 'Lightweight' hikers have base weights – all their gear, including pack, without food, fuel and water – under 9kg, whereas 'ultra-light' hikers get theirs down to less than 4.5kg. Marvel and Quadzilla's gear fitted into backpacks not much bigger than schoolbags.

We all sat on the verandah and watched the shakedown, firing off our own commentary.

'This is the most important thing,' Gonzalo said, removing a speaker from the top of his pack. 'Couldn't live without it.' He pulled out a couple of portable batteries.

'*Two* battery packs?' Marvel, whose name was actually Shannon, asked from the verandah.

'Well, yeah,' Gonzalo said. 'You have to charge the speaker. And one battery pack for the two phones.'

Two phones. This was a lightweight hiker's nightmare, but he argued their case, holding them up and detailing their uses: one with a New Zealand SIM card, Spanish WhatsApp and a headphone jack, but a bad camera; the other with an Australian SIM, Australian WhatsApp, a good camera, but no headphone jack. Quadzilla let him keep them.

Gonzalo held up a small foil packet. 'Condom?'

'OK, yeah,' Quadzilla said, laughing.

'One. Only one,' Gonzalo said.

'Aw, come on,' Marvel called.

'I'm not very hopeful. I'm being realistic.'

Quadzilla diagnosed too many clothes and other sundry items: Gonzalo even had three pairs of underwear.

'You only need one pair,' called one of the Americans.

'I don't have any underwear,' Quadzilla said. Gonzalo was becoming incredulous. He pulled out three pairs of socks.

'Three socks is fine,' Marvel said.

'But not the underwear?'

'No.'

When Quadzilla was finished, he'd removed a heavy load from Gonzalo's pack. He gave it to him to lift.

'That's quite a bit of weight,' Gonzalo admitted. Then it was Quadzilla's turn to demonstrate his own pack and gear, equipment honed over tens of thousands of kilometres, carefully finessed for each new trail. I was aghast. His toiletries barely filled the bottom of a sunglasses sack.

* * *

Another American in his 20s arrived. 'Quite a descent, eh?' I said to him as he walked up to the verandah and joined the rest of his crew; the last hurdle of the trail yesterday had been a drop of 200m in elevation over half a kilometre of slippery, summer-dry grass – a 40 per cent incline. It was fucking steep, in other words. He looked at me and said, 'Young knees,' and walked inside. I rolled my eyes. Of all my various ills at the moment, my knees were not one of them.

I got on better with the tall, 50-year-old American southbounder who turned up later that evening. He'd just walked a tough 50km from Aparima Hut in the middle of the Takitimu Mountains. We gave him and his trail friend a round of applause from the verandah when they arrived and gratefully put down their packs. My spreadsheet had me covering that distance in three days, but they had got up early and blitzed it in one.

This mentality was astonishing to me, and I quizzed him a little on how and why he'd do something like that. You were here

65

to enjoy the outdoors; why rush through it? How did your body handle that? How did you even get to the point of being *able* to do that?

'I don't know,' he said. 'You just get like this towards the end. You've seen enough forest. You're so fit that the challenge becomes something different. You want to see what you can do.'

It had taken me twelve hours to walk 30km yesterday. I was by myself, without much sense of urgency, and certainly mucked around taking long breaks and photos, but I was struggling to get through the distances and days suggested on the official trail app. I could not imagine ever feeling like he did, or wanting to.

* * *

The next day was a 28km traverse of the rolling Mt Linton Station, one of the biggest farms in New Zealand, to a campsite at the base of the Takitimu Mountains. Sunrise was at 6.20a.m. but I left at 7.50, which was early for me so far. Most of the other northbounders were gone when I set off, and I soon lost the trail in the wet, towering grasses, eventually coming to an electric fence with no stile. I had spent twenty minutes trying to find a way around or over it, getting repeatedly shocked, when Marvel and Quadzilla powered up.

'Is there no way around?' Marvel asked, and I told her about my electrocutions.

'I'm just going to jump it,' I said, chucking my pack over and edging up the diagonal stay, the wood slippery with morning dew. I clambered on top of the fencepost and stood, feet jammed together, hesitating.

'You can do it,' Marvel said, in cheerleader mode.

'I am just a little concerned,' I said, 'about my forty-two-year-old knees.' Fuck that guy yesterday for making me feel bad about them.

'You can do it! Yes!' she repeated, and I jumped and it was fine. They went off to try to find an alternate way around but ended up having to jump over too, which they told me as they streaked past twenty minutes later and disappeared over the horizon.

I'd been influenced by this experienced group of hikers from all over the world, the biggest I'd yet come across. The confident and competent Americans had revealed the vast gulf between my lackadaisical, she'll-be-right Kiwi approach and theirs, which was to turn everything into a competition of the best, lightest, and fastest, and was frankly a little intoxicating. I was newly determined to get up earlier and hit the trails before sunrise, to become more efficient, stop mucking around, organise my gear and food properly, lighten up my pack, stop my attention being so fatally split between trail and work, and develop a little more fitness and hustle.

But I was still, unfortunately, myself. That day I did the usual: struggled up the farm hills, took long breaks to perfect a photograph, watched a shepherd expertly herd a huge mob of sheep through a gate, and became concerned about a bleating lamb trapped alone in a fenced-off section of gum trees, pondering the wisdom of trying to grab it and get it through the fence to the paddock, before finally emailing the station owner. The Te Araroa Trust worked hard to build and keep good relationships with private landowners, and one stupid hiker mucking around with stock would ruin it for everyone. The day before, a European hiker had made national news by going off-trail straight into a live forestry operation, endangering access across the entire section.

At lunchtime I sat on a grassy hillside, blazed by the sun, and worked my way through half a block of Whittaker's Hokey Pokey chocolate, half a packet of Cheds crackers and some Tasty cheese while I constructed a hands-free sunshade from my hiking pole, the little silver hiking umbrella I carried and zip-ties. It worked well, and I was pleased, but when I looked at my watch I did notice I'd been sitting there for an hour.

The Takitimu Mountains were growing closer, blue and grey and beige on the horizon. Bad weather arrived that afternoon and I bitched and moaned to myself, getting into a massive funk, as I walked the last three hours in the freezing rain, crossing my fingers that the two rivers I had to cross weren't too high yet. They were fine, though I didn't make the campsite at Telford Burn until 8.30p.m. I walked past the group of Americans camped under a tree in their tiny little tents, as neat as envelopes, and put my pack down under a huge spreading beech tree with Zuzana and the two Kiwis, Elle and an older man called Darren.

But when I went to pitch my tent, the lower section of my hiking pole, which doubled as my tent pole, wouldn't twist home.

It spun uselessly, making the entire thing about half a metre long. I needed it to be able to lengthen and stay up. Shit. It was raining and it was nearly 9p.m. I was cold, exhausted, hadn't eaten, as soaked as though someone had turned a hose on me, and was getting wetter by the second, as was my gear. I really didn't have time for this.

I cast about for what I could use for a tent pole instead, and my eyes fell on the sun umbrella jammed into the side of my pack. I remembered the hiking-pole sunshade I'd made earlier that day. It was a good quality umbrella, sturdy, and it had already withstood some decent beatings from the weather. I still had a bunch of zip-ties. Would that work? I laid it down next to the hiking pole and zip-tied them together, making a reasonable approximation of a tent pole. I pegged down the guy rope. It worked, and I smiled. Good enough. Maybe all my mucking around had some uses.

I hung up my gear on a line strung in my tent and outside under the fly. It wouldn't dry at all, but at least it wasn't crumpled in a soggy pile on the floor. I was too tired to get out my stove and boil water, so I lay in my tent listening to the rain, watching an orange-and-pink sunset through the open fly, eating Cheds, dried apricots, the rest of the bar of chocolate and a protein bar. Thirteen hours. Thirteen hours to go 28km. The trail notes had said eight. I didn't know why I was so slow. Was I actually that unfit? Was my pack too heavy? I hadn't managed to weigh my final gear selection, so I wasn't sure. Was it just that I was by myself and was continually stopping, diverted by fatigue, views, and lunch?

They said the trail would push you in every way possible, but the reality of that was only just dawning on me. I thought I was pretty used to being physically pushed in the outdoors, but this was nothing like regular tramping. Each day seemed like the worst day of a normal tramping trip. It didn't just test your fitness, but also your pain and frustration and hassle thresholds, your ability to change plans on the fly and cope with the unexpected. Gear failed. Rain hit, rivers rose, feet broke down. You got lonely, hungry. You had to keep your things together, clean and mended and functional, solve problems and consider the terrain ahead. Day after day for months. I remembered what I'd heard Marvel say the night before: 'This trail has humbled me.' We'd not even gone 200km, and everyone was finding it tough.

There were not many easy days on trail. It wasn't like a two-night tramping trip with friends and red wine. I was beginning to see how with thru-hiking you needed to get through the day's kilometres quickly so you could give yourself time in the afternoon and evening to recover, wash, dress wounds, dry and mend gear, dry out your feet, sleep properly, eat well and socialise. Or the next day would be tougher and even more disorganised. And if you kept going like that you'd slowly lose gear, health and strength, in a chain of diminishing competence that would end in failure.

I lay there, alternately scolding myself, trying to cut myself some slack and ruefully thinking of exactly how much I mucked around in the mornings. And during the day. And at night, actually. Being too tired to make and eat a proper dinner now, for example, would mean my body was working with less nutrition for the next couple of days. I resolved to try to be a better hiker tomorrow. Again.

* * *

A rainbow appeared in the morning, swelling over the mountains, and we were thrilled and watched it shimmer. The group of young Europeans and Americans strode past us as we packed our stuff, flicking us a silent wave when we called hello. They were aiming for Aparima Hut today, which the rest of us were planning to reach tomorrow. And that was the last I saw of Marvel and Quadzilla.

CHAPTER 4

TELFORD BURN TO ŌHAU

The Mavora Lake sandflies had trapped me in my tent for the evening, but at least I could watch a couple of South Island robins leaping to snatch them from under the tent fly. I'd misread the trail notes and stopped too early, and I was annoyed. It was now a couple of weeks since the rainy night at Telford Burn. I'd struggled through the Takitimu Mountains, and worked in Te Anau, desperate to be back on the trail. Now I lay back on my sleeping mat, bored, and decided on impulse to try for my first long day tomorrow instead of sticking to the recommended days. I'd try to go as fast and as far as I could and get as close to Lake Wakatipu as possible. It was 50km away, and there were four DOC huts between here and the end of the section.

I left the campsite at 7a.m., walked past three of the huts, then in the evening lost the trail for more than an hour, first in a bog and then again in beech windfall that hid the path. I clambered through trunks and branches tangled like pick-up sticks until I just happened to spot an orange triangle on a fallen beech trunk and found the thin path, strewn with twigs and cornflake-like beech leaves. I reached Greenstone Hut 14 hours and 37km later, at around 10p.m.

Here I entered an unfamiliar world of Muggles – trampers from town who went into the hills as I normally did with friends, carrying beers, games and piles of fresh food. I said hello and claimed a bunk and lay down, exhausted but satisfied. I'd really pushed myself. And I'd discovered I liked tramping at night. The world reduced to a patch of white beyond my headlamp. Aside from a few nerves at dusk, I felt safe. It was good not to be cooked by the sun, and my energy surged when darkness fell. I liked seeing the first harbingers of night, Venus or Jupiter, shining in the evening sky as the light faded and the moon took over from day.

I wanted to stay the day at Greenstone, which was basically like a flash city hostel, and talk to people, watch the kea flying around, read the magazines, play a game of 22. But I was a TA walker now and we strode by in a parallel universe. We grabbed at food and sleep like marathon runners snatched water. Summer was waning; I had to keep on.

At 7a.m., I stood at the hut window and ate a protein bar, watching a stag grazing in the blue dawn, then went outside and sat on the hut steps to tie my shoelaces. The sky was clear; it was going to be a beautiful day. I shouldered my pack and walked joyfully on proper walking trails – flat, soft, and well-formed – to the edge of Lake Wakatipu, where the trail paused before picking up again in Queenstown, and I caught a ride into town.

But once I got there, I walked scared, shocked by noise, colour, and humanity. I had spent the past five days alone in the bush, including an extra day in Kiwi Hut waiting out a storm, and the streets were thronged with summer revellers, the shops like a punch. I felt scared by people now, yet craved to be around them. The southbounders were coming through in full force, tanned and fit at the end of their expeditions. I'd encountered dozens of them on-trail now and envied their trail 'families'. My haphazard work schedule had meant I hadn't been able to join forces with anyone. Instead of making my own friends, I sat on sunny hut decks and listened to people chat about their trail mates instead.

'Hugo fell down the Waiau Pass, like ten metres, and he's taking a break from the trail.'

'Did he hurt himself?'

'Yeah, he got totally beaten up. But he's lucky he didn't, like, actually seriously hurt himself.'

'Jeez.'

'Yeah, he went off track in the pass, which I don't think anyone does. It's really dangerous. But then he had a family emergency so he flew back home.'

'Where's Amy?'

'Amy injured her back so she's a couple of weeks behind me.'

'Did you know Rob is just ahead of you?'

'Is he? Ooh, I knew I was close.'

'You'll get him tomorrow.'

'You know what he said, right?'

'No?'

'He said if I catch him, he'll walk the last day in his underwear.'

'Oh my God.'

'That's why I'm on a mission. He's going to suffer.'

* * *

I rarely saw other northbounders now, but outside the coffee cart at Arrowtown Holiday Park I met a group of three, two women and a young man, who were headed over to Macetown that day. I was bussing to Frankton to have lunch and then a work afternoon with my friend and editor Rebekah, but I hoped I'd be able to catch them and make some trail friends at last.

Rebekah bought me a chicken salad and an orange juice, and when I bussed back to Arrowtown that evening I had so much energy I decided to walk the 13km over the mountains to Macetown that night so I could join the trio and leave with them in the morning. It would take about four or five hours, and was an ascent of 938m and a descent of nearly 700m, but I was excited to potentially have company, maybe even for a few days, through the Motatapu Track to Wānaka.

I left Arrowtown around 7p.m. It was a beautiful, still, peachy-blue evening, and I felt my energy soar as I walked the trail. When I got to the tops and night began to fall I felt so good I began to alternate walking with jogging. I trotted along the thin dirt trails, scattering feral goats, then over Big Hill saddle and down through tussocky valleys. Night had fallen and I heard pigs snort and possums scream.

Do boars attack? I swallowed back a stab of fear; nothing was going to hurt me out here. I followed the moon and waded through rivers, water rushing silver in the light of my headlamp.

I got to Macetown near midnight and eagerly cast my headlamp around the campsites, looking for tiny hiker tents and feeling desperate for at least a day of trail conversation, of sharing snacks, laughter, struggle. But after a bit of searching, I realised Macetown was empty. They must have gone on.

I began to cry. In fact, I didn't just cry: I sat down on a log and bawled my eyes out, putting my face in my hands and heaving and sobbing as deeply as a child. I was devastated. And so, so desperate; I had talked to these people for a couple of minutes and yet had planned my entire life around them. I'd just walked for four and a half hours alone through the night on a narrow mountain trail, going up nearly 1km and down just about the same, hoping only to join them.

It was humiliating. They would have gone on that day because they were trying to avoid me. I must have looked wild-eyed and weird when we met at the coffee cart, my urgency for company giving off a palpable whiff. God, I was a loser.

I was getting eaten alive by sandflies. I pitched my tent and got in, still crying, and went to sleep, tears pooling in the inner corners of my eyes. In the morning I felt rinsed and grim, but the trail was delightful; it had become the Arrow River, and I sloshed through its beautiful deep blue pools and grey gravels, wishing there were some people to stop and swim with.

A southbounder approached at midday. 'Hey,' I said. 'Did you happen to meet two northbound girls and a guy recently?' There weren't many of us by now; she would have remembered.

'The Australian and the Dutch girls and the young guy with the drone? Yes, I just passed them.'

'What? Now?'

'Yes, just an hour ago.'

I'd missed them at the campsite the night before. They must have left just before me that morning.

Cloud drifted lower and smothered the ranges. It always made me nervous to climb into cloud, like I was going to instantly die of exposure. I worked my way slowly up the mountain to 1240m elevation and across Roses Saddle, stepping carefully to avoid the tiny skinks skittering ahead of each footfall. I walked down into the stark, dry Motatapu Valley alone.

* * *

77

The skin on my left little toe had filled with fluid and died. In the bathroom at my friend's house in Wānaka, I pulled off a whole, white-skin casing, like I'd dipped it in candle wax. I snipped off the last thread of connected skin and covered the fresh pink toe with Crystaderm, tape and plasters.

It was now 18 February. I'd walked every inch of the 424km to Wānaka, ascending and descending tens of thousands of metres of elevation. But more than half of the last four weeks had been spent working, including spending the past five days in the Wānaka library. I'd stayed with University of Otago friends I'd made twenty years ago to finish it: Joanna and Vaughn, Hannah and Luke, and Elissa and Sarah, with whom I was staying now.

Seeing old friends, combined with the extra rest days, had been good for me. Joanna and Vaughn had given me their son's bedroom in Te Anau. Hannah and Luke had met me at the Glendhu Bay trailhead with ice blocks, drinks and fruit, then walked with me along the lake to Wānaka, which had meant a hard 30km day straight from Highland Creek Hut to the town in one go. I'd barely hung on with them and their dogs at the end, but we made it. Their friendship rejuvenated me.

I was adjusting to the exertion now, as well as trail life itself. I took magnesium at night and my legs no longer jerked as I tried to sleep. In huts, I found I liked to be by the window so I could have the breeze on my face and look at the stars at night, checking how they had moved when I woke in the dark. My hip pain came less often and I was sleeping better on my inflatable mat. I discovered I slept best flat on my back.

I was getting my trail legs under me, becoming more confident and a little more feral. I was starting to challenge myself rather than battle doing the bare minimum and then collapsing shellshocked at night.

* * *

In the last five days in Wānaka I'd rested in the late summer sunshine after work, ambling on the trail around the lake to Hāwea, on one day walking only a single kilometre. I'd gone out for a beer with Elissa's workmates at Snow Sports New Zealand, and even went to the movies. I'd waited for my second pair of shoes to arrive; gorse and blackberry had shredded the uppers of the first, despite my haphazard sewing and the ministrations of a section-walking carpenter from Whangārei who carried shoe glue.

Catching up with old friends had been good for me, but tomorrow I'd leave town, climbing Breast Hill from Hāwea and walking towards Canterbury. I was a little nervous about Breast Hill; a day-walker had fallen and died on it just last month. I'd be walking well into autumn now. The unplanned extra work I'd done meant it was now very late in the season to be walking north, and I was beginning to worry about autumn and winter conditions on trail, particularly snow and ice at the second-highest point of Waiau Pass, near Nelson. My home region was treacherous and had killed many hikers, including two walking Te Araroa. I had to get on.

* * *

Breast Hill looked like it was going to burst into flame. It was mid-afternoon and the sun assaulted me as I worked my way up the steep, dusty, winding track. The track up and over to Pakituhi Hut was about 5km, but it climbed almost 1000m up into the sky over that distance. A southbounder approached and inched past me on the narrow track.

'How is it up there?' I said.

'Hot. Steep. And beautiful.'

I tried to take the advice of an arrogant German hiker I'd met at a hut on the way to Wānaka, when I'd dropped a couple of wry comments about the infernal heat and steepness of the Motatapu section. As usual with some of these guys, instead of smiling and commiserating or offering a joke of his own, he'd decided he needed to instruct me about what I was doing wrong.

'It's all about mindset,' he'd said.

'What mindset?'

'That you love hills.'

'Well, OK,' I said. 'How do you do that? Do you just repeat to yourself "I love hills"?'

'That's pretty much it.'

'I love hills,' I said now through gritted teeth, walking step, pause, step, pause up the track, letting the lactic acid in my legs dissipate every few metres. My pack, which I'd finally weighed for the first time at Elissa and Sarah's, was nearly 16kg today. My base weight was about 11. It was quite a lot for a thru-hiker, though my work iPad accounted for more than a kilo of that.

The problem, as usual, was that I was carrying too much food. I'd dehydrated a lot of my own at home and posted it ahead to myself, but I never ate all of it. So I just kept adding to my stash when I picked up a new package I'd posted ahead. This was stupid, especially because I posted some of it ahead to myself again. But I couldn't bring myself to leave any behind.

I still had fears about running out of food in the wilderness, but I was beginning to get to know my body and energy systems by now. It was becoming clear to me that I was both underestimating how many calories foods such as nuts contained, and overestimating how many calories I needed. Having snacked all day, I hardly ever felt the need to eat in the evening, though I would sometimes wake in the middle of the night hungry, after my recovering body had processed the food I'd eaten that day and wanted more.

I paused on the hot hillside to try to slow my heart-rate. I had to stop my music; it was too intense to listen and cope with the heat. Looking down made me feel sick and shaky. A trip on a shoelace and you'd be over the edge and done. The day-walker who had died, a local named Steve Smith, had fallen 50m.

I sat down on the dusty track in a patch of shade and tried to breathe slowly to calm my heart. I could hear my blood sluicing in my ears and the dizziness was making me feel drunk.

It seemed I had a touch of vertigo. I got out a packet of berry electrolyte powder and added it to my water bottle, but the path was so steep I had to be extra careful so things didn't roll along the dusty track and off the cliff when I put them down.

Summer hung over everything. The lake was a sheet of hot blue steel, opaque, barely shimmering, the breeze painting gentle currents on a surface striped with the thin white wakes of boats and water-skiers. A hawk circled lazily and grasshoppers bounced in front of me. The old wire fence to my right was hand-wound. I could see Mt Aspiring peeking up from behind the ranges, and a tongue of glacier. A young woman climbed up behind me, breathing hard under the weight of her pack.

'It's really fucking hot,' she said. 'Are you going to the hut?'

'Yup,' I said. 'What about you?'

'I'm going to go up a bit further and then fly back to Hāwea.' It was then that I realised her pack wasn't a pack.

'Is that a parachute?'

'Yeah, I've got my wing,' she said. 'It's my first solo flight. I was hoping for a bit more lift from the valley floor – I just saw a guy hanging out up there for ages.' She held her hand high, hovering in the air, then dropped it. 'Hopefully I don't just go plop – straight down.'

I was deeply impressed with this. She was about to jump off the side of a mountain by herself for the first time? When she said goodbye I tried to quicken my pace so I could catch her take-off. Near the summit, I rounded a corner and saw her standing on the steep, grassy hillside in front of me, her giant pink-and-blue canopy flat behind her as she arranged lines. I saw her look forwards, down the cliffs to the lake. I stood on a rock to watch her. The cicadas were deafening, and the wind rustled softly in my ears. When the silk inflated and rose overhead, she faced forward, took a few running steps, and as her feet left the ground I gasped in shock. 'Oh my God!'

She leaned back and slotted her feet into the harness. I stood transfixed and heard her scream in joy as she adjusted lines and soared out and up, adrift on hot summer air, sailing over the blue mountains, the blue lake, the blue sky shot through with beams of light.

* * *

Pakituhi Hut was in shadow when I reached it, a neat and clean eight-bunker with five people already inside. One of them was Anna, a Kiwi northbounder in her early 20s. I was stunned; I hadn't met another northbounder for ages. She pounced on me.

'Are you NOBO?' she said.

She was worried about walking alone; so far she'd walked with people every day apart from two. I had to smile; I'd walked by myself every day apart from two. We decided to walk together the next day. She was beautiful, with dark hair and huge eyes and a coltish look about her long limbs.

I ate my heaviest dinner, a lentil bolognese, and was cleaning the pot at the sink outside when a huge golden coin of a full moon popped over the mountains in the distance. It was so beautiful I gasped, and poked my head into the hut to tell everyone what was happening. We all went out and stood on the deck watching it rise, incredibly fast, until it reached a point in the sky where it looked normal again and no longer astonished us, and then we all filed back inside and went to sleep.

* * *

'I've had a couple of trail romances,' Anna confessed as we walked over the steep, dusty mountains and down to the Timaru River, which doubled as the trail for a while. As we waded through ice-blue water and clambered through small gorges, she explained she'd fallen for a man named Daniel but he was very fast and she'd struggled to keep up. They'd spent a nice few days in Wānaka together, and he'd passed a note down the trail to her, hand to hand.

She liked him but didn't know if he liked her. She was also concerned about walking the trail chasing boys instead of tackling it herself; she was worried that she latched on to guys and followed them, and she wanted to be self-reliant.

'Don't worry about it. It's a thing,' I said. There were actually words for this in United States thru-hiking slang, drawn from 'blazes', the US name for trail markers: *pink blazing* was when a guy slowed his pace for a love interest, and *banana blazing* was when a woman sped up. (*Green blazing*, meanwhile, meant spending much of the hike stoned.)

'I don't have his inReach number and I don't know if he has mine because he hasn't texted,' she said, lovesick, desolate. I had to smile to myself. Constantly checking for a satellite text was the thru-hiking equivalent of waiting by the phone. 'If he hasn't texted me, what does that mean?'

We passed three young men that afternoon and stopped to chat. They leered at her. As they left, one of them muttered something to his mate, who said, 'Oi, steady on.'

'Did you hear that?' Anna said. 'That was disgusting. I got such bad vibes from them.' It occurred to me as we wrote our names in the Stodys Hut book at lunchtime that we always wrote down our full names, and maybe that wasn't safe if someone decided to get obsessive and track us down. Then I got pissed off that three idiots had made us feel unsafe out here, and that took care of my mental space for the rest of the afternoon, which pissed me off even more.

We camped on the flats by the riverside that night, and I walked down to the water in the evening to wash myself and my clothes in a clear, icy pool that the river had dug in front of a boulder. It was so cold I lost my breath, but I sat there for a while and my body numbed and I felt better. I dug my toes into the fine, gritty sand and rubbed them back and forth, then dunked my hair, squeezed it out and walked back up to our tents, brain and body rinsed clean of the day.

'What does P.S. mean?' Anna asked from the tent next to me later that night. She was writing another note.

'Post-script,' I said.

'Oh, so P.P.S. means post-post-script?'

'Yup.'

'How do you spell "appallingly"?'

'Two Ls.'

But in the morning she was quiet, a little morose.

'Daniel made me coffee in the mornings.'

I was obviously not matching him in quality of company. I had no coffee but heated her up some of my dehydrated mocha rice pudding instead and we pushed on up the river.

I slowed down after our afternoon stop at Top Timaru Hut; I was too hot and felt sick, the protein bar, miso and rice noodles I'd cooked sitting badly in my stomach. I never did well in the heat; I preferred the dark and cool of colder months and evenings.

Anna took off from the hut and I let her go, watching her stride up the rocky track towards the 1680m Mt Martha Saddle, on the boundary between Otago and Canterbury. She looked tiny against its mammoth sides, a bundle of sticks.

I went up slowly, taking videos and photos, looking at the grasshoppers that scattered as I walked, trying to figure out the alpine plants and what snow-capped peaks I could see on the horizon behind me. When I crested the saddle I sat there for a minute admiring the Ahuriri Valley ahead and the ranges folded behind it, enjoying the feeling of being right on the boundary between two provinces, the second one finally under my belt. It was the highest elevation I'd reached so far on the trail.

Dark clouds hovered in the distance. I got up and entertained myself for a minute by standing on the Otago side and then stepping over to the Canterbury side, then back to Otago, then finally sat down facing Canterbury and ate some peanuts and raisins and some of my dried fruit leather. I had put currants in this batch, and as I unrolled it the tiny black dots came unstuck and fell everywhere, which was annoying; I had carried those calories. I picked them up off the rocks and ate them, then wandered about on the ridge a little, trying to find the single bar of phone reception that was apparently available here.

I didn't find it, and I didn't look for long, because I heard a huge crack of thunder. I looked a little closer into Canterbury, at the clouds in the distance. They looked quite dark. I could see curtains of grey sheeting from the sky down to the ground. Rain began to spatter the hot stones around me. I realised I was standing at nearly 1700m and a thunderstorm was bearing down, and I was the tallest thing in the landscape and possibly the most conductive, too. I was also carrying metal hiking poles. It was nearing 6p.m., and Tin Hut was still about 8km away.

Shit.

I ran as the sky fell in and soaked me in seconds. I counted the gap between the lightning and thunder as I ran; it was coming closer. I ran down the bulldozer track into the rocky alpine valley as fast as I dared, becoming increasingly more panicked as I realised just how exposed I was. I thought of National MP Maureen Pugh as I ran; she'd been struck by lightning three times, each time in a house, for God's sake, when she was running a bath or picking up the phone. How at risk was I right now? As I ran I tried to calculate it, annoyed at my lack of weather and science knowledge. What would get hit first? Did it depend on the conductivity of the material or height or something else? There were metal route poles here, but I was taller than them. Would the lightning hit them instead? They were topped with orange plastic. Did that make a difference? How conductive was a human body? Lightning hit trees. Did it hit rocks?

There was a huge crack of thunder at the same time as a flash filled the sky around me, and I screamed my throat raw. The air got very hot and surged with charge. I could feel it fizzing in my body, my skin and my teeth. I flung my poles away and ran off the path and across the humped tussock to two enormous boulders, about the size of a car, then threw my pack down, pulled out my tent and flung it over them. There was a cleft between them and I huddled inside it, crying, as the rain pelted down on my tent fly, the sky flashed and the thunder rolled above me in long, crackling booms, pulse after pulse of heavy sound. The rain came down so hard that a river formed between my rocks. The threat was invisible and it came from the sky; I wouldn't even know if it hit me. I have never been so convinced that I was about to die.

I stayed there huddled under the tent fly for nearly an hour as the rain lashed. I was wet but I had left my fleece in my pack, and I didn't want to unbuckle it and get everything wetter, so I began to get very cold. Finally, the storm seemed to be moving away to the west. I shook the rain off my tent, and as I packed it up I saw I'd torn its mesh on the rock. I put on my fleece, beanie and neck gaiter, then shrugged back into my wet jacket. It was nearly 8p.m. and anxiety was still rippling under my ribcage. I picked up my poles and jogged down the track, diving behind bushes a couple more times when cracks and booms rent the air, but they would not protect me from the sky. I had to get to Tin Hut, but it was still a few kilometres away. It started hailing lightly.

The running soothed me, and I soon rounded a corner and saw the hut, then a small group of people gathered in the doorway, jumping and waving. I heard Anna scream 'Coooeeeeee!' I yelled back and waved my poles.

People. They'd been waiting for me. They'd been worried.

The hut was surrounded by a herd of beautiful, glossy young cows, but I was so enervated I was scared of them too, and shouted at them as I walked through, clacking my poles together in case they decided to attack me.

'Oh my God!' Anna said when I got to the hut door. 'I was so worried! I am so sorry! I just took off, and when I looked behind me you weren't there!'

'No, I was going slowly, don't worry.'

'There's one top bunk left. We brushed the rat shit off it for you,' said Ashley, a tattooed, gregarious hiker we'd met earlier that day. 'But you should still lay your mat down on it.'

'And we made you some lemon and ginger tea,' Anna said.

I took the hot cup and sipped it gratefully. 'God, thank you so much.'

At 9p.m. we all went to bed. I ate a Peanut Slab for dinner and clambered up to the top bunk, which required some gymnastic contortions as it had no ladder. My head scraped the ceiling as I adjusted my sleeping bag, then I lay there for a while listening to the snoring and the mice and rats chewing on plastic somewhere below, then somewhere next to my head. My hip ached from running over rocky ground.

The river burbled and cows brushed the sides of the hut. I was cold. I pressed the hot battery pack charging my phone into my stomach. Then I lay there quietly for six more hours, unable to sleep, until I finally dropped off somewhere near dawn.

* * *

Anna had put her inReach against the hut window, in view of satellites, and it beeped early in the morning. She turned to me, her face alive with delight.

'He texted!'

Daniel was a few days ahead and now there was the question of what she should do. She could get to State Highway 8 and then hitch to catch up with him, but she felt guilty about skipping past Lake Ōhau and a section of the trail. She was again full of questions about if this or that was the right decision, and the whole hut weighed in with their opinions. She took on everyone's thoughts and treated them equally, unsure what she herself wanted.

Twenty years ago I'd been exactly like this about boys. I had forgotten what it was like to be in your early 20s. Anna was fast, intrepid, smart, funny, beautiful, kind, and well-prepared, but over the last couple of days I had seen how people patronised her and told her that she should follow their own choices. She told me that when she decided to do the trail, some of her family and friends had been dumbfounded.

'Don't you have to be a good hiker to do that?' a friend had said. Older family members had tried to lecture her on it, as if she hadn't done her research. Because she was open about her fears, people took it as an invitation to tell her she wasn't prepared and maybe shouldn't do it. At 42, I was either ignored or treated like someone's lame mum out here, but Anna was treated like a child, and I felt the urge to bolster her. Undermining a young woman so she questioned herself and her abilities was far more damaging than ignoring an older one. I noticed it but no longer gave a shit; Anna was still on the edge of knowing just how much she was actually capable of, and absorbed people's ill-founded opinions about her and her capabilities. At nearly 500km in, she was still unsure if she could do the trail herself; she had started out with a friend, who had bailed early. I told her only that she was already walking it, and she would finish.

The sun was rising later these days. It was only a week until autumn. Anna left at 7.45a.m., still nervous, and she crept past the beautiful black cows, her arms wrapped around her stomach.

'Bye, Anna!' I said as she walked off. 'You can do it!' I added. She turned and clenched a fist and held it up.

'We can do it!' she said.

'I'll see you for nachos at Lake Ōhau!' I joked. She stopped and turned around, eyes wide.

'Do you think I should go to Lake Ōhau?'

'Just … let the universe decide,' I said. She heaved a big, flustered sigh, then started walking again. A cow refused to move so she gave it a wide berth, then scampered down the grassy track. And that was the last I saw of Anna.

* * *

'Are you the one who got caught in the storm?' a musterer called as I walked down the farm track to the road. 'So weird – it didn't even rain down here on the highway.'

The sun was searing that day, super-heating my skin. By midday I was so tired that after wading the Ahuriri River I stopped to camp in the first patch of shade I'd found, a grove of willow trees next to the Ahuriri's east branch. I had gone just 15km, a half-day on trail, but I tied up my rope, then hung out my wet tent and gear. I let my tent flap in the sun for a while until it was dry, then pitched it fully and crawled inside to starfish in the heat, trying unsuccessfully to get a bit more sleep. Two English southbound women arrived in the afternoon and I greeted them through the tent mesh.

'Did you get caught in that storm?' one asked.

'I did,' I said. 'It was fucking terrifying.'

'I bet,' she said. 'It looked like it was only hitting that valley. We could see the lightning forking down from where we camped.'

'Well, it forked right down on me.'

* * *

The next day I threaded my way beside the river, which snaked like a dropped silver chain. An enormous ridge held my gaze to my right, a steep slope built of grey stones that looked as though they'd been caught falling, suspended in time. The sky was cloudless, powder blue. The trail wound on; in some places the path split into two, southbounders and northbounders each finding the easiest way through the rough terrain. The two trails looped like a double helix, one ascending and one descending through the tussock and Spaniard grass and sharp alpine plants that cut your legs to ribbons. My legs were soon running with blood.

In the afternoon I crested the last hill in stifling heat and felt a ruffling breeze on my skin. I saw Lake Ōhau blue in the distance, a thatch of beautiful beech forest in between. I felt tears pricking my eyes. Ōhau marked the end of this section, which always sparked a rush of emotion. Descending a ridge to see a valley holding a river or lake I had been walking towards for days always felt like a huge achievement, a mountain ticked off.

I broke into a run as I entered the treeline, welcoming the birdsong; with only patchy forest in the last few weeks of trail, I had missed them.

The sun was still a couple of handspans above the ridge when I rounded the corner and saw Aoraki Mt Cook cloistered in the Southern Alps, shining blue and white. The land still held blackened remnants of the fire that had torn through here a few

93

years back, and some of the marker poles carried dripping orange plastic caps, melted then frozen in time.

I was staying at Lake Ōhau Lodge for a couple of nights – a huge treat. I walked the last 6km to the reception desk, where once again I stood in front of a normal person, bleeding from the speargrass stabs on my legs, dusty, sweaty and tired, and tried to recall how to be normal myself.

I'd booked the room and dinner over the phone when I got reception on the hillside, but I'd arrived a bit late for the meal sitting. The staff member I'd called said she'd save me dinner to eat at the bar.

'You're walking the TA?' she said as she checked me in. 'And you're a Kiwi? Why?'

I didn't yet have an answer for this question. 'I don't know,' I said. 'I've just always wanted to.'

'See your own country?'

'I suppose so.'

As she handed me my key and directed me to the bar, I made a small apologetic fuss about my filthy clothes, pack and shoes. She scoffed.

'No one gives a shit,' she said. 'Don't worry.'

And she led me to the bar, where a smiling man brought a hot plate of food, fetched me a knife and fork, and then pulled a tall, cold glass of beer and set it down in front of me.

CHAPTER 5

ŌHAU TO OTIRA

I walked my longest-ever day, more than 40km, on the flat between Lake Ōhau Lodge and Twizel. It was hot, dusty, dry, windy. Around 10am a pack of grim-looking young southbound women strode past, strung out along the lakeside trail. When I stopped to eat some beef jerky, another southbound hiker told me that the group had just about completed a 100km stretch that would finish at the lodge. They'd been walking all night. I was aghast.

Ten hours later I arrived in Twizel hobbling, leaning on my poles, my hips and feet throbbing, tears in my eyes from the pain. Al, a friend of a friend, picked me up and took me back to his house, and fried me up some fresh trout he'd caught, served with potato pom-poms and a lettuce and tomato salad. The first snow had fallen on the Southern Alps when I set off for Takapō two nights later.

After so many days in the sun I wanted to spend some time walking under the stars, and this flat, 54km trek was the perfect chance to soak up the universe. Most walkers cycled it, but I was still stuck on my Every Fucking Inch goal. Inspired by the group of young southbound women, I decided to also walk through the night, just to see how far I could go before I collapsed.

I stoked up on a treat of eggs Benedict for breakfast, then left Twizel at midday and walked through dry plains dotted with wilding pines, the fresh, blue-white Alps like jagged teeth on the horizon. Everyone I passed was delighted by the snowfall. I walked to the edge of Lake Pukaki, where I joined groups of tourists at picnic tables eating fresh sashimi made from salmon farmed in the glacial canals. I walked around the head of the turquoise lake, scaring hares that ran between dead, rustling stalks of lupins. The poplars were turning yellow and the rosehips bowed over, heavy with bright, deep red fruit. A wasp flew into my cheek like a thrown stone.

My shadow lengthened and someone in a car threw a bottle at me. As the hours ticked past I watched shadows play on snow-clad Aoraki, the great ancestor's facets changing as the sun crept across the sky. As night fell around 8.15p.m. the trail had turned into farm track, and the maunga was suddenly enormous, glowing pink in front of me in the last of the light.

But as the darkness settled in, I felt again the familiar tug of fear, and my mind began to run worst-case scenarios. Someone was following me, waiting to pounce. *This was a bad idea. Why would you put yourself in this situation? This is actually fucking irresponsible. No one would be sympathetic if you got attacked out here. It would be your fault. You should be safe inside. Why did you need to do this?*

There was only one legal campsite in this section, and it was far back behind me. It was 9p.m.; I'd walked 26km that afternoon and had 30km left to walk to the holiday park in Takapō. There was nobody around. I *hoped* there was nobody around. Then I glanced at the map on my phone and realised I was way off trail and had been since 7p.m. Kilometres off; I'd mindlessly walked down the wrong farm track, and my phone was nearly out of power. I realised I'd forgotten to charge my battery packs in Twizel.

I zoomed out on the map and saw the nearest place to rejoin the trail was the road running alongside the hydro canal, on private land owned by Meridian Energy. It was too dark to see the ground underfoot and the canal was bound to be fenced; I'd have to backtrack with a dying phone. Fuck. I felt my last nerve twang, and called Doug.

'You're walking through the night?' he said. He was watching me on the GPS.

'I'm scared,' I said. 'I'm out here alone and what if someone is hunting me down?'

'None of those munters are going to be out there in the middle of nowhere looking for people,' he said. 'They're all in Christchurch.'

'I'm lost,' I said. 'It's dark and I went down the wrong farm track and I'm off trail and my phone is dying.'

'I can see where you are,' he said. 'I can see the canal. Can you see Matariki and Orion?'

'Yes.'

'Can you see Taurus?'

'Yes.'

'It's due north right now. Just keep heading towards that.'

'There's no track.'

'Just go towards the start of the canal, it's all farmland out there. Do you remember how to find your way using the Magellanic Clouds?'

'Yes.'

'There you go. You'll always know where you are. I'll stay on the phone.'

I stumbled across the rolling, dry hills, but gasped when dozens of clusters of bright eyes popped out of the dark, caught in the beam of my head torch. Instinct told me they were wolves, watching me pass through their lands.

'There are eyes out there. What animal has green eyes in the dark?'

'Sheep.'

Talking made me relax, and Doug and I chatted for an hour and a half as he drove home from an evening meeting, brushed his teeth, fed the dog and took him for a walk down the road, talking about home, about nothing. I made it back to the trail and approached the canal gates. I was relieved to see that no cars could get down the canal road, and felt safer, so we said goodbye.

Now that it was pitch black and I was protected behind gates and I could walk freely down the tarmac and gravel without rolling an ankle or losing the trail, I felt glee creeping in, then joy. The Milky Way stretched overhead and a few meteors flashed across the darkened vault of the sky. Lights of faraway towns glowed on the horizon and the ghostly shapes of the mountains ran ragged to the west and south. It was bitterly cold in the snow-laden wind, and I layered on extra clothing and turned my headlamp off so my eyes could adjust to the dark. There was just enough light that I could see the white lines on the road in front of me, so I followed them, and followed the stars. The canal was a pale ribbon to my left, and I watched starlight reflecting off it as I walked, enjoying the calm of being alone in the dark with only the universe for company.

The moon rose at midnight. A white plastic public toilet loomed out of the darkness to my right, and I decided to take a break for the first time since my Pukaki sashimi at 3p.m. The loo was perfect for a rest: spacious and seemingly little used, it was clean, odourless, windproof and had a lockable door. I inflated my sleeping mat and laid it down for a rest.

Six hours later I woke with a start, unlocked the door, and staggered out. It was 6.30am and dawn was starting to redden the horizon. The sky and the white-clad Alps began to glow pink as I followed the calm blue canal, watching large trout undulating in the water, but as I got closer to Takapō each step began to drive shards of pain from my feet to my hips. According to the trail numbers I'd walked 55km from Twizel, though I'd fallen asleep in the middle of it and had no idea how many kilometres my unplanned detour had added. I had a ways to go yet to match the effort of that group of southbound women.

My phone buzzed. My friend Kirsty had sent me a $50 voucher for The Greedy Cow, a café in town, and I quickened my pace, gritting my teeth against the pain. When I got there I dumped my pack beneath a table and drank three glasses of water, then ordered a flat white, a kombucha, a cup of peppermint tea, and a huge slab of French toast with bacon, long slices of caramelised banana, maple syrup, crushed nuts and candied orange, all of it nestled on the plate against a towering pile of softly whipped cream.

* * *

For nearly two weeks I walked up Canterbury to Otira, alone. I followed Anna in the hut book. At one hut, Daniel's name was there, just a day ahead of her. At the next hut, she'd caught up, and she'd written both of their names together on the same line and added a single word in the comments box: 'Bliss'.

'Good for you,' I said aloud, and closed the book. Their names stayed together from then on, sometimes in his hand, sometimes in hers.

It was autumn. I hardly saw a mirror and my body had adapted without me noticing. One day I saw my feet were wider, the tissue denser. My heels and toes had grown layers and ridges of yellow calluses. My ankles had thickened. My calves had grown fat and solid. The skin on my legs was covered in dark blue, green and yellow bruising, the skin torn daily by rocks, gorse and matagouri, then scabbing and healing over, then opening again, bleeding once more. The blood and mud washed away in rivers.

I had lost my ass and my thighs were developing a hard curve on the outside, like a rugby player, narrowing above and below my knee until the joint stuck out. My pants were loose on my waist now and I had to keep them belted. The zippered circles of my zip-off pant legs were no longer tight on my thighs when I stepped up.

My hands were sun-dried rough, and new twin moles had welled up at the base of each thumb. My lips stayed chapped. My fingernails were permanently half-mooned with dirt. The skin of my chest was seared and mottled red and had a long, deep wrinkle in the centre. When I did encounter a mirror I looked with interest at the new way my neck skin crumpled when I turned my head. I could see age blooming there, and as my chin and jaw and cheeks sharpened and my upper lip creased and thinned and the edges of my mouth began to sag, I saw my face slipping away. In the mirror was my mother, my aunt, my future.

Two strange new muscles had popped out under my collarbones, and my trapezius and deltoids were hard and swelling. The ends of my hair were split and bleached. A rough patch had erupted on the top of my upper lip; a solar keratosis.

Sometimes my nose bled from the dry air. When this happened at first I fussed and stopped to staunch it, but soon I just let it drip until it clotted, perfect circles of blood falling on grey rocks when I lowered my head to navigate them.

I passed the 700km mark and discovered one of my back molars had a rough edge. I thought I might have chipped it or lost a filling, and couldn't stop running my tongue over it as I walked. I tried to see what was happening in there using my phone camera, then threaded a bit of floss between the molars to see if there was something stuck. Sudden pain and nausea crashed into me and I pulled out the floss, gasping and swaying. I sat down and clutched my head in my hands, groaning in pain. My jaw was now on fire, pain flaring into my ear and temple and the rest of my teeth. I could only take ibuprofen and paracetamol and walk on.

I was faster now, my strides coming as easy as a metronome, as though they were ancient knowledge, which they were. My lower back no longer hurt, but instead gnawed a hole through the pack fabric. I thought of my skeleton, ligaments, tendons, muscles flexing, my foot pushing down and through, rolling off my big toe. I thought of the similar skeletons of my ancestors doing the same thing for millions of years, each of them living long enough to produce the next ancestor, enough of them that I had arrived here to walk these hills north.

I tramped 240km over mountains and down valleys in those thirteen days, across worn hills flocked bronze with tussock, up scree slopes, and down the length of rivers, from left bank to right bank and through the middle, holding my poles loosely and stepping quickly across hot boulders, wading deep pools and navigating shoals of gravel. Some rivers were choked with didymo, some not yet infected. Some days my Achilles would be sore and walking in the cold rivers helped. I watched distant banks of cloud tipping over the ranges; they sometimes left patches of snow behind, but it was fine nearly every day. There was a drought and the rivers were low, and the ground sounded like a hollow drum under my poles. I felt as though I was walking over an eggshell of Earth that my pole might tap through, and the whole thing would crack open and cave in. On a fence near a lake a bird skeleton hung, bleached white, the bones of its foot caught in a twist of wire.

I didn't need to sit down during the day. I ate as I walked. I walked 33km in nine hours straight. Thirty-four. My resting heart rate dropped to 41 beats per minute. My pack became an exoskeleton, its weight irrelevant, like the weight of my hair. Only when I took it off for the first time in eleven hours did I feel the extra lightness, the different sway in my stride.

* * *

The other northbounders were long gone. The world was empty except for the grasshoppers, sometimes a kārearea call, sometimes the sight of a tahr, a few rare southbounders. It wasn't like the world of other TA walkers on my Instagram feed, the young, tanned people who bounded through the mountains with their mates, their links forged in the North Island, doing shoeys at Stirling Point and cuddling up under blankets. One afternoon, the sight of a dusty northbound footprint held by the trail brought me close to tears.

I watched their names appear in every hut book. Each day we travelled along, trains on the same track. Anna and Daniel, together and happy. Michael, a couple of days ahead. Annie and Sylvan, five days ahead. Zuzana, Else, Elle, Marvel and Quadzilla were there, though I saw on Instagram that Elle had finished the trail in the Richmond Ranges and gone home, her heart done with the journey.

Early one morning I heard the creak of bike brakes outside the hut and was shocked to see my friend Simon opening the door. He had biked in from a road end to bring me food. His wife, my old friend Caroline, had packed me black-bean brownies, cherry tomatoes, boiled eggs, three golden queen peaches, a bar of chocolate, a can of Sprite, some cooked bacon and two fresh steaks. Simon gave me some energy chews and his inReach for the mountains to come, which could send and receive text messages via satellite. When we said goodbye I walked away from the hut thrilled and crying, and cooked the steak over the fire that night, holding its blackened edges in my hands and tearing at the bloody, buttery flesh with my canine teeth. I wiped the grease off my mouth with the back of my hand. There was no one around to see me.

The mountains shed gravel. I cut my toenails and taped my heels, held my breath and put my head under the cold rivers and felt the flow tug my hair downstream. Sometimes I was screamingly bored. Other times I didn't notice the day tick past. Sometimes I sobbed or laughed to myself. There was no one to put sunblock on me or make me a cup of coffee. The flashes of anger I had in the beginning were long gone, replaced by a deep, numbing solitude.

Sometimes I was alone in these old musterer's huts and listened to the wind keening outside as I read cheerful messages in the book from warmer, busier days. Sometimes I met people in the huts, and when mice flung themselves about like circus performers we cursed them together.

I had nothing and no one to care for but myself and the potted basil plant I'd bought and nursed along for a few days of salami and salad wraps. I'd been sad when I'd stripped it of all its leaves and left it in a hut; I'd talked to it and said goodbye, giving it a little pat and hoping someone would water it. Each day, I set off alone and walked with no one. I don't remember what I thought about.

* * *

After walking 753km since Bluff, I met four other hikers at Lake Coleridge Powerhouse Lodge: two southbounders and two rare northbounders, a pair of young Australian men, Ethan and Hugh, who had been a couple of days behind me. I decided to take a rest day, my second since leaving Takapō. This was because the lodge's owner, Andy, a warm and kindly man who had walked Te Araroa with his daughter, had blatantly tempted us with his waffles, cold drinks and hot chips. He also invited us to the Lake Coleridge Billiards Club that night, where we could join him for a beer and a chat with a few locals.

'You'd be very welcome,' he said. 'There's a big stone billiards table up there and you can have a game if you want. That's kinda what you do in Lake Coleridge on a Saturday night.'

That afternoon, the four other hikers and I sat on couches and ate our waffles and chatted. A fifth hiker arrived, a southbound American man, and I learned he was famous down the trail for the massive distances he walked each day and for his meals: wraps spread with Nutella and sprinkled with Skittles and M&Ms. The talk turned to injuries. I mentioned my sore Achilles, which had grown from an occasional to a daily nuisance ever since I had spent a rest day schlepping around with my pack on wearing jandals.

'Medical science doesn't apply to thru-hikers,' he said airily. 'You just walk it off.'

The lodge had a massive replica of a track marker, an orange wooden triangle that we could write our names on. Andy planned to photograph it each year and display the photos, then paint over the sign with fresh orange for the new season. We all went over to look at it, slapping at sandflies as we stood searching for the names of friends we hadn't seen for weeks. It was one of the only tangible remnants of us passing through. I wrote my name, the date and 'NOBO'. Chatting to locals that night at the billiards club, I felt oddly out of my body after two weeks alone in the golden mountains and plains, as sparse and temporary as a tumbleweed blowing through.

I set off early the next day and walked through an arboretum of sweet-smelling pine, one of the biggest collections in the world. It was 30km along a gravel road around Lake Coleridge to a campsite near its head. I was rejuvenated from the rest and started off jubilant, music in my ears and unable to stop from dancing in the middle of the road; but when I unclipped my pack for lunch I realised I'd left my food bag behind.

I cursed, but there was no way I was going back. I checked my rations: I had three days through the valleys until I reached Arthur's Pass. I had enough snacks from the supermarket at Methven to keep me going, though it would be lean. I texted Andy a message on the inReach, asking if he'd hang onto my food and I'd send him a post bag when I could.

I camped with Ethan and Hugh that night. Ethan had walked from Bluff, Hugh had joined him at Queenstown, and the two of them were so fast that on this one day I found myself walking with them I couldn't keep up, even at a trot. Their stride was simply too long. It meant they could take leisurely breaks during the day, swimming and napping under trees, and still manage huge kilometres.

Four mothers and around half a dozen children were also at the campground that night. I went over to say hello and found out they were home-schoolers who regularly took advantage of free campgrounds around Canterbury to let their kids run wild. One offered four eggs and some fruit-and-nut dark chocolate, and another gave me a quick tour of wild plants in the area: dandelion, for salads; yarrow, good for cuts; burdock to aid digestion. The kids ran around throwing balls and riding bikes until 9p.m., two hours after Hugh, Ethan and I were in bed. But I was OK; a friend I met in Methven had given me a pot brownie, and I ate half and went to bed heavily stoned at 6.20p.m. It was the best sleep yet on trail.

I woke to Hugh and Ethan bickering, their Australian twangs ringing across the campground in the early dawn. They bitched and carped at each other like an old married couple, from the moment they woke up in their separate tents and someone called out the first insult, to well after they laid their heads down at night. One would complain about the other stealing food or wrecking a piece of gear, and they'd embark on a long routine of complex banter and inside jokes, secure in their own world of mateship. They mocked each other ruthlessly, set up dares and punishments, threatened to fight, then fought.

This morning they were arguing about who had ruined whose headphones and whether they should settle it with a fight. At 8.30a.m., frost hard on the ground, I sat on a fireside log and boiled up the eggs as they faced off over their half-packed gear.

'That's truly unfortunate,' Hugh said. 'So now we both can't be fucked fighting each other.'

'I'd still beat you though,' Ethan said, after a pause.

'No, you fucking wouldn't. Fuck off.'

'I've got a second pair of headphones. So I'm good.'

'They're shit.'

'Which ones? No they're not.'

'So they're just going to stay in your ears while we're fighting, are they?'

'Yes!' Ethan said, and made some martial arts moves. 'It'll be like a full-on movie trailer.'

'Or are those fucked too, cos you dropped them in the mud?'

'*You* dropped them!'

They were still going when they left 30 minutes later. Ethan was doubled over in hysterics as he walked. Having won the argument, he had made Hugh carry the large fireside log a kilometre down the road, across his shoulders. This was some form of payback for Hugh having made Ethan swim in a freezing river the day before, and I heard the home-schooled tribe cheering him as he passed. I buckled my pack, picked up my poles and set off as well. The kids were sitting at camp tables, contentedly eating breakfast while the mums packed everything down like stagehands.

'Goodbye, nice to meet you, good luck!' the kids chorused as I passed, and I smiled. So nice.

'Hope you don't die!' a boy of about nine called.

The others whipped around. '*Josh!*'

* * *

I walked up the Harper River towards Arthur's Pass and stayed that night in Hamilton Hut. A few other trampers were there and they told me Ethan and Hugh had arrived in the afternoon, spent half an hour arguing about whether they should go to the next hut or not, and finally left, still launching insults at each other. I was sorry they were way too fast for me to stay with; I liked listening to the labyrinthine conversations that reminded me of high school, and I envied their companionship, their ease. And their long legs.

I walked up into the beech forest, clambered up a riverbed for a few hours, and then climbed to 1200m near Lagoon Saddle before descending steeply to the state highway and hobbling to the Bealey Hotel, where I made up for my forgotten food bag with roast lamb and beer. My tooth was throbbing again, and so was my Achilles, but I took more painkillers and ignored them.

I checked the weather as I ate. There was a storm on the way, but it was only two more days to Otira, where I was planning a couple days' rest with Doug at the Stagecoach Hotel; he was driving from Nelson to meet me. I'd had only two days off in two weeks and 240 mountain kilometres, but the trail to Otira descended the entire length of the Deception River from its headwaters at 1070m Goat Pass. I needed to stay ahead of the rain.

I camped that night on the flats where the Bealey River joined the braids of the Waimakariri, but it was so cold I couldn't sleep. It was nearing the end of March and my sleeping bag was no longer warm enough. At night I was now so freezing that I cinched the hood shut and found stuff I needed – headlamp, water bottle, beanie – by jamming an arm out the hole, flailing about like a sandworm. When I couldn't sleep, I played my Te Araroa playlist and sang to the dust, the spiders, and the mice.

Hoping for a warmer night, I stopped early the next day at the tiny, two-bunk Mingha Bivvy, which I knew had an open fireplace; the next hut, at Goat Pass, did not. But again I lay awake for five hours, shivering, snatching only a couple of hours' sleep near dawn. The fire had been too smoky to light. You needed to keep the hut door open so it could draw, but it was too cold for that, and I didn't want to waste firewood; it was all damp, anyway. I let the fire die down, but the wind then came down the chimney and blew ash into the hut, smoking it out. I woke up at 4a.m. feeling like I was choking when my head shifted away from the tiny, smoky airhole I breathed through.

At 5a.m. I decided I might as well just get up and walk, and make the best of the day's weather in case the rain arrived early. The Deception was not to be messed with. Its trickling headwaters were tumbled with huge boulders, and its lower reaches were wide and swift. If there was any rain in the tops, I didn't want to be traversing it alone. I had seen only one other hiker the day before.

I slid home the bolt on the bivvy's door and made my way up through dark bush and into the alpine scrub. The Coast to Coast adventure race came up the Deception and down through here, and as my feet thudded on boardwalks installed to protect the track, I thought, *This trail is like a months-long adventure race.* It wasn't just covering 20–40km a day. It was that but with no sleep, poor food, bad weather, rough tracks, no tracks. Living on the cheap, never enough time for recovery. It was not just a one- or two-day race; the event went on for half a year. I wondered, again, what I was doing out here alone.

I heard whio whistling and wheezing far down in the river below, sounding exactly like the foot pump on an air mattress. Goat Pass was hung with cloud. Walking into it made me nervous, but it was scudding swiftly across the saddle, and the rest of the sky looked clear. It wasn't meant to rain yet. I kept going, pausing at Goat Pass Hut to write my name in the book. There were shoes outside. I poked my head into the bunkroom; several huddled forms were still sleeping. They would be the only people I'd see that day.

The Deception's rocky upper section was fun, like being at a water park, and I clambered through icy water, swinging over giant grey boulders. I saw a pair of whio flying low above the river beneath the immense valley walls, settling further ahead to surf and whistle in the rapids.

As I got lower, the river became harder, wider, swifter. Now as I crossed I had to jam my hiking poles firmly into the riverbed. In one spot, my pole began to vibrate in my hands urgently, like a tuning fork. I was startled; was it an earthquake? The Alpine Fault rupture that Doug had worried about? Then I realised it was the river. The water was flowing against my pole so violently that it was shaking. I fell in, then recovered, but I was now soaking wet. I gripped the poles and crossed slowly, choosing the best places, testing and settling and strengthening one foot and pole at a time. The river was fresh and strong, but there had been no decent rain for weeks. This was about as low as it could be.

I crossed again and again, accompanied by flitting ngirungiru, pīwakawaka and korimako, which sent up a beautiful chorus as the evening drew closer. Eventually the river widened enough that I could wade through the pools and stumble over shoals of gravel and boulders. I climbed over slips and smelled sulphur, a hint of a hot pool somewhere. I ducked through broken riverside bush on barely-there tracks, all the way down the Deception to the highway as the rain clouds threatened to the east.

* * *

Fat, black, spiny blackberries were growing on the side of the trail and I feasted on them, plucking as many as I could reach. I had run out of food; I hadn't wanted to waste time resupplying in Arthur's Pass before the coming storm. My tooth was now too sore for me to eat much anyway. I was trapped between bouts of pain by the maximum recommended adult dose of paracetamol.

Doug texted me when I was nearly at our meeting point of Morrison Footbridge, which crossed the Ōtira River to State Highway 73. The car had broken down in Murchison, nearly three hours away, and he had to wait for rescue. He'd be there when he could. I'd have to walk 6km along the highway to the Stagecoach Hotel.

My Achilles was really burning now, making me limp. I walked in the middle of the railway tracks, then decided that was a bad idea and left them. Sure enough, minutes later a humming began, then a train clattered past. I walked along the gravelly highway shoulder, but it disappeared and soon I was clinging to a crumbling metal barrier, orange rust rubbing off on my palms and jacket, each footstep slipping down a loosely-packed scree bank as cars and trucks roared past a metre away at 100km an hour. I could have touched them.

Another bad idea. I felt like a target. I felt like a maggot.

I realised I should have hitched back at the footbridge parking bay, because now the road was so narrow there was nowhere for cars to stop. When the highway descended to a side creek, I saw on the topo map that there were large transmission towers marching towards the village, and reasoned that following them would be the straightest and quickest path. I left the highway and crossed the river and walked below the towers, hobbling over rough rocks, pushing through gorse and weeds on the overgrown service track. My Achilles burned with every step.

At least it was quiet here, away from the maddening car noise tearing my peace apart. There were pīwakawaka cheeping. I hoped I wouldn't stumble into an old gin trap, or someone checking their dope plot. It was that sort of place.

CHAPTER 6

OTIRA TO ST ARNAUD

He had brought me my dressing gown. My cotton tracksuit pants, fruit and fresh socks. Easter eggs. More Voltaren 75. Doug and I stayed at Otira for a couple of nights as I rested my Achilles, letting the throbbing in the soles of my feet subside and the loneliness and fear of the last few weeks sink into memory. Across the highway, the daily freight train arrived every afternoon, crouching like a breathing beast, until at midnight it powered off to Christchurch with a scream of clashing iron.

I had walked 850km from Bluff and now I was stuck. The storm had rolled in and was forecast to last for three days, and the rivers would be high for at least a day after that. I needed good weather to turn west again and walk up the Taramakau River to Harper Pass. Being alone and only 165cm tall, I had to be conservative. People died crossing rivers. My personal horror was getting in trouble and not just ending up the subject of a scalding post on the Te Araroa Facebook page, but that a LandSAR volunteer would die while looking for me.

'I'll just get a backpackers' or tent somewhere here and wait it out until the rivers drop,' I mused, tapping through the pink-and-blue MetVUW forecasts on my phone. Doug looked incredulous.

'Aren't you forgetting something?'

'What?'

He pointed to himself. 'Free ride home to free accommodation?'

No. Absolutely not. 'No, I don't want to go home. I want to stay on trail.' I had already picked up the American practice of calling it 'trail', as though it was a proper noun, a singular place; and to us, it was. But Doug got his mutinous look.

'That makes no sense.'

'It's a *zone*. I want to stay in the zone. Thru-hiking is about staying on the trail and ... walking through. That's the challenge.'

'You're here now. Otira is off the trail.'

'Otira is allowed,' I said. 'I needed to resupply and there was no accommodation left in Arthur's Pass, where everyone usually goes.'

'Allowed by who? You can't go anywhere in this weather, and it makes no sense to pay for the YHA when you could stay at home for the same time for free, and you have a free ride there.'

'I just ...' I faltered. I'd loved the idea of reaching Rocks Hut in the ranges behind Nelson and walking off trail and through my front door after months away. The vision had sustained me for nearly a third of the trail. Going home now by car when there was no emergency? That would be failing.

Doug's was an argument of practicality applied to a feat of romance. But it was only romance that was getting me through. There wasn't much that was practical and logical about walking every inch of the trail. It was entirely arbitrary, a line drawn on a map that was sometimes very inconvenient, and it changed each year, sometimes at the whim of property owners, or as slips fell and riverbanks got washed away or DOC closed sections. The Line was not run through the most beautiful parts of the country; it had other factors to contend with, such as pushing walkers to legal campsites each night, with water at least once a day, through towns roughly each week at least. The trail I was following this year would be different the next; the exact route existed only one year at a time. But I didn't want to leave it.

How could I explain the magnetic pull of the path ahead, the satisfaction of the miles unwound behind me, the urge to follow it unbroken? Hikers leapfrogging, strung out like beads? At night as I tried to sleep, I felt the trail's wonder as I mentally zoomed in and out of the hills and saddles and valleys, my steps invisible behind me like footprints on melting snow. At night I flew back down the country, near the treetops, following my path. It was my trail and everyone else's, thousands of us. I had not yet got over the magic of crossing the country on foot in one unbroken journey. Despite the suffering, I had only become more attached to the idea over time. I wasn't sure if anything had ever grabbed me as hard as Te Araroa. It had calcified in me.

I was finding it hard to explain this to anyone who wasn't drawn to walking it. It sounded so ridiculous. Normal people shook their heads and asked questions like, 'Are you finding yourself?' or 'Are you buff yet?' or 'How much weight have you lost?' Even most of the Kiwi trampers I'd met over the past decade weren't interested in the TA.

It was also hard to explain the privations we thru-walkers suffered. How to explain that you walked every day for weeks in searing pain, by choice, for no particular reason? To be so scared, so low, so afraid for your life, and then so high you'd cry over a pair of whio whistling in a lonely river at dawn? It was at once too universal and too personal to put into words, an experience of awe and devastation known only to those who shared it, a bit like parenting.

Only my fellow walkers got it. But from what I'd seen, even most of them didn't care about the line as much as I did. Many wanted to experience the trail's highlights and pick up other spots like Aoraki Mt Cook and Cascade Saddle and Mt Taranaki along the way. There was something faintly embarrassing about walking every inch, suffering the horrible roads and the sections of farmland as well as the wilderness tracks, as though you were too earnest, a lingering super-fan of a '90s pop band. But I was smitten, gripped by this idea long ago. I was determined to see it through.

'I need to stay on the trail,' I said lamely. I had no other argument. But then Doug played his trump card.

'You could go to the dentist and get your tooth fixed and you could eat properly again.'

Fuck.

* * *

'I cannot believe I am leaving trail,' I said as we drove past the glaciated spurs of the muscular West Coast. 'This is not right.'

'Just think of me as your trail angel.'

The drive home seemed to be at an obscene speed. It would take me two weeks of battling to walk this. As we drove I tried to explain what I'd been through, to articulate the thru-hiker culture I'd discovered.

'It's like a travelling summer camp,' I said. 'But you suffer a lot.'

Trail life was a circus, a carnival, a Contiki tour bus on foot. It was tramping, but it wasn't. In all the tramping I'd done, I'd suffered, sure, but I'd never starved like I had on trail. I'd never been in so much pain. I'd never walked through the night to see the stars and because there was nowhere to camp. I'd never kept going through shit weather because it was seven days to a resupply point. I'd never gone beyond boredom to a place of blankness and peace.

Thru-hiking felt to me like clinging to the outside of a train on a cross-continental rail journey. You had a dirty swag on your back, you were whipped by weather, you slept on the ground and jumped off at stations for fuel. You grabbed a roadside apple and caught the next train north.

The trail carried us. There was no rule book. You had to leave it sometimes, to stay alive. But you had to jump back on and keep moving.

'Getting off trail to the nearest town to wash your clothes and binge-eat is OK,' I said. In fact, it was a reason for living. 'If you're with your trail fam, you have a tent camp or share the cost of a motel room so it's cheaper, and you bond and stuff.' I was wistful. The lack of this connection on my lonely northbound journey still hurt.

'I presume you're allowed to get medical care for emergencies,' he said. 'Broken ankle?'

'Fine, obviously. You couldn't walk.'

'Sprained?'

'Debatable. You could strap it and keep going.' I told him about the American I'd met at Lake Coleridge who'd informed me that medical science didn't apply to thru-hikers. 'You just walk it off,' I repeated happily, still entranced with the idea of cheating weakness. Doug rolled his eyes, just a little.

'I suppose replacing gear is allowed?'

'Fine.'

'Covid?'

'They can fuck off out of the hut if they have Covid.'

'No hitching?'

'Not for me.'

'What if you get giardia?'

'I heard about this one guy who tried to starve it out,' I said, and told him about the skeletal European who'd staggered into the Wānaka medical centre, his bowels laden with the parasite he'd tried to kill by spending days not eating.

'Jeez.'

'Flip-flopping' between walking sections north or southwards was fine; section-walking over twenty years was fine. So was skipping a bit to walk the Routeburn Track in one day, or hitching to chase a trail romance, or shuffling dates and sections to meet up with family and friends or escape flood or fire, as had happened with a small blaze near Takapō last month. Pausing to work along the way, whether fruit-picking like the young Europeans or holing up in huts and libraries, like me? We all needed money to hike. When anyone argued that something like this was 'cheating', someone would say mildly, 'Hike your own hike, man.' Everyone had families, jobs, health problems, time limitations, injuries, gear blowouts, personal goals and mishaps along the way. The maxim of HYOH covered it all. The lone pedant who argued about cheating would sit in furious self-righteousness while the people happily skipping bits of trail to keep up with their new friends laughed and shared chocolate and played cards.

We all had little rules we drew up in our heads to keep ourselves going, and they were entirely our own. I'd followed TA safety recommendations and not crossed the Rakaia and Rangitata rivers on foot; they weren't part of the official trail and I was too cowed by the story of one woman who'd been heli-rescued in blue-sky conditions from the Rakaia's braided channels, the river flash-flooding around her as rain hit the ranges hundreds of kilometres to the west and barrelled downstream.

I was both obsessed with the trail and embarrassed about the obsession. It was hard to justify such indulgence to the person I'd shared my finances with for a decade, and who was working this whole time. I'd saved and was working while walking, sure, but I wasn't pulling in anything equal to what he was.

To his credit, Doug was avoiding any allusion to this. He knew I knew, and he didn't have to say anything. And although I'd joked about the avalanche of marriage points he was saving up, he knew I'd support him in something he wanted to do in the future, which would help balance the scale of loneliness and hassle I was putting him through this year.

Now, though, he drove smiling, just happy we were together. We passed the Richmond Ranges, the blue backdrop that anchors Nelson's western side and spears south, thrust up by the sheer number of faults in the region that we all avoid thinking about.

'You'll be up there soon,' he said. 'I can't believe you've walked this whole way. I am really proud you've come this far. *I* couldn't do it.'

It *was* a long way, though there was still more than two-thirds to go. It was good to be home and have a little pause to think about it.

We drove along Rocks Road. I marvelled at the sparkling bay I hadn't seen for months, and realised that although I'd thought the trail had been the only thing in my life so far that had caught me and fascinated me, trapping me in its grasp, there were actually three other things that had done the same.

Journalism was one; nearly twenty years ago it had sunk its teeth into me and shook me with its curiosity and challenges. Nelson was another. Nestled between wilderness, the sun and the sea, it was Doug's home, and it had taken me into its heart and refused to let me go. And, a little while later, so had he.

* * *

Someone had cancelled their appointment so I managed to get to the dentist two days later. The dentist showed me a photo of the giant, crumbling, red crater that had sent me into stratospheric pain on the grasslands of Canterbury.

'Oh my God,' I said, staring at the screen, looking through the remainder of my tooth at the fleshy hole. It looked like the centre of the Earth.

'That's what happens when you eat muesli bars all day,' he said cheerfully. I grimaced; I did love my cranberry OSM bars. All the dentists at this clinic seemed to be mountain-bikers – it was Nelson – and they played slideshows of their sunny antics above the examination chairs. He said he had had the same issues when riding on expeditions. 'There's not much you can do about it when you need the fuel.'

'I've got months to go,' I said. 'What can I do? Brush my teeth after eating?'

'That's the worst thing you can do after eating acidic foods. It can damage enamel. You could go keto to avoid carbohydrates.'

I blanched. 'Ew, no.'

'Or chew gum.'

He wished me well on the trail and told me to help myself to the mini toothpastes. I thanked him through my numb mouth with its brand-new filling. Then I went to the supermarket to resupply for the next section, filling my basket with the usual trail food, the stuff I could still stand the sight of: apples, crackers, cheese, salami, cherry tomatoes, a capsicum, a cucumber, wraps, cream cheese, peanut butter. I still wanted the OSM muesli bars. At the checkout, I added three packets of gum.

My mum drove Doug and me back to Morrison Footbridge two days later, on 29 March, Good Friday. I felt fresh and fizzy after seven full days of rest. I had waited out the bad weather and high rivers, eaten fresh food, had an interview for a summer writing fellowship, sorted out my tooth, rushed through filing my freelancing taxes, bought a warmer sleeping bag, dug in the attic for winter clothes, and arranged food for the next sections.

Doug had been wanting to walk with me on trail at some point, so he had decided to join this section and traverse the 105km over four days to Boyle Village, near Hanmer, where my friends Caroline and Brittany were meeting me. I was excited to see them and thrilled I would pass the 1000km mark and reach Nelson in their company. It would be the start of a couple of weeks of walking with friends; from St Arnaud, I was going to tramp with Lauren through the Richmond Alpine Route. Then Mum, Samantha and Virginia would join me for the Marlborough Sounds section, until I reached kilometre 1313.4 and finished the South Island. I had walked with other people for just four full days on the whole trail so far. The next month walking near home was going to be very different to what I had done so far.

My Achilles didn't hurt at all as Doug and I walked across the bridge and back onto the trail; it was a half-day's walk of about 14km to get to the hut by evening. This was once the main route between the west and east coasts for Māori trading pounamu, and as we threaded up the Harper Valley, the range's grey-red rock folded the highway behind us, the valley walls feathered with tall beech. The high cirques were still empty, their smooth bowls holding only a dusting of snow.

The storm had passed over and it was a brilliant blue day, but the Taramakau was fast, high and milky. I was surprised that even now it was still too swift for me to cross alone without losing my footing on the shifting stones, and I clung to Doug to keep my balance. We both nearly tipped over, but made it. We walked on through golden plains of sun-bleached grass.

Doug, a keen tramper his whole life, was getting a crash course in the specific peculiarities of thru-hiking. When we sat down for a snack, I offered him some peanut butter from my ziplock bag. He recoiled.

'What is that?'

'It's peanut butter, it's fine,' I said, scraping out the warm mush with my long titanium spoon.

'That's disgusting,' he said. 'No thanks.'

We got to Kiwi Hut at nightfall, and as we took our boots off at the door I heard a familiar boasting twang.

'It can't be,' I said, but I opened the door and it was. Ethan and Hugh were back on trail in full swing, bickering this time over who had stolen whose chocolate. They'd waited out the Arthur's Pass storm at Deception Hut, halfway down the river. They'd been a few days behind me, because once they'd gotten to State Highway 73 they'd hitched to Christchurch to fulfil their trail dreams of all-you-can-eat waffles.

'If you ate eighteen in one hour it was free,' Ethan said, once we'd gotten through the remarkable serendipity of meeting up again nearly two weeks since we'd parted.

'I was *this* close to getting my name on the board,' Hugh said, pinching his thumb and forefinger together. 'And they walked up and said "Time's up!" And I had like two squares to go, and I was spewin'.'

'Felt so crook afterwards,' Ethan said.

'The rest of the day I was in a coma – we had to do shopping and stuff and I was walking around like a zombie. Got back to the hostel and went to bed for the afternoon.'

'Some maniac's eaten seventeen of them before,' Ethan said, shaking his head. 'And he had his name up there like three times.'

'They were *yuge*,' Hugh said. 'And that thick and sturdy you could slap the table with them.'

'Oh, they'd break the table.'

'Ethan was putting maple syrup on them and enjoying them but I was like, "Nah, I'm getting on that board,"' Hugh said. 'I smashed the first four without putting any toppings on but after that I lost the enjoyment and it was just trauma. Pure trauma.'

The hut was cosy and full. Ethan and Hugh climbed onto their bunks. Ethan pinched more of Hugh's chocolate and they argued about it for approximately twenty more minutes. Another Australian, an eighteen-year-old named George, poked his head over the bunk and asked about the river crossing we'd done that day. He was an appealing chap with the look of a pug dog, his round, wide-set eyes staring over a cute nose and smooth, adolescent jaw. He chatted continuously without stopping, or indeed blinking. He had just seen snow for the first time in his life, on Travers Saddle in Nelson Lakes National Park.

'It was crunchy,' he said. 'I didn't realise it would do that.'

George had started walking south from Cape Reinga in November and reckoned he'd developed scurvy by the time he got to the Richmond Ranges.

'I was eating only two-minute noodles,' he said. 'I don't know if it was the wind and cold, but I started getting these nosebleeds ...'

* * *

Doug and I crossed Harper Pass and walked through beech and grasslands to Hanmer, where we said goodbye and I welcomed Caroline and Brittany, friends I'd known since my twenties. They got on well, and we rambled for three days through the grasses of the St James Walkway. It was the roar, the breeding season for red deer, and the huts were full of hunters. They were stocky, swarthy and silent, and when a harrowing stag call echoed in the bush they cocked their heads to listen. They took over the huts, piling delicious town food on the stainless steel benches, and they left deer heads outside, propped against the deck, sometimes covered in black plastic rubbish bags, sometimes not; the stags' tongues lolled from stilled mouths. The hunters may have been gruff, but they were generous with their venison, offering us seared, seasoned slices with quiet pride.

I forgot about the loneliness I'd felt earlier on trail. I was busy with laughter, years of memories, problems to sort through, landscapes and birds to admire, knowledge to share. Who was that person who'd marched so many solitary kilometres? I left her behind in the vast autumn tussocklands of Canterbury as beech forest began to crowd the trail and I turned my head towards home.

Brittany and I farewelled Caroline at Waiau Hut and set off for three more days of walking to St Arnaud. It would be a reasonably tough ten straight days of tramping for me: 201km from Otira, over several rocky mountain passes, with no rest days. I'd worried for most of the year about snow and ice on

Waiau Pass and Travers Saddle, two of the highest passes on Te Araroa, at 1867m and 1787m respectively. But in the end, there was none; just a clinging fog that fell over us as we climbed hand over hand up the rocky south side of Waiau Pass to slip over the border of Canterbury into Tasman district. I stood on the saddle for a while and watched fog thread the rocky tops and roll down the valley, and a swelling rose in my throat. I had walked home at last.

But although we'd slogged up a sun-blazed trail just a couple of hours before, it was cold and damp on the pass and getting late, and we had to get to Blue Lake Hut with enough light to traverse the exposed and difficult bluff above Lake Constantine, where Andy Wyatt had fallen and died. We made it, scampering back down to the treeline with relief, but had to walk the last half-hour to Blue Lake in the dark.

I felt like an animal these days. I belonged to the dirt. The smell of wet earth and moss was in my nose, cold water on my feet, dappled sunlight in my eyes. When I closed them at night, the beech forest unrolled before me. As I drifted off to sleep the vision swelled; I was visited by myself transfigured into an ancient creature, covering mile after mile, leaping boulders, roots, swinging off trees, splashing through rivers, breath coming hard in my throat.

On our last day we stopped for lunch at Lakehead Hut on Lake Rotoiti, having tramped 22km that morning, down the valley from Upper Travers Hut. I'd walked 1051.6km from Bluff now – still obsessively counting every inch of the trail. There was just another 11km to go to St Arnaud today, where Mum was collecting us. I'd go home for a couple of days before returning to St Arnaud and tackling the Richmond Ranges, meeting Lauren halfway through them.

Daylight saving time had ended in the night. Winter was nearly here. I was feeling good as I got out my stove and pot to make a special treat of Indomie Mi Goreng noodles, which I'd been saving for the last day. Brittany had found a sleek new tramping skirt left behind in one of the huts, and I'd tried it on and liked it. It had cute little inbuilt shorts. It felt amazing to walk so freely, to step up on logs without heavy hiking pants or shorts constricting my movement. But I'd been hobbling a little on the last few kilometres, and my feet felt raw and burning. I'd changed my thin toe socks for woollen ones, and I thought the wool might have been abrading my skin after all the river crossings.

I ate my noodles, then took off my socks to inspect my feet and gasped in horror. Both feet and all of my toes were swollen, misshapen and weepy, covered in a red and pink rash. Bright red pustules covered the base of some of my toes. Red dots swept across the tops of my feet towards my ankles. Between and underneath my toes, there were tiny, red, painful slits, and the skin was peeling away in strips. It looked like the end-stages of a 19th-century disease.

The cold air made the pain even worse. I tried to get my socks back on and groaned in agony. Why did everything always hurt worse when you stopped?

Just then, the spicy noodles began to revolt in my stomach, and I knew I needed to get to the toilet pronto. I couldn't untie my Crocs from my pack quickly enough so I hobbled across to the hut toilet on my raw, bare feet, but they were too sore and the toilets were too far away. Brittany was outside talking to some other trampers, but I could only limp past her, whimpering. I forgot that the cute little tramping skirt I was wearing had cute little inbuilt shorts. I forgot it had a fashionable, fiddly, invisible zip in the back.

I didn't make it in time.

I screamed for Brittany.

'There's a water taxi arriving soon,' she called from outside the toilet door, once she'd stopped laughing. 'And I think we should take it.'

'Please!' I shrieked.

'But he's about to leave.'

'Stop him!' She ran down the track to the jetty while I recovered from the devastation as fast as I could.

We climbed into the little boat and shot across the lake. There was a cheery group of tourists aboard, including an entertaining young Frenchman who'd bailed on his tramping trip. He'd conducted a passionate argument with his friends, insisting he was returning to town to drink beer as they harangued him,

Gallicly, from the shoreline. But I couldn't enjoy it. I was mute with horror.

'I was going to throw myself off the boat if you didn't make it, so he'd have to wait,' Brittany told me as we sped across the silky water to St Arnaud.

'You,' I croaked, 'are a true friend.'

CHAPTER 7

ST ARNAUD TO MERETOTO SHIP COVE

A soft and soaking rain began to fall as I left St Arnaud and climbed through mist to Red Hills Hut. It was the middle of April and evening was falling early now. The heavy cloud brought the darkness closer. I dropped my pack to put on waterproofs, then climbed a rough forest track in the dimming light of my headlamp. The rain crept down my neck and soaked my shirt as I got to 1300m and walked through twisted beech and along a puddled ridge, sensing shorter alpine forest and empty air beyond the glow of my headlamp.

My jacket was no longer keeping the rain out, only holding it in, and my limbs slowly chilled and went stiff. I was so wet and so cold that I sensed I was on the edge of trouble. At least my Achilles no longer hurt; I'd apparently managed to walk it off.

The hut was near, however, and soon it loomed from the fog, dark and silent. It was only about 7pm, but hikers went to bed with the sun. I briefly shone my red light inside to see if anyone was there, and saw at least one sleeping body. There was clothing and gear on every surface. It was a small hut and I couldn't face walking in and disturbing everyone, but I had to eat and get warm. I stayed on the wet verandah and began rooting through my soaked pack. My hands wouldn't work properly but I managed to change clothes and socks, and slipped into my hut Crocs.

It was five days since Brittany and I had left Lakehead Hut in the water taxi. During the week, a storm had downed trees and blown snow over these ranges. I'd waited out the weather at home while my feet healed from their nasty fungal infection, then returned to Lakehead and walked on. I now carried a large tube of antifungal ointment with hydrocortisone.

I got water from the hut tank and squeezed it through my filter, then sat down on the step to boil it, to make a Thai green curry. I put the hot meal inside my down jacket, sealed it and hugged it to steal some warmth while it soaked, staring out into the drifting mist and thinking how good and strong the curry smelled.

In fact, I realised after a few minutes, it smelled a little too good and strong. And come to think of it, it was also a little too hot. I unzipped my jacket and saw that my numb hands hadn't managed to reseal the top of the packet properly, so most of the curry had oozed out over my only set of dry clothes: top, leggings and all down the inside of my down jacket, including somehow getting inside its internal pocket.

I sat back against the hut wall and groaned. Now I had no dinner and nothing dry to wear. I ate what was left of the curry in the bag, then scraped it off my goddamn merinos with my spoon and ate whatever I could. Then I squelched over to the hut's water tank, stripped off my clothes, wrenched open the plastic tap and rinsed off the worst of the curry with as little of the frigid water as possible. It was a mud-bath under the tap. For a second I was entranced by the stream of water sparkling like tinsel in my headlamp, but then noticed it was soaking through the holes in my Crocs onto my sole pair of dry socks, which made me hiss a final, savage 'Fuck's *sake*.'

I'd been out on the verandah for probably half an hour, trying to keep my hapless clattering to a minimum, but now I hauled my gear inside to claim a bunk. I was cold to the bone and beginning to shiver. It was all of 8p.m. And it was then that I met Lea.

A shadowy body popped up from the far bottom bunk and exploded into conversation. 'Oh my God, hi!' she said. 'Why were you out there!?'

I slung my sleeping bag on a bottom bunk and willed it to loft quickly. 'I didn't want to wake anyone. Are you the only one here? God it's cold. Is there no fire in here?'

'No. You should have come in! You were out there for so long.'

'I thought there were at least three people in here.' I began hanging up my wet stuff around the hut. It had a small table, a stainless steel bench and six bunks. It was a tidy, clean, newish hut, but it was bloody freezing.

'No! It's just me,' she said. 'I'm Lea. What is your name? Are you on the TA? You were so brave to walk in the dark and cold!'

'Brave or stupid.'

I got into my sleeping bag in my damp clothes and we swapped trail stories for a while, but eventually I had to cinch the hood shut to try to keep the heat in.

'Goodnight,' I said into the dark. 'Look forward to actually meeting you in the morning.'

'Yes, Naomi, I look forward to seeing your face!'

My limbs were still icy to the touch and I'd started really shivering, shaking uncontrollably in my cold sleeping bag. I had the vague sense that this wasn't a good thing, but I was so tired. The rain pushed against the windows. Lea and I drifted off and slept for ten hours.

* * *

I woke when the sun breached the ridgeline and shone into the hut windows, and realised I was deeply, deliciously warm. It was 7.30a.m. I lay there for a while, luxuriating, then sat up and greeted Lea properly.

She turned out to be a German woman in her late 20s, a northbounder like me, but walking only the South Island. She

136

had a winning smile and two dark blonde braids, which she was freshly twining now, sitting up on her bunk in a black thermal top and leggings.

She made coffee and breakfast and chattered about the trail, the people she'd met and the side trips she'd done over the past few months. Then she slipped into her shoes and disappeared across the clearing to the long-drop while I got up and fussed over my own meal. After a while she came back into the hut and stood by her bunk, rubbing her lower tummy. Her pep had vanished.

'I have to tell you something, Naomi, and it is a little personal, as we have just met,' she said, furrowing her brow. 'I have not pooped for four days.'

'Oh dear,' I said.

'What is the word?'

'Constipated. Well, you'd say that you are constipated, or you have constipation.'

'I am constipated,' she repeated. 'I have constipation. This is not English I wanted to know.'

Lea told me she was normally a vegetarian and ate a lot of fresh foods, but had just spent a few days in Nelson with a guy and had indulged in potato wedges, fried foods and too many bananas – which, as everyone knows, she informed me, can really block you up. Yesterday, she'd truly started suffering.

'I felt so awful last night when you arrived that I couldn't get up, so I was shining my torch and calling out, trying to tell you to come in out of the cold.' Well, I thought. I wish I'd realised that before I'd stunk out my clothes with Thai curry for the next nine days and given myself stage-one hypothermia.

We put our cold and wet clothes back on, packed up our gear and set off for Hunters Hut at a very late 8.45a.m., immediately squelching through a cold, muddy bog. Lea walked ahead, saying she was determined to adopt a positive attitude and walk through her pain.

'The trail gives, the trail provides. It is always like this,' she said. 'Every day is a new challenge and you need to solve it.'

'You can do this,' I said, grimacing as I struggled to extricate my back foot from a deep bit of bog. 'You can poop.'

'I am a strong, independent woman. I can cope!'

* * *

Te Araroa skirts the border of the Dun Mountain mineral belt, a desert-like patch of bright red and orange rock pushed northwest from Fiordland along the Alpine Fault. We walked through sharp flakes of iron- and magnesium-rich rock, clambering over broken outcrops and fording the streams that tumbled into the Motueka River, which feeds so much of Tasman's fertile plains to the northeast.

After a couple of hours, Lea's pace and conversation slowed. She sat down on the side of the track and requested a bathroom break.

'I will try again, OK? Do you want to go ahead?'

'OK,' I said. 'Good luck!'

'I hope I will have a good review.'

I walked on a bit then sat on the side of the track to wait for her, admiring the stark divide between the two types of vegetation growing on the different rock bases. One side was lush beech, the other a range of short, spiky and stubby alpine plants, the only species that could survive on the poor soil.

Lea staggered up the path a little while later. 'Any luck?' I said brightly, like I'd happened upon her fishing from a wharf.

'A tiny bit,' she said. 'I worked hard for it. But it's better than nothing.'

We walked on, chatting about the side trips she'd taken off the TA. Before she'd gone to Nelson and ruined her bowels, she'd walked up Mt Misery and fallen into the sublime; she'd had the tiny four-bunk hut to herself, with its beautiful view of folded ranges.

'It was the best sunset I'd ever seen,' she said. 'I could poop. Everything was nice.'

'The dream,' I agreed.

But what had been a bit funny in the morning slowly became more alarming as the day went on. Every hour or so, poor Lea would double over in pain, grasp her stomach and call for a break. By mid-afternoon the light was waning and the mist settling in, and as we picked our way over an enormous shattered riverbed of orange rock, I started getting worried about her. She looked awful.

We weren't going to make Hunters Hut before dark; thankfully, Porters Creek Hut was nearby. I started wishing I had phone reception so I could Google horrible terms like 'impaction' and find out what to do. Could you hurt yourself by not pooping for four days? How long was too long? I mentally rifled through the first-aid kit in my pack, but the only digestive cure I had was pills to stop diarrhoea. What could I do? I pulled out Caroline and Simon's inReach and laboriously texted Doug, who had an ecology degree and knew a bit about rongoā: *What plants are good for constipation?*

'I wanted a physical challenge,' Lea said at another stop. 'But not like this. What do you call the painful stuff before birth? It comes in waves.'

'Contractions?'

'Yes. I have contractions.'

'Jesus Christ.'

'I feel like such a burden,' she wailed. 'I'm usually really fast and fit and I'm slowing you down. You should go on.'

'We've been through too much already,' I told this crippled, beautiful woman whom I'd known for nineteen hours, ten of those mutually unconscious. 'I can't leave you when you feel this bad. What if you need help? And you've been in so much pain all this time – I need to stay and meet the real Lea.'

'You know when people drink bad water,' she said. 'I need to do that. Maybe I'll go and drink out of that river.'

'I wonder if constipation merits the PLB,' I said, only half-joking; she did not look well. Then a thought occurred to me. 'My friend Lauren is coming in to meet me the day after tomorrow.' I held the inReach aloft. 'Should I text her and get her to bring laxatives?'

'Oh my God!' Lea said. 'I will take anything. I will take pills or something you put in your ass. I will take anything. I don't care how much it costs.'

I sat down and sent a message to Lauren, who responded saying yes.

'Say thanks very much to her and she's an angel!' Lea called from behind another bush.

It was getting quiet out here. Neither of us had seen anyone else on trail in the last day. The Red Hills Hut book showed only Ethan and Hugh had been through recently, as it snowed and stormed on the ridge, along with Isaac, a Kiwi guy Brittany and I had met in Blue Lake Hut. Ethan and Hugh had apparently met him too, because Isaac was now a part of their interminable circle of banter.

Where are you, Isaac? Scared of a bit of snow? Ethan had written.

Is that why you guys hid here for two days? Isaac taunted back two days later, though of course they'd never see it.

*　*　*

We crossed a last, glassy stream to make it to the six-bunk Porters Creek Hut, and called it a day. We'd walked just

11km, but it was nearly 4p.m. and rain was threatening. Lea immediately stripped naked at the hut's tank and washed herself in the freezing water.

'I have nothing to hide from you now,' she said.

I lit the fire and we hung up our gear and made some meals, then I huddled in my sleeping bag as Lea tried different concoctions: caffeine gels, water, dried fruit, my vitamin pills, my magnesium tablets. She lay back on her bunk, massaging her belly.

'In Germany we have a phrase: "Small steps lead to Roma", and I think it's a bit like this,' she said.

Doug had also replied on the inReach, saying koromiko tea might work, but even if a stunted version was growing on these toxic soils, I didn't know the plant on sight and would be too unsure to identify it without access to the internet.

The tiny hut grew warm enough that our clothes dried and we could lounge about wearing only one layer – a total luxury. The wind blew hard all night, lashing rain against the windows. Mice cavorted in the woodpile. I woke up a couple of times and heard the rough weather beating down the glass and worried a bit about how Lea would cope tomorrow. I was thankful that the dicey Richmond Ranges were blessed with huts every few hours' walk.

The next morning, the clouds lifted and Lea pooped. All her ministrations over the previous five days had finally worked. I was making breakfast when I heard a whoop from outside, and she burst into the hut, clutching her hand sanitiser and toilet paper and beaming with pride and delight.

'I did it!'

'Yes!' I said, and we hugged. I was nearly as relieved as her.

* * *

It was in the Richmond Ranges that I began to remember my dreams again. The nights were longer, falling now at 5.30p.m. I was finally sleeping more, and with greater ease and peace; I was in bed at 6.30p.m. now and asleep by 8. I'd be comatose until midnight, then lie awake for a couple of hours until I fell asleep again and woke to the sun rising over the mountains. My main joy was my winter-weight sleeping bag; after each day of battling the indifferent landscape, I took deep pleasure in the moments it settled over my sore, chilled body, comforting me like a pile of laundry fresh from the dryer.

I'd left behind the feverish summer days of rushing through golden southern landscapes for fourteen hours. Now my exposed skin was always cold to the touch, and in the mornings, climbing the scree or a dirt slope, I saw thousands of tiny trunks of thrusting ice crystals, each bearing a clump of soil, breaking down the mountain as it was pushed up from below.

Lea and I met Lauren at Mid Wairoa Hut and the three of us walked for two days along the alpine route, the toughest part of Te Araroa, ascending and descending thousands of metres in a day. When we dipped down to Hacket Hut near Nelson, we went our separate ways: Lauren back to the normal world, Lea to rush ahead and catch her flight overseas, and me to finish the last two days of the Richmond Ranges alone. It was the first time I'd been by myself since Otira, which was now one month, two storms and more than 300km behind me. It had been another tough ten days tramping 139km of alpine terrain, relief found only in the views, the companionship, and my cold-skin dips in clear rocky rivers, so blue and beautiful I could hardly believe them.

I got to Rocks Hut, my 'home' hut, the one closest to Nelson, opened my food bag for a snack, and found laxative powder everywhere instead. Lauren had been true to her promise and had packed in Molaxole for Lea, and I'd added it to my first-aid kit. Somehow it had torn and coated everything in my pack, even wedging itself into the corners.

I laid out everything at the end of the hut bench to wash it. It would get cold soon, and the sun-warmed hut would chill quickly. I lit the fire. There were coffee rings and chocolate crumbs on the table; Lea had been here this morning and had a snack. I recognised her almond Whittaker's. I pulled a cloth off the hut wire and wet it to wipe down the table, then paused. Next to the crumbs, curled in a delicate C, was a single golden hair.

* * *

I walked slowly through the Marlborough Sounds with Mum, Samantha and Virginia, enjoying a bit of a holiday along the Queen Charlotte Track. We spent an evening watching blue-green phosphorescence bloom around the jetty at Mistletoe Bay, and then Mum and Virginia returned home while Sam and I walked on. I farewelled her at Furneaux Lodge, standing on the jetty as the water taxi pulled away. I held my arm in the air for a long time, waving. From now on I'd be by myself again.

It rained on my last two days in the South Island. Resolution Bay Camp was deserted, and as I descended to the bay from the Queen Charlotte Track I wasn't sure if I was in the right spot. But I could see small cabins arrayed down the slope, a collection of older huts with their backs to the hillside. A thread of smoke curled from a chimney down by the shore, and I headed towards it as I realised it was the reception building, and that everything in the sounds faced the sea.

The water was calm under a layer of evening mist, reflecting the deep green of the bush. When I eventually found Simon, the proprietor, he told me it was the 49th year the place had been running. From the shelf in reception I bought a packet of salt-and-vinegar chips, a pilsner and a packet of two-minute noodles for dinner. Simon, his uncle and I appeared to be the only people in the whole place.

Simon showed me to my little cabin, handing me two lanterns and pointing out the shower across the way. I said goodnight and closed the door. Small, wooden and painted white, the cabin felt half-sized, like an old yacht. There was a kitchen/dining room and two tiny bedrooms – as small as berths, really. A diminutive gas oven, but no heating. A massive tree outside the window was dropping yellow leaves.

I hung my wet clothes lavishly around the cabin, and noticed my merino T-shirt was getting threadbare across the shoulders. It was only 5p.m. but the encroaching gloom pushed me through my small daily tasks: wash, make dinner, air my gear. I boiled the noodles, then put on my headlamp and walked down to the wharf with the beer, hoping for more of the phosphorescence we'd seen at Mistletoe Bay. But heavy rain was coming and the water was disturbed, with mist still hanging low on the dark coves and headlands. The other cabins were cold and shuttered, the camp grass growing long. Several fat and unconcerned possums chewed fruit on the ground as I walked past, and a weka screeched and darted into the bush.

The waves were breaking more insistently now, and when I walked onto the wharf and shone my headlamp onto the water the surface fractured into mottled, bubbly glass. I stood there in the dark and drank my beer and listened to the wooden steps down to the pontoon knocking in the swell and the cries of paradise ducks flying low overhead.

Tomorrow I would wake in the dark and pack my still-damp clothes and walk two hours to Ship Cove to finish walking up the South Island. I would catch the 10a.m. Cougar Line boat to Picton, then the evening *Strait Feronia* ferry to Wellington, and then bus to Waikanae so I could meet Zuzana, the Czech hiker I had met at Birchwood. We were planning to catch a good weather window to walk the Tararua Ranges that week, before I'd return to Wellington and walk the city north. At Furneaux

Lodge, I had texted Zuzana someone's trip report on the Tararua section, with a cheery note, and now in a slice of reception at the wharf I picked up her response: *That article is terrifying. It sounds worse than the Richmonds.*

Did it? I had saved the story offline, and read the first line again now: 'Friends, when was the last time you felt like you were taking your life in your hands and preparing to fling it away like dust in the wind?'

Oops.

We will just have to keep an eye on the weather, I replied lamely, but the message didn't send before the rain began to hammer down.

I ducked back to my cold little cabin and got into bed with the tiny lantern, holding it above a book I'd found. I was wearing my beanie and down jacket. The rain beat on the roof like a drum and dripped heavy outside my window. It was as black as pitch out there, and I thought of the raw yellow gashes of landslides I'd been walking past all week.

It was 6.30p.m. on Wednesday, 1 May, and I wanted to go home. An earthquake had woken me the night before, and the stab of fear had stayed with me that day. Usually when the weather heaved down or the wind roared and I was suddenly scared of landslides or floods or an earthquake, Doug would be there to tell me why we were safe.

I had walked more than 1300km along the spine of the South Island to the very outer finger of these drowned river valleys and was now at the end of the line, just a few bays back from the heaving mass of Cook Strait and the North Island beyond. I had already spied it, seen the cool blue cone of Taranaki from the top of Mt Starveall and the shores of the North Island from the ridge between Kenepuru Sound and Queen Charlotte. At the beginning, I had loved seeing the land ahead. I'd been so excited to sight the Takitimu Mountains from the top of Bald Hill in Southland. But now I simply felt tired.

I still had 1715km to go. It did not seem possible that I'd be able to walk it, and I didn't want to. I had been more than four months away from home and I wanted my life back. I wanted to wear an old cotton sweatshirt hot from the dryer and tear the foil off a fresh tub of yoghurt and stand at the fridge spooning it up. I wanted to mow the lawn and eat bread and butter and drive a car and fold the towels nicely and put my slippers beside the bed and set out cups of coffee for my friends, with biscuits on a plate.

'Come home,' Doug had said. 'Winter over with me. Go back in the spring.'

But I couldn't. I couldn't even explain it. I felt possessed.

I stared at the white tongue-and-groove walls and into the blackness beyond the narrow doorframe of the tiny bedroom. I closed my eyes and went out of my body and flew back to Furneaux Lodge and beyond. The line unfurled again in my head, as it did each night while I waited for sleep: back through the beech forests, tarns and farmland, glacial terraces, the whio and state highways and sunlit ranges and scree, the parched earth of mid-Canterbury and summer snow above Queenstown and a blue dome of Southland sky, all of it a whole season ago, a quarter trip around the sun.

I felt myself back in the body that had seen those things, my little toe pinched between boulders in a shimmering river, my poles vibrating in its flow; my breath coming ragged on a pass, my feet throbbing so much I cried and my skin slimy with sweat, swearing at speeding utes on a gravel road, stepping quietly over roots in dappled forest light.

As much as I didn't want to walk the rest of the trail, nothing short of catastrophic injury would stop me now. The rain would cease, the world would turn into the morning sun and I would get up again, pack my bag and go. I had to finish. I had to follow the line. But it meant there were months more risk, pain, cold, fear, hunger and solitude to come.

* * *

The rain had cleared by the morning, and I was on the trail at 7.30a.m. to meet the water taxi. I put my poles away and ran some of it, anxious that Simon's estimate of two hours to Ship Cove would be wildly off and I'd miss my boat. When I got to the crest of the last hill before the rocky clay trail wound down into the bay, I saw the horizon and Motuara Island framed by ferns, a sentinel at the entrance to Cook Strait.

The sun was steaming off a wooden seat overlooking the bay, sending white spirals into the air. Every few steps the breeze shook loose drips from last night's downpour, and they hit my face as I followed a stream past nīkau and mamaku, rounding a corner to see a long wooden jetty extending into the bay. I walked as though in church over manicured lawns, past the carved pou, over a small bridge, and then saw the hulking white concrete Cook monument I'd thought about every day since I started.

I stopped dead and stared at it, unable to approach. I walked up to it and dropped my poles, then rested my head and hands on the concrete and cried. For the pain and loneliness I had endured to get here. For the uncertainty and fear to come.

The bay was empty aside from a scuttling weka. I dropped my pack and took off all my clothes and edged over the rocks into the sea. I waded out and ducked under, emerging with a gasp from the shock of the cold. On the beach I pushed the water off my limbs with the sides of my hands and dressed, shivering. As I walked back to the jetty, the *Sounds Navigator* chugged up and tied off, and groups of walkers poured out, setting off into the hills. I boarded for the two-and-a-half-hour journey back to Picton, stowed my pack, and sat down and looked out the window as the boat plumed away from the bay.

A pod of tutumairekurai, or Hector's dolphins, sliced through the water, one of them as small as a puppy, and we all craned to see. The sea salt dried on my skin. In a few hours I'd be back on these waters, heading north, with 1313.4km under my heels and the rest of the country to go.

CHAPTER 8

MERETOTO SHIP COVE TO TE KŪITI

I tripped over a rope of supplejack lying across the track and smacked into the ground, my face landing on the handle of my walking pole. It split my lip and I felt the shock reverberating in my teeth. I got up, brushed the leaf litter from my pants, tasted blood.

'Just *fuck* this!' I burst out. 'I hate this so much! I just HATE THIS! I just want to sit on a couch and watch TV with some fucking popcorn and some fucking M&Ms!'

At that second, a young man with a moustache, wearing a stylish beige rain-jacket, rounded a corner on the trail above me. He was out for a run. He was the second person I'd seen all day.

'Oh hi,' I said. 'How are you?'

'Yeah, pretty good,' he said. 'Yourself?'

'Fucked off.'

'Yeah, it's not the most fun track.' He smiled. He must have heard me bitching.

'At least it's not raining,' I said.

'Oh, it's about to.'

Great.

It was the first day of June, of winter. It was my second day in the Tararua Ranges. It was the third time I'd tried to tackle them. Zuzana had bailed on our original plans while I was on the bus on the way to meet her, and then I hadn't wanted to walk them by myself. They were notorious, it was winter, I'd not been up there before, and there was no one else on trail. The ridge-tops were in cloud nearly 80 per cent of the year. The wind could be abominable. People often got into serious trouble up there, and even died. Walkers talked about crawling on their hands and knees along the tops – and that was in summer. I wanted as little risk as possible.

A couple of weeks of work had come up in the first half of May, so I spent the last month of autumn walking Te Araroa from Wellington to Whanganui, putting easy road and city kilometres under my belt. I waited for a good weather window to walk the Tararua Ranges, and for company to magically appear. But as May turned to June, I had to accept I'd need to walk them alone before winter set in too deeply. This first week of June the weather looked good, so I'd decided to go for it.

I wasn't in the best frame of mind. I was nervous about the trip ahead, and tired. My lips were permanently chapped, my skin dry. The white half-moons on my thumbnail beds were weird; they were pierced with pink, and white spots bloomed on the rest of my nails. My hands had grown calloused from the hiking poles, and when I took a break from the poles to walk these roads, the skin began to peel.

The North Island had felt like a chore so far. A high point had been staying with my friend Noon and spending a morning walking the city with her, but otherwise I'd trudged next to highways and across hills stuck with windmills and singing transmission pylons. When I'd pitched my tent for the first time at a busy city holiday park, I found a yellowed South Island beech leaf cornflake in its corner, and I'd felt very sad. I picked it up on my fingertip and put it in the tent's side pocket to keep.

Now that holidaymakers were long gone, I was regularly bailed up by single older men in holiday park kitchens while I was sitting there charging my devices. They leaned back on the bench as the kettle boiled for their tea and crossed their arms and asked why my husband had let me gallivant around the country alone like this. They always said 'gallivant'. And then they always asked: 'Aren't you afraid?'

'Of what?' I'd reply. But they never said: 'Men.'

* * *

The only bright spot in the North Island so far had been meeting trail angels for the first time, a Te Araroa phenomenon that was more common here than in the South Island. These were people who hosted walkers for a night, for koha or a small fee, and they had all been delightful. Nicky and Fergus had left me an avocado chocolate tart in the fridge. In Feilding, Abby's daughter showed me her Sylvanian Family collection. I saw the 10 May aurora, one of the strongest in the past five hundred years, with Megan and Lance, who excitedly drove us around the hills looking for the best view of the pink and green streaking through the sky.

I'd also enjoyed talking to more people in general. At the Palmerston North BP, I had gone down the back to eat a pie at their bench and sat next to a woman and a man in trackpants, eating ice creams.

'You walking?' the man said, indicating my pack. I told him a bit about the past few days on trail. The woman smiled. 'You don't know who you're talking to.'

It was Gerald Manderson, a retired dairy farmer and one of New Zealand's greatest long-distance walkers. Gerald was a New Zealand Centurion, one of just fourteen people in the country who had qualified as such by walking 100 miles in under 24 hours. In 2001, he'd walked 500km in four days and 19 hours. He'd walked 200km in 40 hours in 2010. His national walking records had held for decades. Gerald looked about 65. He was 81.

I chatted to people who sat at bus stops with me on weekday mornings. One man wandered up holding a mug and sat down on the bench. Then he said, 'Excuse me, I appear to have forgotten to put a teabag in my cup,' and left.

Another was Gwen. She had had a hard life: she was diabetic, had married an alcoholic, and was struggling to live on the pension. We bonded over a real-life soap opera we'd witnessed while we waited for the bus in Waikanae. A teen boy had got out of a police car holding a red New World bag full of clothes, crying. The cops drove off. A girl approached him, shouting that she wanted her EFTPOS card back.

'Fuck off, you crazy bitch!' he shrieked hysterically. 'I'm not supposed to have contact with you!' She began kicking over road cones, then picking them up and hurling them at him. I was impressed; this would have taken quite a bit of strength.

He ran off, and she chased him down the street, screaming. *'Give me back my fucking EFTPOS card!'*

'The trouble is, there's nothing for the young people to do,' Gwen said. I appreciated this magnanimous mindset. She was wearing a white woollen beanie with diamantés on it. I offered to get her a drink from the dairy.

'Sprite Zero,' she said immediately, and I walked off, jangling the coins in my pocket. 'Or a Diet Coke!'

* * *

I trudged from Waikanae to Parawai Lodge, the first hut I'd encounter in the Tararua section. I'd been walking in towns for a month and I felt the relief of being in the bush, back to my familiar rhythms. The muscle memory of checking my pack, my tent, clipping things closed, helped remind me of the person I'd built in the South Island. But I'd made a big error in Waikanae: I'd forgotten to buy gas for my stove. I hadn't been actually tramping in the North Island so far – I'd been road-walking between dairies, and it had slipped my mind.

This was a grim development. I walked along, justifying continuing without the gas, instead of wasting a day going back to buy it and potentially losing my precious good weather. I tried to ignore the little rush of unease and think logically. Many thru-hikers walked stoveless – though probably not as many in winter as in summer. I was lucky in that I hadn't packed dehydrated meals for these four to five days through the Tararuas. For a change, I'd brought along heavier, pre-cooked pasta meals. Instead of using gas, I could heat them up slowly on the hut fireplaces, I reasoned. The forest was infernally damp, but I was hoping there'd be at least a bit of firewood around. If not, I'd just eat the food cold. I had plenty of calories in the form of chocolate, nuts, cheese, muesli bars and all the rest. Plus I had the calories I'd stored all over my body for years.

But it gave me a bad feeling to have forgotten something, to be venturing up here without a way to make something hot quickly, which would help in case of threatening hypothermia. Not just for myself, but to help others, too. Was it an ominous sign? In the bush, alone, it was harder to avoid this anxiety trap of paying too much attention to imagined signs, premonitions and warnings. I felt closer to my ancient ancestors here, and visions sometimes came very strongly. At those times I was witnessing the neuroscience of spirituality in action, parts of my brain that had lain dormant in my godless life so far. The bush brought them out.

I'd had it with the voice in the Longwood Forest. I'd had it again when washing naked by a South Island river. I'd felt a giddiness come over me as time ripped open and I was transported back thousands of years. I was suddenly in the body of my ancestor, a woman, doing just as I was doing. Washing in the bush, in the sun, with a piece of rag, on the riverside sand. She used the same water. She had the same body. The same thoughts. The same peace. Maybe she had thought of her own ancestors this way, too. It was fleeting, but I was there with her.

With only my senses to rely on out here, everything seemed loaded with portent. And there was nobody else's senses to use, either. After being alone for so long, I now had a deep knowledge of how and why humans banded together. I let the signs come. They meant something; they were keeping me safe. I tried to respect them, to allow them to touch me while thinking my way around them.

I could do without gas. Avoiding hypothermia didn't depend on a hot drink. I could eat my food cold. I'd keep my sleeping bag dry. There were enough huts up here. I could wait out bad weather for ages. I had my PLB. I had my tent. People were watching my GPS tracker. I could send a 'Safe' signal via a button on its case. I kept on.

* * *

I walked the valley floor, admiring the glossy, green, cup-like ferns climbing over everything. At Parawai Lodge I met Andrew and Rebecca, who were on an anniversary tramping trip. The sun had dropped behind the ridge at 2.45p.m., and everything was mildewing. Andrew and Rebecca spent some time deciding what to have for dinner. They had spread a nice array of dehydrated meals on the table.

'We usually have couscous, but since it's our anniversary we decided to branch out,' Rebecca said. 'We thought we could go to a hotel and spend hundreds, plus breakfast, but instead we got some ten-buck standard hut tickets and saved ourselves nine hundred bucks.'

In the late afternoon I was already in my sleeping bag when a hunter came in, leaned his firearm against the bench, and said, 'This is a nice cosy hut. This hut could tell some stories.'

His name was Dave, and he fell into conversation with Andrew and Rebecca. He inspected the fire Andrew had lit and told him how to lay a good one, then picked up a few of their dehydrated meals and proceeded to instruct Rebecca on how to best cook them. He dropped his cup, and it hit the floor with a metallic clatter.

'Whoops,' he said. 'Every animal within a hundred k will have heard that.' He told us about his days deer-culling in these hills. 'We'd spend two weeks up there, go into town to collect our pay, get on the piss, find a couple of floozies, and back into the bush again. That fire's smoking a bit – has it gone out?'

Rebecca asked if she could look through his night-vision hunting monocular, and Dave was only too happy to oblige. He took her outside and showed her, and then I wanted to have a look, too. I went out and Dave showed me the land, newly bright in the dark. My breath misted.

'Take a look up on that ridge,' he said. I tried to get the angle right. I saw the pit toilet nearby, glowing white with the heat generated by human excrement. I saw rocks glowing white, still warm from the day. Then I saw the birds, small white shapes sitting in trees. And then I saw the possums: large, white, round silhouettes sitting there, their tails hanging down. In tree after tree after tree.

Dave had two firearms with him: one for deer, and one to take down the possums.

'I'm going to crack a few tonight,' he said. 'They need to go. If I see one, they're gone. Give DOC a bit of a hand. Only good possum's a dead possum.'

* * *

I stayed at Waitewaewae Hut the next night, and ate my cold, wet tomato pasta; there was no dry firewood. I got into my sleeping bag at 3.30p.m. again. Some students arrived and filled the hut with chatter, and I silently welcomed their presence.

'What's "tanobo"?' one young woman said, reading my entry in the hut book.

'That's me,' I said. 'TA NOBO. Te Araroa. Northbound.'

The forecast had been for fine weather but it had been overcast and drizzly the whole time. The rain really started sheeting down at 5.30p.m. It was forecast to blow more than 100km an hour up there on the ridge tonight, and I could hear the wind roaring in the treetops.

In the morning the students and I stood around outside, looking up at the cloud on the tops of the ranges and debating. I was going up, but they were headed back to town.

'A storm is exciting,' the young woman said. 'Be cool to be up there in a storm.' Mired in my fear, I hadn't thought of that. I patted the hip pocket containing my PLB, by now an automatic gesture. *I can always turn back.*

I spent the day climbing from the valley floor up a long, steep ridge to 1462m Mt Crawford. I walked through rainforest, admiring pīwakawaka and miromiro leaping among the dripping rimu, mataī, mamaku, the trees laden with huge balls of moss, the ground covered in ecstatic bursts of crown ferns. Spiderwebs caught between trees were glistening with diamonds of moisture, shivering in shafts of white-misted sunlight. I could see lines of other, further ridges through tiny breaks between the trees. This low light changed everything. It hit one thickly moss-covered tree and I could suddenly see the tree's real shape, its skeleton, strong beneath its fuzzy green exterior, illuminated like a pair of legs through a sunlit skirt.

I walked along the blustery, exposed ridge, on the way to

descend to Nichols Hut at 1156m. It was cloudy up here but it wasn't heavy and settling; it was white, airy. I realised these misty tops didn't scare me as they had in the South Island. I no longer felt I would immediately die of exposure as it began to cloak me. Every one of my inhalations became laden with cold beads of moisture. I was breathing in clouds.

* * *

There was a stag and a hind grazing near Nichols Hut when I arrived. I scared them away as I descended from the ridge, and watched them crash into the bush. There was no dry firewood again that night, and I got cold. The next day I quickly got colder, wet and tired, and stayed that way. Tired of the mud, my pants heavy with it; tired of pushing against the wind, of wiping away the tears it whipped into the corners of my eyes. I was gashed and bruised. My shoulder ached and so did my legs, from the slips and falls and stabbing of broken branches in the last few days. My knee had twisted and gone dangerously backwards on one fall, and it was swollen and sore, seizing up.

Walk it off.

Drained of energy, I stopped very early at Dracophyllum Hut, a two-bunk bivvy at nearly 1100m, and got into my sleeping bag to eat – a lot. The hut was mildewy and smelled damp. No fire. It was just an emergency shelter; there would have been no dry firewood anyway. It was tied down with wire cables at all four corners, securing it to Earth against the roaring winds.

I thought of Doug's system of firewood stacks at home: night logs, day logs for when we were home, day logs for when we weren't home, spring logs, and big, dense, hardwood winter logs. God, he was good at lighting a fire, I thought. Somehow he filled the entire firebox and set it roaring in seconds, a skill I'd never mastered.

There was so much I had longed for out in the bush. But shivering in these damp, cold huts, in my winter sleeping bag, wearing my down jacket, two merino tops, merino socks, merino leggings, possum-merino gloves, fleece hoodie, wool beanie and fleece neck gaiter, I thought constantly of the luxury of our home fireplace and the fires Doug lit. The baskets full of newspaper and cardboard and the pinecones I'd gathered, the firelighters and hearth brush, and most of all his precise stacks of split pine and beech and blackwood and oak, the edges squared and the tops covered with corrugated iron, and all of it so dry it blazed into life with a single match.

Having spent the previous seven years in a damp icebox of an ex-state house, we loved that fire. In winter we would retreat upstairs to the tiny mezzanine and lie about like lizards in the rising heat. This hut had only my body heat to warm it, and I was having trouble just heating myself.

I lit some candles, which helped with the drear. At 5.15pm I saw streaks of pink in the sky and unzipped the bottom of my sleeping bag to shuffle outside and see the world transformed. I walked up to the helicopter pad and stared about in wonder. The mist had finally left, with just a few wisps caught in the valleys, and a clear, darkening blue sky fell from horizon to horizon. The peaks I had ascended over the last few days cascaded back to the south. I could see dark mountains shadowed in pink, far on the horizon, and knew it was the South Island and the mountains of Blenheim and Nelson, of home.

I saw why people fell in love with the Tararuas. They were hard-won but the rewards were remarkable, more so for being fleeting. As the sun lowered, the pink and blue faded and merged and glowed stronger. I stayed out until my hands froze, still wrapped in my sleeping bag, walking around the helipad taking in the 270-degree view. Darkness fell at 5.30p.m. I wanted to watch the stars come out, but it was too cold. I went back to the hut and burrowed into my sleeping bag and slept for thirteen hours.

I woke at dawn the next day, feeling better. The weather was still clear, fine and beautiful, with sunrise painted above rows of ridgelines. I had got my rare, clear day in the Tararuas, and it was energising. It was mostly downhill from here. I'd stopped too early the day before, so I decided to make the most of the good weather and walk two days in one, straight out, past two huts, to the Poads Road end and then hitch to Levin Holiday Park.

I sprang across the ridgelines and tramped up and down through the forests of twisted, ancient beech, thickly cloaked in green moss. But the 21km to get off the muddy, rooty ranges took longer than I thought and I walked into the winter evening, tired and cold. And hungry. I had eaten more than I thought on this chilly trip, but I'd had nothing hot for days. I had only 2 per cent phone battery left, so I rang Doug to ask if he could organise some kind of food to be waiting for me at the Levin Holiday Park. I broke down when he answered.

'Maybe the owner has a spare can of baked beans or something,' I said through tears, feeling desperate. 'Toast.'

He did better than that. Thirteen hours after I left Dracophyllum Hut, Doug had his friend Alice waiting for me at the road-end.

'I hear your husband's worried about you,' she said as I walked up, tired but happy to be out under the stars and with the prospect of food closer. She drove me straight to McDonald's.

* * *

I had already walked the road sections from here to Whanganui while waiting to enter the Tararuas, so Alice drove me there from Levin and I struck out on fresh trail. Going northbound, I couldn't paddle down the Whanganui River as southbound Te Araroa hikers normally did, and no tourist boats were operating this time of year, so I was walking the 70 km up it, on the river road. At Pipiriki, where the road finished, I had decided to leave Te Araroa for the first time and walk on the road to Ohakune, then around Mt Ruapehu on the Round the Mountain Track to reconnect with Te Araroa at Waimarino. It was a puzzle. There was also no accommodation along the river right now; it was essentially closed for the season.

Doug's ancestry includes Te Ātihaunui-a-Pāpārangi, an iwi on the river, so I was grateful when his relative Frances offered me a bed in her home at Rivertime Accommodation. She organised me a place to stay on the second night as well, in a cabin next to Matahiwi Gallery, also closed for the winter. But then I got a bit stuck. Most walkers on this side of the river would stay at the old Jerusalem convent, but when I emailed enquiring, they replied that there was a group booking and they'd have to check if there was a spare bed.

I didn't hear back and there was no phone reception up the river, so I decided to pop in to see if I could find out. It was raining as I walked from Matahiwi, and a stream of cars rolled past. Every second one paused to wind down their window and a woman would say, 'Are you all right, love? Do you need a ride?' I thanked them and waved them on. I was still walking every inch.

I arrived at the convent about 2p.m. and went looking for an admin person, but the rooms were full of people preparing for a wānanga rongoā that weekend, a class on traditional Māori medicine. This must have been the group booking.

'You look like a drowned rat,' a woman said. 'The jug's on – go and have a cup of tea and sit down in front of the fire.'

I could do with drying out a little if I had to walk on today. I took off my wet jacket and pants and steamed in my damp underlayers, sitting near the fire with a cup of tea and keeping the blaze going. I picked a book off the shelf and slung on a blanket, trying to warm up, as I spent so much time doing these days.

I was so accustomed now to solitude, to my small tasks of self-preservation. I had become used to plugging on alone, reliant on only my own mood and energy.

But this was no life. It wasn't even what I desired; I'd originally wanted to find a trail family. But I knew loneliness now, and how it sat in your gut as a yearning, a hunger, a twisting, radiating pain that on the worst days would make me stop on trail and double over in agony, gasping heaving sobs. I was desperate to lock eyes with another person, to have the relief of talking, of being perceived and understood.

But while I craved attention and connection from others, I was finding it harder to be with them; each fleeting encounter reminding me of how much I was losing by being so alone. I had forgotten how to be human. I simply felt estranged and awkward everywhere I went now, an oddity out of season, as unwanted as a housefly, and I was becoming pathologically averse to relying on people. Visiting the trail angels was intensifying these feelings; even though they were listed in the trail notes, even though I paid the koha or fee, I still felt the burden of unmatched generosity. On trail and out of society, I couldn't reciprocate kindnesses easily, especially serendipitous ones.

And yet the line pulled me on. I could no longer stay in one place unless I had to, to get food or to rest something aching, or wash my filthy, thinning clothes. The craving to walk overwhelmed all. My main solace was my Te Araroa Trail Mix playlist, to which

I added every good song I heard in a dairy or booming from a passing car. At 70 hours, it was getting long enough to entertain me indefinitely.

It took two whole hours to warm up, for the chill to leach from my bones. I spent the afternoon reading *The Double Rainbow*, about how Ngāti Hau had supported James K. Baxter's Jerusalem dreams, and the changes that the commune had wrought for both iwi and hippies. As I read, people bustled back and forth. I was better one-on-one than in a group; I talked for a while to a woman who had been a te Tiriti negotiator, and she told me the new government could expect a fight.

'They want to mine stewardship land?' she said. 'Whanganui will fight. All these women are here for rongoā. The health system is crashing. What will we do when the forests are gone?'

Across the hall, peals of laughter and song rang out from the wānanga, and when the door opened and closed I caught glimpses of rocks and plants on the floor. They were making chest rubs and cough syrups today. But although I still craved fun, relaxation and company, I was too shy to open the lounge door and go in, even though they'd invited me.

The ākonga streamed back and forth. They sat down and asked me what I was up to, where I was going.

'Faaar! Don't you miss your family?'

I said I did.

'You can stay and have a kai with us.' They had turned on music in the kitchen and begun singing while preparing food.

'You're going to have a kai with us later, eh?' a man named Jessey said, bringing in wood for the fire. 'You're staying here with us, eh? It's hosing down out there.'

The teacher came past, holding a bundle of greenery. 'Will you have a kai with us?' It felt rude to decline, rude to accept.

'I have some food ...' I started, but she was having none of it.

'Come on. Plates are over there.'

I filled my plate with potato salad, sushi, buttered bread rolls, French bread, pizza, salad and macaroni cheese. I sat there with the others, holding a cup of warm water with herbs floating in it, tearing at a soft roll. The ākonga talked about the Native Land Act 1909's impact on whāngai (adoption by a family member), and thus traditional practices of breast-feeding and wet-nursing.

'You can tell who's been doing their homework, eh,' the teacher said to me with a sly smile.

* * *

Jessey told me there was wifi outside, and pointed me to a picnic table under cover. He was from Ātene, downriver. I remembered seeing Ātene on the topo map; the settlement was nestled beside an ancient meander of the river that had once encircled a large hill, which stuck out like a keyhole. Jessey told me Ātene was 'the eye of the world'.

I went outside. A teenage girl, one of the students' daughters, joined me and we sat together in the dark, me checking messages, weather, map distances and accommodation further on while slowly downloading episodes of *Bridgerton*, and her chuckling at TikToks and reading me the current temperatures in various parts of the central North Island.

'It's fourteen degrees,' she said, looking at her phone. 'That's warm! It was two degrees the other day in Ohakune.'

'Yikes, that's cold. I'm headed there,' I said. As I couldn't travel on the river at this time of year, I watched it instead, from the road. I wanted to notice it and remember. How it swung around the bends, its upwellings, eddying out on the corners, slowly moving down towards the sea.

'Are you going around the Ruapehu track?'

'Yes, then doing the Tongariro Crossing, then walking north.'

Her whānau were from here, as well as Ohakune and Ruapehu. She sat on the narrow bench, untangling her silver necklace in the dark and showing me photos on her phone of the snow-clad mountain I was heading towards: Ruapehu, whom she called koro. 'He has his blanket of white now.'

She came to all the wānanga, she said, and was learning rongoā by osmosis. She was helping her mum with the reo. She asked about the trail.

'It's cool you're still motivated to keep going after all this time being alone,' she said, and her young voice became laden with compassion. 'Don't you miss your family?'

'The trail is kind of pulling me along,' I admitted. 'But I do want to go home.'

We fell silent, attracted to our bright phone screens like moths, and soon we both got too cold to hang around. She went back inside, to sit in the warm, fun room with the rest of the rongoā whānau that I was too shy to join, and I went uphill to try the door of the chapel. It was open.

I took off my shoes and walked the aisle, admiring how the ceiling was vaulted like an upturned boat. Empty of its people, it was cold inside, and damp. I dug out some cash and put it in the donation box, then found some koha for the meal they gave me, maybe for some tea and packets of biscuits for their next weekend workshop.

Of course they offered me one of the spare beds upstairs that night. The narrow nuns' beds had curtains that pulled around them, and heaters were scattered on the wooden floors. I was grateful to accept.

* * *

For the next week and a half, I walked up the Whanganui River to Raetihi and Ohakune, then traversed the central North Island mountains in the ice and snow on the Round the Mountain Track and the Tongariro Crossing, snatching the good days from a run of bad weather that brought rain and snow. I went home for a few days at Matariki to see my family. Doug was nearing mutiny as my trip ticked over six months; I'd said vaguely that I'd be done by now, and he was over the whole thing.

'Take a break,' he begged again. 'Stay with me for winter.' I still couldn't. But the day after I got home I was immediately knocked out by a flu that seared my throat, muffled my hearing with swelling and left my body weak and aching. I had to delay my return to the trail to lie on the couch staring at my pack, collapsed in the corner of the lounge. I was sick of the sight of it, sick of the layers of raw fabric on the pack's base where it had spent 2000km rubbing against my spine. I hated its smells of protein powder and jerky.

Most of all I was sick of its contents: the sad little pile of ziplocks patched with duct tape, the lumpy, compressed sleeping bag, the creeping mould on my sleeping mat, the mismatched tent pegs. I couldn't imagine hoisting that pack; the muscles that had been growing for months were melting into the couch fabric.

For two weeks I recovered, flattened by a hacking cough, living off my main cravings: toast, fresh coffee with cream, and oranges. Mum came around and made me my other craving, a 1990s childhood special I hadn't been able to stop thinking about: Coat'n'Cook chicken pieces baked in the oven, exploding with hot, savoury juices when I bit into the meat.

My illness at least solved Doug's sadness about me being away for so long. He came home from work each evening to find me ripe with nausea and crushed by exhaustion, laying my head on my folded arms at the dining table, complaining about my cough and making him assess my swollen neck glands.

We clashed a little, navigating each other again in our tiny cottage. I pointedly pushed in the dining-table chairs he left strewn about every time he got up from the table, blocking the house's narrow thoroughfares; he informed me one day that I always tilted the shower head up when I showered but never put it back down, so that for the entirety of our marriage he'd gotten sprayed with cold water when he turned it on; but that he, gentleman that he was, had spent eight years quietly tilting the shower head back down and not saying anything.

After two weeks of this he declared himself ready to face the next couple of months alone at home again.

'We've caught up,' he said. 'You get this trail done.' The morning we parted he said, 'Hey, you might see southbounders again soon.'

I was startled, but he was right. A few hardy walkers occasionally started at Cape Reinga in August, and by the time I'd clawed my way back to Waimarino to pick up the trail at the end of the Tongariro Crossing, it was 11 July. I still had more than 1000km to go, and I'd returned to trail with a lingering, tiring cough.

I spent ten days walking from the volcanoes to Te Kūiti, through Ōwhango and Taumarunui and over the Timber Trail in the Pureora Forest. Near Whakamaru I stayed with my childhood friend Becky and her family. Her six-year-old daughter Emma had written about me in her notebook. 'Noami is wlcing around the wld,' she'd written, 'wis no wan.'

I sounded out her phonetic spelling, then read it again, startled at her perceptiveness.

With no one.

I did walk alone. I didn't see anyone else on trail apart from a couple of cyclists. I had heard that the track through farmland to Te Kūiti wasn't well-formed, so I waited in my tent for two days for the heavy rain to cease so it wouldn't be as wet, then walked it carefully.

The rumours were true; in some places the trail was barely a goat path. About 10km from the town, edging down a grassy bank above the river, I slipped and fell off a little cliff. My right leg dropped and my left leg stayed on the track. I fell a metre or so into a cradling nest of blackberry and gorse. Not too far, but far enough to be scary. I lay there for a while, my hand on my PLB, waiting for the pain to set in. I didn't know if it had just been a branch, but I'd heard a snap.

The slippery slope was near vertical, but once I felt OK to stand I peeled the blackberry vines off my skin and clambered back up to the path, holding onto a tree with one hand and dragging up my pack with the other. I tested my knee; it hurt, but I could walk. There were just 10km to go and I needed to get myself out of trouble.

After about twenty minutes of stumbling and grimacing, I met two men walking towards me.

'Naomi?' one said. He was named Mike. And the other was also called Mike. Before I'd started the section, I had enquired with a local trail trust member, Peter, about the condition of the trail; he'd said it was a bit dodgy and they were fixing it, and to let him know when I had made it through. But I didn't get that message – I'd gone out of reception and then heavy rain had trapped me in my tent for two nights. He'd become worried and sent the Mikes in to look for me.

'We thought we might find a body!' Mike said cheerfully. I was glad they had not.

I walked out to their car. Mike offered to pick me up at the end of the trail and give me a bed for the night and dinner with him and his wife Jackie, plus a trip to the doctor's the next morning. They drove off, and I managed the last 5km alone, wincing when my knee twisted on slippery leaves and mud.

In the morning, Mike drove me to the doctor's, but I couldn't get an appointment for a few days so decided to bus north to stay with my aunt Lynda in Auckland and find a physio there. I limped up to a café window and the barista, Toops, asked what had happened to me. He gave me a flat white on the house. I booked a bus for that afternoon and sat in a café with an egg sandwich to wait.

I poked the straw into a chocolate milk and thought how touched I was by the spontaneous kindnesses of the last few days – and once again, by the joyful serendipity of the trail. Both of the Mikes' wives were named Jackie.

CHAPTER 9

AUCKLAND TO PĀKIRI

Mum happened to be visiting my aunt that week. She picked me up from the SkyCity bus terminal and we went back to Lynda's house in the Waitakere Ranges. Lynda made up the couch for me and they all listened patiently to my trail stories.

I described the cacophony of being in town; the lights, smells, and noise; of reeling when walking past people smelling strongly of shampoo, the bright colours in the shops, every sound feeling too loud.

'It's all green and brown and farm sheds out there, and then you come in here and it's full-on colour,' I said. 'It's a total sensory overwhelm.'

'It sounds like being on LSD,' Lynda, a child of the '60s, said to Mum in a stage whisper. Mum laughed.

'They're using that for mental health stuff now, aren't they?'

'Mmm,' Lynda said, floating around folding blankets and putting a side table and lamp next to my couch. 'I don't necessarily recommend it, actually.'

* * *

I got a physio appointment for the next day at Urban Athlete in Auckland's CBD, so Lynda dropped me off at the train into town. Jen diagnosed a sprain of my MCL, the medial ligament on the inside of my knee. She instructed me to keep off it for five days and then she would reassess.

The trunk of a huge kauri took up most of the view out Lynda's living-room window, and the Sky Tower glinted on the horizon. We watched the Olympics while eating peach crumble made from last summer's harvest. I remembered the places I'd been on trail where last summer's sun had struck me. Te Anau. Mavora. Among the dust and lizards of the Motatapu.

For five days I ate proper breakfasts, lunches and dinners. The rain cycled over in bursts. A ruru called at night, always from the same place. A man walked his dog past the dining-room window each day at 8.40a.m. I hobbled past the tall and silent kauri out the living-room window, grimacing in pain, not sure I'd be able to continue the walk. My hard-won calluses peeled off my toes. I would suffer getting them back.

But by the time I went back to see Jen, the pain and stiffness had reduced. There was a large photograph of what looked like a Timber Trail suspension bridge hanging in the examination room, and I stared hard at it, trying to place myself back there, under the sky and forest and light.

Jen manipulated my leg and pronounced me OK to continue walking if I put on an articulated knee brace, and kept surfaces even and my pack light. So I walked Auckland packless, in shorter chunks, starting at Tom Pearce Drive outside the airport and following the line threading through the city and over the volcanoes, past rough red-black volcanic walls, drowned mangroves, blackbirds scratching under trees, gutters scattered with nitrous oxide canisters and Monster cans, strings of Pita Pits and City Fitnesses and everywhere the smell of exhaust fumes, or garlic frying in butter, or honeysuckle, or the sea. I sat near the summit of Maungawhau and ate a chicken and avocado sandwich for lunch, admiring the weathered boardwalks and platforms that had been installed since I'd last been there, sharp against the glinting city skyline.

Ten days after I'd sprained my knee, I felt it was better enough to venture away from the safety of my auntie's and back to the trail proper, wearing my full pack. But I could still feel my knee complaining on downhills and when the ground was uneven underfoot. I decided that instead of returning to the slippery mud and grass tracks further south, I'd keep walking Auckland for a while to see how it went.

In Devonport, I worked up the courage to email Te Araroa founder Geoff Chapple to ask if I could buy him and his wife, fellow trail-founder Miriam Beatson, a coffee or lunch. He replied inviting me to stay the night. So I knocked on his blue front door the next afternoon. A fabric patch reading TRAIL ANGEL was affixed under the brass knocker. It was something an American would sew to their shirt while they were handing out sodas on the Pacific Crest Trail.

Geoff opened the door with a smile. He was just the same as the photos in his 2002 book that had inspired my journey – fit, energetic, lots of lively red hair. He showed me to the cosy space downstairs where they often hosted hikers, sometimes even plucking them off the beach and bringing them home: a bed, shower and kitchenette. Miriam was making dinner, and she greeted me with a big hug; they'd heard me rabbiting about the trail on Radio New Zealand earlier in the year. 'You made it!'

She'd baked walnut balls in a roux with broccoli, cauliflower, potatoes, pumpkin and kūmara from the garden, followed by feijoa crumble and vanilla ice cream. Geoff, a librettist as well as a journalist, found a recording of the trail song he'd written and performed with Don McGlashan and Annie Crummer in the early 2000s.

It was a funny thing that he was the one who had taken on the trail, Geoff mused, adding, 'Miriam was the walker in the relationship.'

'But he sat up in the bath one day and said, "I'm going to walk the whole thing",' Miriam said.

'It's my wedding anniversary today,' I confessed after a few hours' talking, and Miriam shrieked and clapped her hands together. 'Why didn't you tell us!?' She broke open a bottle of Deutz and some pita chips, and I told them about Doug's last words to me before I started the trail, about how if the Alpine Fault went I should stay out of the rivers in case a rockfall dammed them and then broke apart.

'There won't be much of the rivers left if that goes,' Miriam said. Geoff brought out his guitar and sung a song he and Miriam had composed about the Alpine Fault, and it reminded me of Otira, the West Coast's strong and muscular gorges.

Finally, at 11p.m., Geoff said, 'I notice you're yawning'. He had to be ready at 7.30a.m. for the grandchildren, and Miriam gave me some feijoa crumble and ice cream to take downstairs for breakfast. There was a Mt Somers Station wool blanket on the bed, and a bunch of fresh pink camellias on the dresser.

I lay in the little room, feeling awed at the thought of the dozens of hikers who had sheltered there before me, aware I was under the roof of the very people who had conceived and birthed the trail half my lifetime ago. It was the work of their lives, and all I had to do was enjoy it. I couldn't believe my fortune at meeting them, at being here at all, warm, fed and tucked into bed on the shores of volcanoes.

In the morning, Miriam called downstairs early as I was eating my breakfast ice-cream.

'Naomi! Would you like me to make you a sandwich?'

They took me walking on the trail around Maungauika North Head, Geoff humming to himself. We walked onto Cheltenham

Beach, and they showed me the haunts of a happy family growing up in the 1980s and '90s; the children's birthday parties and their wedding on the sand, where they strung bunting in the trees.

'Thank you so much,' I said when we parted. 'You've been so kind.'

'You're very welcome,' Miriam said. 'This is how the trail is kept alive for us.'

* * *

I walked the footpaths north of Auckland, past hedges cut as tight as stone. The skyline dipped and soared, full of large homes, many wrapped tightly in white plastic for construction or renovation. I ate $2 lolly mixtures and pies from bakeries and brushed showers of pastry from my jacket. I walked past pockets of neighbours with small white dogs, gathering to mutter about other neighbours.

I walked past seawalls of volcanic rock, temporarily protecting multi-million-dollar homes from the encroaching sea, sending the wave energy off elsewhere. I heard how the waves echoed, the sound bouncing back at me from the stone walls along Milford Beach. Hunks of thick sea foam wiggled loose and blew along the sand. I delighted in encountering one of the most personable young men I'd ever met working the checkout at the Torbay Four Square. I waded low tides and got stuck in thick mangrove mud, which I washed off outside a boat club. I walked into the welcoming arms of a Domino's.

Near Ōrewa, I stopped at the home of trail angels James and Cynthia Mackenzie, who turned out to be the parents of a friend's friend. They were involved with the local Forest & Bird – in fact, James's ancestor had been involved in the society's inception – and had spent many years planting trees on an old family farm overlooking the sea. I stayed the night in their cottage and then decided to have a rest day the next day too, as the tide wasn't favourable to get around the coastal rocks in time to walk a full day.

In the morning, I went up to meet them and have a cup of coffee. James invited me to sit in the La-Z-Boy, and I sat back and put up the footrest.

'My God,' I said, stretching out. 'This is the life.'

James quizzed me about my next moves. There was a kayak section to Puhoi, and he searched his phone for his neighbour's kayak business, but they were shut until spring. 'It's no bother,' I said. 'I'll walk the road alternate.' I sank into the La-Z-Boy with my coffee, still enjoying the novelty and sensation of my feet being suspended above the earth. Cynthia brought in some cheese and crackers.

'Have you got a PLB?' James said, then smiled at himself. 'I'm in dad mode.'

That night, their son Andrew and his partner visited for dinner. Andrew was an engineer and a director of a parks infrastructure company called reNature. He told me about the work he did on tracks and bridges, and when he mentioned some he'd done that were along the TA, I sat straight upright.

'Those are my favourites!' I said. 'I loved them!'

This was a subject very close to my heart. Well-built tracks, bridges and platforms were among my most treasured encounters on a trail that could be so rough it sometimes took an hour to go a single kilometre. Andrew had worked on the beautiful suspension bridges vaulting across entire valleys on the Timber Trail, and the wood-and-steel platforms at Maungawhau Mt Eden, among much else. I was delighted to meet him; his mahi helped open up and protect the bush and waterways, and freed you to look up and around at the world, rather than spending the day staring at your feet slopping through mud.

The next morning, I packed to go, then walked around the property with James and a young man who came to help him with trapping. We spent a couple of hours traipsing through the kauri forest, and I saw some of Andrew's handiwork in the bridges he'd built from scrap timber. Finally, the tide was low enough for me to creep along the rocky coast. I sat down on the cottage's concrete steps to tie my laces and say goodbye.

'Would you like me to make you a sandwich?' Cynthia said.

* * *

At the Mackenzies' cottage, I'd decided to continue all the way to Whangārei Heads where my friend Kirsty's family had a bach. My knee was a little sore every now and then, but largely OK. I then planned to return to Te Kūiti and fill in the section north to Auckland, so I could tackle the treacherous Mt Pirongia with stronger knee ligaments.

The first night out from Ōrewa, I was planning to stay at Stu Bennett's, a trail angel who had walked Te Araroa himself a couple of years ago. He hosted TA walkers for koha at his Puhoi woolshed, about a kilometre off the trail.

But the road alternate to Puhoi was confusing. It said to walk along the state highway, but all I could see was a giant new motorway. The road funnelled me into it and I ended up walking along it, staying on the far side of the barrier, confused. The cars roared past. I studied maps and apps as I walked, switching between my three Te Araroa notes and map apps, the topo map, Google Earth, Google Maps and Apple Maps. Surely this wasn't the actual trail alternate to kayaking the wetland and estuary? Then I saw where I'd gone wrong, and the terrain, the water, the road resolved. The trail and topo maps didn't have the new motorway on them yet. Only on the satellite image could I see the old state highway running next to a fresh construction site: the motorway to come.

All right, I just had to get off this thing. The trouble was, I really had to pee, and I was now crossing a long bridge spanning the wetland. I quickened my pace, then dashed down a bank and crouched as far out of view as I could, desperation overcoming modesty. As I started back up the bank, buckling my pants, a policeman pulled up alongside the barrier, got out of his car and stood there, arms crossed, looking down at me.

'We've been watching you on the traffic cam,' he said. 'Did you know it was illegal to walk on the motorway?'

* * *

He told me to get in the car and he'd drop me at the bottom of Stu's road. I tried to joke around behind the plexiglass, but he was having none of it. He told me there was a $500 fine, and I was choking back a swear word when he said he'd let me off with a warning.

'We could see you were confused, and that you were staying outside the barrier,' he said. 'Don't do it again.' He stopped at the bottom of Stu's road and I stupidly tried to open the door.

'Kiddie lock,' he said, and came around to open it. I dragged my pack and poles out of the back seat, apologised again and said goodbye, but I was still so flustered I immediately set off the wrong way.

'That's a driveway,' he said, pointing to the actual road running uphill next to it. 'And you're holding up that car,' he added, pointing up the driveway to a waiting sedan.

The sun had set by the time I knocked on Stu's door. He opened it and I immediately adored him; he had long, greying dark hair and a wild energy. His house was perched high above the eastern coastline, and I exclaimed over his view.

'Yeah, mate – come and look at this,' he said, and brought me up onto the deck to show me the stretch of coastline out to Te Hauturu-o-Toi, Little Barrier Island. 'When those pine trees are gone, you'll be able to see the Coromandel as well.'

He'd put a roast of lamb in the oven, then showed me around the woolshed he'd cleaned up and turned into a thru-hiker's paradise. It was a huge, two-level space with a pool table, beds, tables, a wood-burner, a stack of nature books, a huge set of couches, a kitchenette and a sound system. He'd even provided the little white Lightning and USB-C audio dongles for iPhone audio jacks. I was delighted.

I decided to sleep on the comfortable fireside couch instead of a bed, so shook out my sleeping bag to loft and returned to the house. Stu's lamb and roast vegetables were delicious, and he plunked down the fancy brand of mint sauce. Over dinner we spent a good hour engaged in the classic New Zealand pastime of figuring out the people and places we knew in common, eventually landing triumphantly on the fact that he'd just got a job with my high-school friend's hiking company, Walking Legends. I texted Brad to say he'd found a gem of a new employee who made a great roast lamb.

Wicked, yeah we're stoked to have him on board, Brad replied.

Having closed the circle, Stu and I could now conclude our conversation with one of us making the customary observation that it was, indeed, a very small world, and we could then sip our tea and retire content. But Stu went one better.

'I'm actually in Geoff Chapple's Te Araroa book.'

'No! Really?'

'Yeah, mate. I met him in Nelson Lakes and we went over Waiau Pass together. And I defined nature for him,' he said modestly.

'That was you!?' I grabbed my phone and searched Kindle for Stu's name in my bible, Geoff's 2002 book; and there he was, more than twenty years younger. He'd been a volunteer hut warden at West Sabine Hut in Nelson Lakes National Park when he'd encountered Geoff scouting Te Araroa. They'd walked from West Sabine to Blue Lake Hut and over the pass, and then parted as Geoff continued south. Stu was the memorable warden who'd energetically cleaned all the hut windows, discussed a new vocabulary of New Zealand nature for the early 21st century, and cursed out trampers for damaging the forest next to the tracks by walking around the muddy bits instead of accepting their fate and going straight through.

'I guess trampers haven't gotten any less annoying in twenty years,' I said. We'd had the same conversation earlier.

It was past hiker midnight. I went out to the woolshed and put split dry logs on the fire and got in my sleeping bag and pulled it around my shoulders, grateful that the couch's cushioned back and armrests were keeping me warmer than usual in the chill dark. Te Araroa was still so new that it was comforting to think back along the years to a particular summer evening when I was still in my teens and Stu and Geoff were standing on a deck outside West Sabine Hut, the pair of them cloaked in the mountain night, Geoff holding a toothbrush and the pair of them considering an Aotearoa bush language. Stu had suggested its first word: *raw*. I lay on my couch, watching the silent flames flicker, and heard a ruru screech and then call its melancholy lullaby. I thought I was about as happy right then as I'd ever been in my entire life.

The next morning I went up to the house for a cup of tea to have with my muesli bar, and Stu and I watched the sun rise together over the eastern coast. Stu pressed six oranges on me as I packed up.

'Ooh, are these from your tree?'

'No, they're from Pak'nSave,' he said. 'I'm not a fan of these ones but I know you hikers will love them.'

I broke into one and ate it as I walked up the road. I passed the turnoff southbound to Puhoi, the section I'd skipped thanks to the policeman, and paused for a minute, tempted to ignore the missing 14km and go on north; then sighed and turned left to walk downhill to reconnect the line. As I made my way towards Remiger Road and Puhoi, I saw a tall figure with a pack walking through the gate towards me, northbound. I stopped, incredulous. Another TA hiker? A local wouldn't be out on this walk wearing a pack. Had there been another TA walker a day behind me this entire time?

We stopped to chat. His name was Stefan, and he was from Germany and had arrived in Auckland a few days ago. He was walking to Cape Reinga, then planned to look for work and walk some more of the trail. He seemed to be about 25 and was tall and good-looking, with mossy green eyes and thick, sun-blonded brown curls spilling from under his cap. He was planning to camp further up the trail, past where I was aiming to get to today.

'We might see each other on the trail later,' he said as we parted. I took in his long legs and easy frame.

'I honestly doubt I will be as fast as you, but maybe,' I said, and walked down to Puhoi. I stopped at the Puhoi Cottage Tea Rooms, back on trail, and downed fresh scones with cream and jam, a coffee frappé and a Lift, feeling pleased. It was so good to meet another hiker, and I realised with a start that he was the first TA walker I'd met since Lea at Red Hills Hut, 1400km to the south. In fact, except for the handful of students in the Tararua Ranges, the few walking the Tongariro Crossing and a couple at Ruapehu, he was the only tramper I'd met in the entire North Island. I'd been alone on this thing for months.

I stopped on the highway adjacent to the motorway, where I'd been picked up by the cop, then caught a ride back to the turnoff on Stu's road to continue north. I camped that night on a flat, grassy tent site a farmer had bulldozed for TA walkers, but there was no water supply. I'd walked nearly 30km but had drunk less than 1 litre the entire day, so I wandered about in the dark looking for a tap but could only find muddy, rusty rainwater puddled in an excavator bucket. It was getting on towards 8p.m. and I didn't want to disturb the farmer, so I ate all five of Stu's oranges in the hope that'd do. It didn't; I was so thirsty I couldn't sleep, so at 5a.m. I gave up, packed up my dew-wet tent and set off in a glowing dawn for Pākiri Beach. It was a tough 27km away, mostly through slippery, muddy, steep forest tracks, and I could only hope I'd find water soon.

North of Warkworth, State Highway 1 burst from the farmland with a shattering roar. I crossed it gingerly, overwhelmed at the twin streams of rushing traffic, and walked up the driveway of the former Dome Café, where someone on a hiking app had said there was a walkers' water tap outside the owners' house. I tried it. It was dry.

I sat on a retaining wall for a bit, feeling hopeless. It was only 7.30a.m. and I was so desperate for water that I decided I'd have to wait until someone in the house came out and then beg them for a refill. Presently a woman appeared carrying a laundry basket, and she asked her little girl to fill my bottles. I thanked them and drank gratefully, then headed up the track to the Dome lookout, which had a platform with a fine view reaching back to Auckland. I watched the glinting cars heading south on State Highway 1 as I shook and hung my saturated tent to dry, called Doug, made breakfast and coffee, washed my face and brushed my teeth, then brushed and braided my hair and sat back to admire my high little treehouse.

I could see the Sky Tower from up here, and consulted the topo map: it was 60km away. I marvelled at the clarity of the New Zealand winter air, highway traffic and all.

A couple with a dog emerged from the forest, and I was talking to them about this when Stefan walked up and stepped onto the platform.

'Naomi,' he said, smiling as he unclipped his pack and lowered it to the ground.

'Stefan,' I said, smiling back. 'The only other hiker on the trail.'

He'd ended up camping a few kilometres behind me last night, on a kind person's beautiful, soft lawn. He asked where I was headed, and when I mentioned the TA discount at the Pākiri Beach Holiday Park he borrowed my phone to make a booking himself. I began gathering my things to go; the man I'd been talking to about the Sky Tower had begun telling me about magnetic fields and frequencies and I felt the familiar approach of a deranged conversation. I could see Stefan having the same thought; he caught my eye and winked, and my heart dropped past my feet.

I stood up. 'I better get going,' I said, shouldering my pack. 'It's past 10a.m. and there's nearly 30km to walk.'

'I'll walk with you,' said Stefan, and I said OK and went off down the trail quickly.

The track to Pākiri was slower, steeper and slicker than I'd thought; perfectly suited, in fact, to destroying my healing knee ligament, which I tried not to think about. We walked all day through kauri forest and tree ferns, over muddy paths, through forestry blocks, up and down slippery bush tracks, and past lifestyle blocks. Stefan chattered nonstop. He'd left home on the same day I'd left the South Island and had travelled through Indonesia as I walked up the North Island, and now he was here for a year on a working holiday visa. He'd been to New Zealand ten years before and had yearned to return ever since.

'I will tell you, I cried when I got to Auckland,' he said when we stopped for a moment to look up into the kauri. 'I was so happy and grateful to be here.'

As we walked, he marvelled at how the moon and constellations were upside down here, how new this land was and how much it was still eroding, how unusual the plants and animals were, how close the sea on all sides. He asked me why we didn't have the right to roam like in Europe, and what were paper roads, and why we still clear-felled pine, and how long radiata took to grow, and why we weren't all fluent in te reo Māori, and why we were still a constitutional monarchy, and why DOC didn't have enough money to do its job with that much country to look after, and what Peter Jackson was up to these days, and what plants were poisonous, and what huts and tracks I liked in New Zealand, and what were my favourite science and nature books.

He asked about jobs and surfing and houses, and he couldn't hold in an incredulous laugh at the former journalism salary I'd once thought reasonably good, nor a wistful sigh at the apparently bargain cost of even an Auckland home, compared to Germany. He asked what was the bird that sounded like R2-D2, and I thought perhaps it was a magpie.

'And how young are you, Naomi?' he asked after a few hours, and I smiled at his practised charm. I told him and he said, 'That's good. I spent some time with a woman in Indonesia and she wouldn't tell me her age.' He was 30, and he had a deep voice and his cheekbones held a glow of pink above his dimples and dark stubble and sharp jaw, and his teeth were straight and white, and soft crinkles formed around his eyes when he smiled and frankly I could see exactly why the poor girl had fumbled something about age being a limiting social construct.

But I hadn't walked with anyone since Sam had farewelled me in the Marlborough Sounds three-and-a-half months earlier, and I'd forgotten how nice it was to simply have company to share the joys and pain and decisions of the trail. At one point a car crept up next to us on a lonely back road, and I realised I didn't have the little jolt of fear I usually felt, when my hackles went up and I put my shoulders back and tried to look brisk and purposeful and disappear as quickly as possible. I'd even let Stefan take over navigation; while he consulted the TA app I stood idly by, leaning on my poles and staring into the bush, temporarily relieved of the responsibility I'd carried alone for so long.

'It's so relaxing to walk with a man,' I joked as the car pulled away. But he stopped, suddenly serious.

'Naomi, you know I am not going to walk the whole way to Cape Reinga with you,' he said, and outlined his plan for his trip. He'd recently managed to extricate himself from serious depression and was an introvert, he said, and had come here to walk alone, to sit with himself, to be quiet. He'd even asked his family and friends to avoid contacting him. In fact, he wanted to walk the last week in total silence. He was so direct and earnest and concerned that I ducked my head to hide a smile.

'It's OK,' I said. 'I'm only going to Whangārei Heads, and then I'm going back to walk Te Kūiti to Auckland.'

'OK, this is good,' he said. 'We can walk there together.'

My sprained knee was sore and I'd not slept since waking up on the couch in Stu's woolshed, two days and 50km earlier, and I was beginning to feel a bit crazed. The first sign of this was when I cried at the sight of daffodils in the hills above Matakana, flowers I thought of as belonging to my godson, Sunny, who had turned three a fortnight earlier.

'Sorry,' I said. 'It's just been so long.'

'It's all right,' Stefan said, briefly resting a hand on my arm. 'Showing emotions is healthy.' I smelled mown grass and saw insects. Birds mated. There was an extra half-hour of light at night. I saw my first game of lawn cricket. Spring was coming.

The sun was setting. When we got to a busy road and I saw the last couple of hills we had to climb and descend, my resolve to walk every inch began to falter for the first time.

'Maybe we should hitch,' I said. If I was alone I wouldn't have considered it. But gaining permission from someone else was tempting.

Stefan looked stern. 'No. You have your goal. We're walking.'

We walked. We had watched deep orange creep across the dark blue sky from high on the Dome in the morning, and then as night fell we were still climbing through sticky, cold mud, still kilometres away from Pākiri.

I was sliding constantly. Every time I slipped, Stefan leaned down a hand to pull me back up. 'Be careful here, Naomi. Watch your knee.'

It was aching from all the slips and twists, though the brace was doing its job. We stopped for a break and I lay on my back on a concrete helicopter pad, groaning with how annoying the trail was, and spent a few moments staring at the white stars glinting through the trees before heaving myself up and going on.

We walked and crawled and climbed down a fixed rope and ducked and slid, and although Stefan was in New Zealand to walk alone, he told me there were some things he'd been wanting to talk about, about past girlfriends and behaviour he regretted, and how he'd tried to put it right. I could already see how hard he was on himself, how black and white his thinking, and the strength of the strictures he'd built to manage the black hole that had stolen a chunk of his 20s.

We crested the hill at last, and I sensed the horizon opening up in the syrupy dark. We couldn't see the big, beautiful bay stretching past Mangawhai and Waipū to Whangārei, but the void of night beyond the bright green of the grass lit by our headlamps held its own beauty and drama. There was a yellow crescent moon and the stars were thick enough that the constellations had melted back into the sky.

Stefan had revealed a deep love and knowledge of Tolkien, and I put on the *The Lord of the Rings* soundtrack for morale.

We sang along to that and the dwarves' Misty Mountains lament from *The Hobbit* and whatever else we could think of as we searched for the path in the dark. I'd managed to come this far on trail without too much Tolkien, but it appeared it was now time to lean in, and we threw movie quotes at each other as we picked our way down the steep paddock. He was thrilled that a friend of mine and Doug's had played a dwarf in *The Hobbit*, but I couldn't for the life of me recall which one.

'I remember watching the first movie in Dunedin when it came out,' I said. 'It was such a huge deal here. Everyone stayed behind and pointed out the people they knew in the credits.'

'I'm so jealous you got to see it in the theatres.'

'That's because I was twenty when *The Fellowship of the Ring* was released and you were – how old were you?'

'Eight.'

I smiled into the dark. I was old enough to be his – well, his babysitter.

It was nearly 10p.m. when we reached the holiday park. We marched the last 3km along the road in hoots of delirium, obsessing over the food we'd buy from the small camp store the next day. We retrieved our cabin keys from the after-hours box and made it through the gate and shouted in relief. Stefan put his arm around me for a hug. We staggered to our cabins and the bathroom and the kitchen and the laundry and back to our cabins and agreed on a rest day tomorrow. Then I collapsed under my sleeping bag and stared at the bunk bottom above.

I'd now been awake for more than 40 hours, during which I'd tramped 60km. There had been plenty of sleepless nights and long days like that on trail, and fortunately the impact was far less these days. I still couldn't believe how each day could be so thick with surprises, and how quickly intimacy developed in the hills. I'd been walking mostly alone for the whole trip, had met Stefan less than a day ago, and now we'd shared stuff we'd never told anyone else, and would spend the next week together, walking and eating and talking.

I knew this was just the immediate, short-term closeness of strangers thrown together for a short time, like summer camp or a theatre production; but I also knew I was in trouble, because when he'd winked at me that morning something below my ribs had broken open for the first time in more than a decade.

'You're just lonely and tired, and he is just there,' I told myself. This was just what happened when you traipsed through mud and hills with a stranger who by the end of it was a friend, except he looked like a cuter Henry Cavill but with a nicer nose, actually. I was pissed at myself for immediately liking the only charming guy with a wink to wander along the trail. But it was too late now; he'd felled me, like a tree. And then a heavy sleep fell over me like a Lothlórien cloak.

CHAPTER 10

PĀKIRI TO WHANGĀREI HEADS

The good thing about being 2500km into the trail was that every morning now I woke with the previous day's agonies forgotten. I was up before 7a.m. and walked down to the beach to watch the huge orange ball of the sun rising over the sea. I saw a figure in the distance practising sun salutations; I knew it was Stefan but left him alone.

The little shop opened at 9a.m. I watched the clock, and at 8.55a.m. strode over and bought a large frozen pizza, a bag of salt-and-vinegar chips, two Moro bars, two Almond Golds, a coffee for me and a hot chocolate for him; somehow I knew he did not drink coffee. I loaded the pizza with more cheese and cooked it in the kitchen, and when I brought it over, hot and bubbling, I saw he'd also been to the shop and come back with three more frozen pizzas, two more Moro bars, and another bag of salt-and-vinegar chips.

We sat at a picnic table and picked up slices. But now we were facing each other, and our eyes kept locking for too long, and to my horror I found this intolerable.

'I like that you eat pizza in the morning too,' he said, watching me.

'Who could turn down pizza?' I said lightly, but I couldn't hold his gaze and felt myself crumpling, turning sideways on the seat and drawing my knees up and fixing my eyes on the laundry I'd hung to dry on the cabin deck. He handed me a Moro and I peeled off the wrapper and pulled at the sticky river of escaped caramel with my teeth.

The next day, we left in the tangerine dawn to walk the 23km along the beaches to Mangawhai, an easy day. I looked for one of the only 49 fairy terns left in the world, which nested here in the dunes, but spotted none. We walked and talked and each bent at the same second to pick up a shell that had caught our eye, his a large blue fan, mine a small peach one. He turned to me with a questioning look.

'A scallop,' I said.

In Mangawhai, we sat outside AJ's Bakery. I drank a strawberry milk and we shared a family bag of peanut M&Ms while Stefan worked his way through a packet of caramel Tim Tams. I sat sideways again and tried to avoid his gaze, again.

I noticed women in cars swinging through the roundabout and keeping their eyes on him as they drove past. He seemed oblivious to the attention; it must be normal to him. He watched me and I chewed my lower lip and watched the traffic watching him.

I'd found us a place to stay with some trail angels, who offered walkers a cabin for $10 a night, and we walked footpaths to their garden. It was another TA paradise – a swing set, mandarin trees, a solar shower, hens and a little cabin with books and fairy lights and two single beds. We settled in for the evening and I drank a beer and we ate chips and read and mucked about with playlists and went through photos. Stefan sat on the floor and heated baked beans, humming to himself and cooing at the two inquisitive hens pecking at the door sill.

'How do you pick them up?' I showed him. I'd noticed how he liked animals; he'd swooned over every dog and cat that approached us. He finished his baked beans and said, 'Do Kiwis have any hiking songs?'

'Not really,' I said. 'What are the German ones?' He picked up his phone and found a children's version of 'Das Wandern ist des Müllers Lust' on YouTube; bouncy and quick, it was about a miller who loved to hike, as restless as the water that drove his millstones. Stefan sang along, thumping his leg with his hand. 'And then, like, everyone sings it, you know?' He beat his knee some more. 'You see? It's quite a pace.'

'I would definitely struggle to maintain that speed up a hill.'

He kept up a happy chatter as darkness fell. 'Have you heard of the mantis shrimp? How it punches its prey to death?' I hadn't, so he sat beside my bunk and showed me YouTube videos with titles like 'Mantis Shrimp Punches Crab's Arm Off' and 'Mantis Shrimp Unleashes Deadly Hammer Attack'. He explained how its strike was so fast and hard that the water actually vaporised when it hit, creating cavitation bubbles that collapsed and delivered an additional devastating blow, and also, for a second, created light and sound and heat.

'What is your favourite animal, Naomi?'

I told him about the kārearea I'd once seen attack our hens. She'd alighted on a power line nearby and the hens had squawked a very specific alarm call and buried themselves under a thicket of tradescantia. The kārearea sat on the line for a while, holding up one furled yellow claw, then glided down to perch on a stump. I got downstairs and outside in time to see her stalking across the ground and launching herself at a hen. I was awed by her yellow eyes, her claws, her power and audacity.

'Mmmmm,' he said appreciatively. 'I think mine is the mantis shrimp.'

When darkness fell, I turned on the fairy lights and we began to doze off. Out of the gloom he said, 'Do you like to read aloud?'

'Yes,' I said. 'It's cosy.' He told me how he used to like to read books to his girlfriend at night in bed. He liked to hold her and read quietly to her until she fell asleep in his arms.

At this I swore under my breath.

'You like to hold your girlfriend and read aloud to her until she falls asleep,' I said incredulously. 'That is – that is fucking dreamy, Stefan.'

'Mmmm. It's very nice, you know?'

I covered my eyes and pressed the heels of my hands into my cheekbones and silently begged God to release me from this nightmare, then dropped my hands to my sternum and felt my pulse under my fingers and watched the fairy lights glow softly against the ceiling. He was quiet. I turned the lights off and we fell asleep.

I woke once in the night, and across the room I heard him sleeping, his teeth grinding against each other and his breath rippling through the dark.

* * *

Before we left the next day he took a photo of me in front of the cabin.

'Cute,' he murmured, to which I, obviously, attached zero significance. When I found out his favourite movie was also *Interstellar* I couldn't cope anymore and texted Doug in guilt and panic. I knew he would be OK about it; months earlier we'd discussed the possibility that I might meet someone on trail, and although I wasn't keen on potentially derailing our marriage, his wish was that I simply return home to him, no matter what. And I knew he'd understand my attraction to Stefan; *Interstellar* was Doug's favourite movie too, and both of them had studied forest management at university and liked animals and hiking and trees and *Lord of the Rings* and nature and science and feelings and listening to film scores, and both had a habit of embarking on long monologues about politics and philosophy. Doug would actually probably know more about mantis shrimps, though he was less into German techno.

You should go for it, he texted.

He doesn't like me, I replied.

He's being polite, he wrote, with the conviction of a man who missed his wife.

He's not into me. And I absolutely will not go for it, I said. *I don't think you realise how much you would hate that. It would ruin us.*

You've been alone for a long time.

He doesn't like me anyway.

We'd be OK.

After a steep climb to Waipū, we stopped on a high hillside and lay in the grass. I looked for ants as Stefan scrolled through photos on his phone. Eventually he chuckled and showed me a particularly geeky one of him in his high-school days.

'Wow,' I said. 'You've had a glow-up.'

'Yes,' he said modestly. 'The girls at school were quite surprised when I went back for our reunion. What about you?'

'Digital cameras weren't a thing when I was at school, mate.' I showed him some that I had in my phone anyway, then looked at them myself. I felt a spark of tenderness for this scatterbrained, romantic 21-year-old, an idiot trapped behind glass. She had sun-bleached hair, wore head-to-toe Glassons and put on a big smile to hide the crippling anxiety there was no word for back then.

'Aw, you look the same.'

I absolutely did not, and couldn't help laughing at him. He grinned and we fell silent for a while. I lay back on my pack and plucked blades of grass as I looked out at the green hill and the sea, songs and sounds bursting in my head.

We'd been quoting movie dialogue back and forth all day again, and now I broke the silence with *Gladiator*: 'Father to a murdered son,' I growled. 'Husband to a murdered wife.'

'And I will have my *vengeance*,' he shouted.

'*In this life or the next!*' I yelled.

'AGHHHHHH!' he screamed, then laughed. 'I always felt weird to do this.'

'You don't have to feel weird,' I said. 'There's no one else around.'

* * *

A landowner had set up a beautiful free campsite 300m above Bream Bay, with a giant view of the sea and sky, and when we discovered it we decided to stop early. We sat side by side at the picnic table, making dinner. The movie lines we'd been quoting all day had made me realise I hadn't watched one for seven months, and now I looked at my iPad and saw that *Gladiator* was about to leave Netflix.

203

'I'm going to destroy my data and download *Gladiator*,' I said. Stefan was practising yoga in the camp shelter.

'I'd like to watch it with you,' he said, which immediately made me start to fret, because it was getting cold and windy and dark and there was only one way to watch movies together. 'Where are we going to watch it?'

'It'll have to be my tent,' I said, and marched off to tidy my stuff. Stefan dragged in his mat and sleeping bag and we lay down next to each other and I propped up the iPad and managed, finally, to relax. It was so nice to just hang out with another person again, to do something so normal yet so elusive on trail: to be cosy, and companionable, and be distracted by a screen, and not be hungry or cold or in active physical pain.

When the movie was over, I shut the iPad with a slap. There was a long, heavy pause as we both stared into the dark.

'What will you do now?' he said quietly and, true to form, I panicked and sat up in a rush.

'I think I will go to sleep,' I said. It was all of 7p.m. He gathered up his things and left. I stuck my head out into the night and called 'Goodnight!' far too cheerfully, and zipped up the tent door far too aggressively, and sat down on the floor and put my face in my hands. I cursed how unchill I was. I cursed my husband for laying a tripwire of permission. And most of all I cursed Stefan for his stupid dimples and dark eyebrows. Outside in the velvet night I'd caught a glimpse of how his shadowed body cut a hole in the stars.

The trail carried us 38km along roads and sands and into the lights of the Marsden Point oil refinery. We crossed the glinting sea in a local's boat and found the bach. We decided to take a couple of days' rest. I had some work to do, and Stefan's foot was injured; he wanted to spend the day making chocolate-chip cookies and pizza dough. I stretched out on the window seat and watched him cook across the room. He'd put on his Mark Knopfler playlist and tugged up the sleeves of his tight black thermal top. He took the dough out of the bowl to work it and I watched the tendons in his long, tanned forearms ripple and flex as he punched and kneaded it on the countertop, and saw how his cheekbones fell in and out of shadow as he softly sang Dire Straits' 'Why Worry?'. He was completely absorbed, his mossy, dark eyes cast down and his hair falling forward on his forehead.

For long minutes I concentrated instead on looking out the window, studying the heavy limbs of the huge macrocarpa by the shore, carefully running my eyes along each edge and following the branches back to the trunk. Then I looked at the gentle sea, then at the oil refinery, and then back down the beach, towards the headland. I glanced back at the kitchen. Stefan was still absorbed in his task, still rhythmically kneading and humming, but 'On Every Street' had begun to surge around the kitchen and he was moving his shoulders as he worked now too, turning and kneading the dough to the beat of the music. I looked at my work and read the same sentence over and over because the words would not go in.

Later, he told me he'd come to some decisions.

'I met this girl two weeks before I left home,' he said. 'Greta. Yesterday I realised I've never felt this way before about anyone. I decided I'd text her and tell her I really like her. It makes me not want to have anything casual.' He glanced at me. 'You know?'

I got it. 'You don't want a facsimile,' I said.

'A what?'

'Like … a copy. A fake version of the real thing.'

'That's right.'

* * *

His gazing had stopped now. On our seventh and last day together I had arranged to meet Whangārei hiker Mike Lim for an article I was writing on ultralight gear for *Wilderness* magazine. Mike had walked Te Araroa a few years back and was planning to tackle it again this summer with his new kit. Other than Stefan, who was only walking for three weeks, I hadn't talked to another TA hiker since Lea in the Richmond Ranges. Mike's energy reinvigorated me for the trail to come.

That night, when Stefan and I were doing the dishes, he said he'd sent his text to Greta about how much he liked her and she'd replied, but it wasn't the answer he was looking for. We sat down at the clean counter. 'I'm feeling really homesick,' he said. 'I have been having this feeling for a while. I want to go home. I want to be with the people I love, and I want to love them. But I have this whole year planned, this working holiday visa, and I only just got here.'

He talked on for a while, then fell silent. Eventually his head was hanging so low and he looked so desolate my heart went out to him. I sat there awkwardly for a moment and then said, 'Would you like a hug? A friend hug?'

His face crumpled into a pained smile. 'Yes. Please.' It was nearly a sob. We stood and hugged and he didn't let go. It was the longest, closest hug I'd ever had with anyone … ever, actually, and it went on for so long that I started to worry. Was I causing this? I experimentally loosened my arms, but he still held me. He rubbed my back and shoulders and sighed a bit, and hummed a bit, and swayed a bit, and when we eventually broke apart he seemed a bit lighter and we sat side by side and scrolled through our photo albums on our phones and showed each other pictures of our friends and family and homes. He laughed at his friends' stupid poses and told me about their antics – the good friends whom he'd told me he needed to cut communication with on his trip, so he could be with himself. He showed me the farm where he grew up. I showed him Doug's perfect woodpile stacks, and he said he had kind eyes and looked like he had a good heart, and I said he did.

I showed him the Te Araroa selfie I'd taken in 2015, the me that had been just a couple of years older than he was now, and who'd been so determined to walk the trail one day.

'And now we are here,' he said.

'Yup,' I said. 'Two homesick people too far from home.'

'I thought about flying home to surprise Greta for Christmas,' he said. 'But the flights are too expensive. Maybe for her birthday.'

'When is her birthday?'

'October.'

I had a feeling he'd be there well before that, despite the working holiday visa and the trail plans, but said only, 'She would love that.'

'I'm sorry for consuming all your time talking about her,' he said. 'Thank you for a good week. I came here to walk alone but it's been nice to walk with you. Thanks for the company.'

'I enjoyed walking with you. I like you,' I said with a shrug and an embarrassed smile. He broke into a grin.

'I like you too,' he said softly. We sat there and kept smiling at each other and I didn't have to look away.

* * *

The next day the sun was out. 'There's that bird again,' Stefan said. 'The one that sounds like R2-D2.'

'Oh!' I said. 'It's not a magpie, it's a tūī.' We watched the black and green and blue feathers flash into a tree and dart off again.

'I can't believe it's only been nine days since I got here,' he said, collapsing into a folding chair on the porch. 'It feels like months.'

'That's pretty much life on the trail.'

At 10a.m. sharp he stood up and opened his arms and beamed as he walked towards me. 'OK, Naomi,' he said, and hugged me again in the same way as the night before, which is to say he hugged me forever.

'Thanks for being the only man to choose to walk with me in two and a half thousand kilometres,' I said into his chest, by way of a general apology.

'No,' he said. 'Really?'

'Really,' I said. And he chuckled and kept rubbing my back. But it wasn't quite true, I realised. The other man to walk with me on the trail had been my husband.

'Be safe. Keep your good spirit, OK, Naomi?' he said, then offered the classic line that has disappointed women since the dawn of time: 'You have a beautiful soul.'

I went inside the house so I did not have to watch him walk away up the steep driveway, then rang a relieved Doug, and we debriefed like girlfriends. Then I caught a bus south to Te Kūiti and picked up the line where I'd left it.

CHAPTER 11

TE KŪITI, AGAIN, TO AUCKLAND

Some of the trail was closed for lambing from 1 August, so I walked on lonely roads on my healing knee next to the trail, trudging on gravel through heavy rain, listening to Dire Straits, for God's sake. My treasured Te Araroa Trail Mix playlist was nearing 85 hours long. On the roads near Waitomo, an older man pulled up next to me in his car and said, 'Where the bloody hell are you going?'

I stopped and peered in, smiling when I saw his long white hair and green-and-yellow motorsport jacket. He was wearing fetching white leather gloves to drive a Honda Odyssey.

'Cape Reinga,' I said.

'You're not!' he said. 'What are you bloody doing all the way up here in the hills? Do you need a ride? Where did you start?'

'I came from Bluff. I like your gloves.'

'Bluff oysters! The world's greatest. Now listen,' he said, suddenly serious, 'I admire your courage. Have a good day.'

'Thank you,' I said. 'You too.' He drove off and I walked on, grinning. But a couple of hours later, a storm blew in, and in the sudden burst of intense rain I became unusually cold. I pulled out my tent and tied the fly to a fence, pulling it over my head and anchoring it with my pack to make a small green cocoon. But it had been a bad decision to stop; I was soon even colder.

'Where is this transcendence that was meant to happen on trail?' I muttered, and decided to fully pitch the tent and wait it out. But I wasn't in a good spot. As the afternoon waned into evening the wind turned my tent into a walloping sail. Around 11p.m., I felt like a ship tossed in a storm. I began to worry about the integrity of the hiking poles holding the tent up, and sat up in my sleeping bag holding them apart, determined to do so all night if I had to.

By midnight the wind had whipped a couple of guy ropes off pegs pushed badly into the hard, gravelly ground, though I'd managed to tie others to fence wires. The tent collapsed. I'd gotten soaked twice and let rain in on everything when I went out in the storm to put the guy ropes back on and beat in the pegs deeper, and I'd torn the tent inner struggling to put a wild pole back in its pocket. Now the wind was shrieking with such an unearthly, off-key wail that the pitch was making me feel deranged. I felt my heart pound as I became very scared of three specific things: that

211

the tent fabric would rip or a pole would snap, in which case I'd be fucked; or that a tree limb or sheet of corrugated iron would fly through the night and land on me, in which case I'd be dead.

When another guy rope whipped off a peg and one of the walking poles holding up my tent bent, I'd had enough. I shoved my stuff inside my pack liner and went out in the dark and rain to pull out the remaining pegs, swearing and fumbling for long minutes in the cold to undo the knots in the guy ropes I'd tied to the fence wires, which had gotten so wet and tight it was like they'd been glued.

I clamped the sopping tent bundle under my arm and pushed on down the trail, head down against the wind and rain, face muffled in my fleece neck gaiter. I was looking for the cluster of houses or sheds I'd seen as black squares on the topo map earlier that day. I felt better now I was on the move, doing something, although I couldn't really see anything; my headlamp illuminated only a white patch on the fog a half-metre ahead.

I talked aloud to myself, agreeing the wind was indeed very loud; a shrill, demonic screaming straight from the bowels of hell, in fact, but if I considered reality I was actually safe and OK, and see how I'd put my waterproof pants on and my legs were warm, and my pack was actually keeping my back from getting cold? How good! There would be shelter soon, I said to myself. There were people not far away. I could always knock on a door, or keep walking to stay warm. And that was all true, and it became truer as I repeated it. I already knew I could walk all night if I had to.

I came to a gate with a blue RAPID number, meaning a house lay beyond, but it was locked with a chain, so I struggled against the wind to open and close another gate nearby that I could see led to a different black square on the topo map. A woolshed finally loomed from the fog, just metres ahead. The night and mist was so dense that I nearly stepped into a deep, water-filled concrete hole near the door, probably an offal pit. The wind had blown off its corrugated iron cover. My headlamp began giving out, flashing its low-battery warning.

It was 1a.m. I thanked God that the padlock on the woolshed's heavy sliding door was unlocked, and I hauled it aside and entered the gloom. There was no power, so by the light of my headlamp I picked a patch of floor that was less covered in bird- and sheep-shit than the rest, inflated my sleeping mat and shook out my sleeping bag. Every last stitch of my clothing was soaked, and I suddenly realised I hadn't been walking in my usual merino tee, which was the only top I'd worn during the whole trip. That was still in my pack, stretched and threadbare. Instead, I'd been wearing a new lightweight synthetic top, which was why I'd gotten so cold and had stopped to huddle under my tent in the first place. I couldn't believe the massive difference the fabric change had made.

I strung my rope across the shearing area to try to dry my tent and clothes, realising I'd lost four tent pegs along the way. I got in my sleeping bag as the wind screeched and wailed and hurled rain against the iron like handfuls of gravel. I lay there and sung the first song that came into my head, which happened to be DD Smash's 1984 hit 'Whaling'.

I bellowed the first lines into the wind, and spent the rest of the night staring at the darkness, listening to the wind howl them right back at me.

I stayed in my sleeping bag the next day and then all the next night as well. There was no water supply, but in the morning I went outside and found I could drink the rainwater that was pouring from an unmoored drainpipe. After my clothes refused to dry, I put on one wet thing at a time and huddled back in my sleeping bag to steam it drier.

As the day went on the storm strengthened and the wind thumped the massive sliding door, sending it clanging in a regular, deranged beat. The gusts macerated the banks of daffodils outside and worried at the iron on the roof. I spent a few hours watching a corner of it lift, daylight cracking through, and thought about trying to find the farmhouse that the woolshed belonged to. But the rain didn't stop and my clothes were still wet and it was so cold it felt dangerous to be outside.

Later in the afternoon the wind direction changed, and it now blew straight through the walls onto my patch of floor, ruffling the bottom of my sleeping bag and sending my tent and clothes swaying on the line. The temperature dropped so much that I shuffled my emergency bag over my sleeping bag, though in the morning both were wet with condensation.

If I went outside and stood in a specific corner of the paddock in the rain, I had a single bar of 4G reception. I'd been texting my friends Kylie and Richard that week about walking with me, and now they offered to drive two hours to get me, tempting me with meals, beds, hot pools. I was touched. But I thanked them and refused. The storm was crazy up here. It was too intense to drive in, and I'd only have to somehow return to the same spot to keep walking. There were clearer days coming. And, actually, I could keep warm and had water, so I was fine.

I thought of Stefan, 400km in front of me, far up the line, his long, tanned legs walking alone across the empty beaches of Northland. He'd expected it would take about two more weeks to reach Cape Reinga, and had planned his last week to be totally silent. Despite what he'd said, I knew that as soon he got to the cape he would ditch the rest of the trail and the job idea, and go straight back to Auckland to fly home and see that girl.

Did all Germans do that fucking intense eye contact thing that had so unravelled me? I went out in the rain again and stood there and googled it. They did. It was even called the Germanic stare-down.

I went back inside, sat down on my sleeping bag in the cold and heated up some tuna and rice noodles. I realised that after a few months of being alone, I hadn't been able to cope with the intensity of someone simply perceiving my existence.

* * *

It was still raining the next morning, the wind thrashing, but I had little food left; I'd planned to resupply in Pirongia a couple of days earlier and had gotten a bit casual about carrying two days' extra food in the more populated North Island. I put my head out the sliding door to assess the weather. It was still raging but had slackened, and my clothes were drier. I decided to get on.

I walked through more rain and staggered against the whipping wind racing across the low hills, bracing my poles to stay upright in the gusts, and putting my arm up to protect my face from sudden hail. I sunk up to my thighs in a mossy bog and struggled out, lying on my torso to spread my weight so I could inch across the muck on my elbows. When thunder and lightning hit that afternoon I ran down the trail, terrified, the storm coming closer each time I counted the seconds between flash and boom.

I landed wet and shivering and hungry at Casey and John's house that afternoon, two of the precious trail angels on this section. I felt tears sting over the chicken and broccoli bake they gave me, and the gifts of the use of a washing machine and dryer, shower, fresh water, a beer from the fridge, and their two clean and smiling faces. They cracked jokes constantly as they moved about their rambling old home, a view of the sea to the west. I couldn't warm up, so John filled a hot-water bottle for me. I tucked it under my down jacket, which was now so thin it was useless, a mere nylon shell.

The next day I planned to climb Mt Pirongia, a 959m peak that needed to be taken seriously. I had to get food, so Casey said she could drop me in Pirongia village the next morning as she drove through on her way to work. Early the next day, John gave me a huge bowl of his hot, sugary porridge. I eagerly dipped my spoon into it and ate a few bites, then stopped and said 'Whoaaaa!'

After going hungry in the woolshed for a couple of nights, and despite dinner the night before, the carbohydrates hit my bloodstream like jet fuel, filling my depleted reserves like rain on a dry riverbed. I had never felt this sensation before in my life, nor eaten anything so good. I felt my brain fizz. Wordlessly, I put my head down and concentrated on the porridge, scraping the bowl clean, then put it down on the table and said, 'Holy shit!'

'Good stuff?' John said.

'*Shit* yes.'

I washed my bowl, brushed my teeth, collected my pack, left koha on the bedside table, then got in Casey's very nice car. It was 7a.m. and I was full of delight, the woes of the last few days forgotten. I rolled down the window to say goodbye to John, who had come out to give the chickens some leftover rice.

'That seat warmer will fuck you up,' he remarked, deadpan, and I broke into hysterical giggles.

Casey and I kept laughing as we drove down the road towards Pirongia, the velvet green hills scalloped and misty. She dropped me at the Four Square and I ate a pie and an apple and drank a strawberry milk and a kombucha, then filled my pack with fresh food and stood outside to hitch back to the trail and climb Pirongia. But after an hour of standing on the side of the road in in spitting rain, I realised it was already 8.30a.m. The weather was forecast to be iffy tonight and if I didn't get on, I'd run out of light to get to Pāhautea Hut. I knew my habits by now and felt the approaching haunt of torpor, which would mean giving up on the day and finding somewhere to stay in Pirongia instead.

No: momentum beats perfection, I thought, and went to a bakery to buy a Coke and an egg-and-lettuce sandwich and sit down to consult the topo map on my phone, out of the rain. There were several routes up Pirongia from this side, and I saw I could walk from town, up O'Shea Road, go through a farm, head up the southwest side on the Wharauroa route, then meet back up with the TA to stay at Pāhautea Hut. It would the first time I'd willingly deviate from the official trail, but with the inclement weather coming I had to get up there before dark.

I strode the 7km from town with music in my ears and walked across the sodden farm. It was lambing season, but a sign on the fence said it was OK to walk through if you stayed to the track. I met the farmer on the way up. She was wearing a long oilskin and carrying a knife and a crook.

'I'm walking around with this knife, but don't worry,' she joked, and stopped to tell me a bit about the trail ahead, warning me it was slippery. We talked about the storm over the last few days.

'It's been a shocker. We lost fifty lambs,' she said. 'There's lots of triplets up there, but if you see any dead lambs, just ignore them.' I said goodbye and set off again, but after a few steps she turned and called back to me, 'Sure you don't want a cuppa?'

It was now 11a.m. and I really did, actually. But I had to get up the mountain before dark. She agreed that was sensible and I pushed on.

I saw wet and cottony lambs freshly strewn on the grass, dead after the storm, before I climbed for the next five hours, hand over hand, up rocks and roots to the top of Pirongia. I listened for kōkako but heard none. Cloud slunk into the ranges and I went over hard on my left ankle, bringing tears of pain. I slashed my gloves open on branches and waded through deep pools of mud up to my hips, and had to start up my self-talk again as I felt cold and fatigue approach and the wind began to whip. At one point I thought I'd reached the summit, and rejoiced; but if I knew anything about tramping by now, it was that what goes up must keep going up, and I was still a way from Pāhautea Hut. I got there at about 4p.m., once again too cold and wet, my limbs filthy, bleeding, iced and heavy. The hut was clean and empty, and someone had left a fleece blanket on a bench.

I stripped off my clothes and left them puddled on the hut floor, then went outside and washed myself at the sink, shivering naked in the fog. I rolled up my top and dragged the water off myself, then got straight into my sleeping bag and ate an apple and half a block of Whittaker's Creamy Milk for dinner. I had a bar of 4G reception and all my battery packs were full, so I called Doug and we talked for four hours into the dark. But I couldn't stop the sense of deep cold in my torso; it felt like my body heat wasn't enough to warm my sleeping bag. I eventually had to say had to say goodbye to concentrate on getting warmer. I fetched the fleece blanket, cinched my sleeping bag shut around my face and flexed and moved my limbs, hands and feet, willing myself to warm up.

* * *

The next day I woke toasty, but it was raining and my clothes were still wet, and the memory of the deep chill of the last few days remained in my bones. I didn't think it was wise to put the wet clothes on and walk down the mountain in this whipping wind and fog, so I decided to wait it out in the freezing hut for another day and night, wrap myself in the fleece blanket and eat a lot. I constructed hummus, cheese, salami, avocado and salad wraps and boiled up multiple hot chocolates, and hung my sopping clothes on the verandah when the rain stopped and the sun came out for brief periods. The clothes dried a bit as the day went on, before once again I put them on over my hut gear and got in my sleeping bag to stare out the window at the cloud until everything steamed dry.

The next day, the weather felt safe enough to get down the maunga and as close as I could to Hamilton, 50km up trail. I was staying with my friend Isobel's parents, Alison and Mark, in Tamahere, and was curious to see if I could make the whole 50km after the extra rest I'd had this week with the unplanned weather stops. I was on the trail at 6.15a.m. and caught pink rays pushing up from the horizon at Pirongia's summit, which spread into a deep orange sunrise. I could see the blue of Auckland's volcanoes to the north, and I looked to the south to trace all the land I'd traversed since Ruapehu.

I walked down through the forest and along country roads and past the swelling lemon trees of the Waikato. The sun came out and I closed my eyes and tilted my face up to its warmth. In Whatawhata, I stopped for a scone with extra butter at the Village Café, but when they started putting up chairs and hustling me out at 3p.m. for closing, I went across the road to the petrol station, the scone still clenched in my fist, and bought a bag of short-dated gummy worms. I ate them next door at the Backyard Gastropub with hot chips and a pint of raspberry and Coke.

Alison was at a pest-trapping meeting, so she'd organised their friend, Marius, who'd walked the trail with his wife Linda, to pick me up and deposit me and my filthy gear at her home. He was waiting for my text, so I abandoned my 50km idea and decided to make it a round 38km, walking another 5km across a farm through golden evening light and meeting him on the outskirts of the city. I gingerly put my pack into his clean car, although he had sensibly laid a blue tarp in the boot. I privately wished he'd laid one on the passenger seat as I eased in. He drove me to Alison and Mark's, then said goodbye at the door; this good deed for a total stranger must have taken a couple of hours out of his day, and I didn't know how to thank him enough.

Alison and Mark's son Jack was home, with his girlfriend Sophie and her father, Murray, and he poured me a glass of sparkling water. When I dispatched that in seconds, he put the bottle in front of me, and I finished the litre. The family were outdoors people, and Jack directed me straight to the washing machine, hose, rubbish bin and shower. I ate good cheese and crackers, and when Mark and Alison came home, she was bearing the remains of a large cake celebrating a successful run of pest trapping, sporting large chocolate Afghan rats. We ate Moroccan lamb and roast vegetables, and drank wine, and ate Alison's tangerine cake with cream and warm oranges, and I went to sleep in fresh linen sheets, gazing across the dim room at Isobel's collection of childhood novels, their spines blued from the sun.

The next morning Mark made me coffee and Alison made me toast and eggs with homegrown avocado. 'What size gumboot are you?' she asked; Isobel had instructed her to show me the gully and its eels. Alison took me at a quick pace down into the gully to show me the beautiful wetland they'd created, the steep, grazed valley sides turned rich and lush, with blue-eyed eels looming in the dark water, birds in the trees and countless kahikatea seedlings planted. Neighbours were joining in too, with more planting and smarter trapping planned. Alison gave me an Afghan rat in a ziplock bag and a fresh orange from their tree and dropped me back to trail.

I walked to Ngāruawāhia and rolled my sore ankle again on the Hakarimata Walkway and broke a pole in its mud, then strode hard tarmac to Auckland. I was on the city's edge when Stefan texted me, and I lost my breath.

Greetings from Reinga :) How are you doing?

I stopped dead and stared at my phone, my heart starting to pound in my throat as a cascade of notifications and photos flooded in. I saw Ninety Mile Beach at night. A far-off light in the dark. The lighthouse. The bristling yellow sign I'd been walking towards the whole year. A video of the cape at sunrise; his slow, even pan around a wide band of orange on the horizon. And him smiling, tall and bearded and tanned. He'd finished that morning; he'd walked 88km on Ninety Mile Beach in 21 hours, then napped in the sun behind the lighthouse. I asked him to tell me more. He sent a euphoric, ten-minute voice message describing his day and night and dawn walking with the sands and tide and sky.

The next day he texted: *Will be in Auckland next days if you wanna meet :)* It was Monday and he was flying out on Friday. I said how about dinner, then a couple of hours later we both admitted we were too tired and said we'd catch up tomorrow.

But in the morning he sent me a long voice message, apologising. He'd changed his flight to make it home for a friend's going-away party and was leaving today. Now, actually. In the background I heard the scrape of the plastic chairs in the food court and the bongs of flight announcements and replied *oh wow no way haha no worries*. We sent a couple more voice notes but then there was only one grey tick on WhatsApp, and I could see he'd boarded, or just turned his phone off.

I hadn't thought I'd see Stefan again, and hadn't realised how much I'd wanted to until I was about to. The sudden loss of him hit me like a sickness.

There was only ever one thing to do. Walk. I went outside and ignored the spears of pain in my sore ankle and strode the last of the Auckland section at a blistering pace, stepping into the shadow of my past self on the corner of Tom Pearce Drive at Auckland Airport. I stopped at the waypoint for a minute to feel her standing there, squinting at her phone, checking her map, about to set off north through the city. I felt her purpose, her lightness. She had no idea of the maelstrom she was walking into.

The planes buzzed and roared. He was around here somewhere, or already gone. I let him fly up and leave my airspace. The year had been full of these intense, fleeting connections and goodbyes, and Stefan belonged under a different sky. I belonged to this one.

That night, awake and alone in my hostel bunk, a thought occurred to me and I texted Doug.

Do you know about mantis shrimps?

Yes, he replied. *Why?*

Do you know what they do?

They are a crustacean with a very powerful strike from their claws, faster than the speed of sound, he wrote dutifully. *So powerful the shockwave can stun their prey.*

I smiled into the dark.

Amazing, isn't it?

CHAPTER 12

WHANGĀREI HEADS TO RUSSELL

I bussed from Auckland back to Whangārei and began walking from the city to rejoin the trail at the bach. As the day waxed I began to sweat and get sunburned, and the traffic pouring along the winding narrow road chafed my nerves as I stood on the white line to let it pass, half a metre from my chest. I was about halfway back to the trail when a woman pulled over on a gravel driveway, wound down her window and leaned over the seat to call out to me. I jogged up to her passenger door and peered in.

'Do you need a ride?'

'Bless you,' I said, slinging my pack on the back seat and swinging myself into the front.

'I saw you when I drove into town and said to myself, "If she's still walking when I come back, I'll pick her up".' She eyed her mirrors and pulled back into the traffic.

It was a relief to be free of the tight roadside. I watched the hills and sea and shore unfold as we drove, the harbour a sparkling, faceted crystal twisting and swaying in the rear-view mirror. We talked about Whangārei, the tropical fruit of Northland, the heat of the sun, the beauty of these scalloped bays, and who owned them. She told me about a local Pākehā couple who, after she'd once said 'Mōrena' in greeting, had engaged her in a conversation that concluded with them insisting their family home was their marae and the land their tūrangawaewae.

'People here can get very defensive,' she said. She'd been living in Australia for most of her adult life, had only just returned to New Zealand, and had noticed a marked increase in cultural temperature. More racism, to put it bluntly.

'Jacinda said: "Come home", and I did. But I wish I'd never left Australia.' She'd become a recluse out here; it was too easy to do in Whangārei, she said, but at her age she lacked the energy to pack up again and move back across the Tasman.

The tall, craggy outcrop of Manaia, the ancestor of many Whangārei iwi and hapū, came into view on the left, and soon we were at the bach. She pulled into the driveway and I thanked her, retrieved my pack and waved her off, feeling as though I'd met a friend. I felt like that a lot these days.

I walked along Whangārei Heads Road feeling hollow, and eventually realised it was because I was following in Stefan's footsteps. When I strode past the Manaia Tennis Club and saw two couples playing doubles in the sun, their friends relaxing in the stands, it finally occurred to me that I was lonely. But it was different from the loneliness I'd felt in the deep south, so I hadn't recognised it this time.

Back in autumn, as I walked the 600km between Te Anau and Otira, I'd craved to be around any person at all. Although I hadn't met another hiker on the trail in the North Island, I'd encountered my first trail angels and far more Kiwis than in the empty wilds down south. The week Stefan and I had spent together had sparked something that had been lying dormant: the memory of friendship.

Now I saw people often, but I craved real companionship; the satisfaction and love of long friendship; the chance to share twenty years of memories, inside jokes and banter; that mutual, voiceless understanding. I wanted to belong.

I realised that since meeting Stefan I'd remembered how to be around people again. I'd shed my sense of alienation and was now increasingly chatty, honest and open. I seemed to have lost a layer of concern over how I appeared to people; the absence of human interaction had made me more eager to simply connect.

I was also no longer afraid. At the beginning of the trail, I'd been scared of my own shadow, thinking it was someone hunting me down. I knew there was still a risk, but I was no longer walking along expecting to be attacked. Instead, everyone I had met had wanted to help, and I now expected everyone I met to be good.

Only one or two cars had rushed me or made me feel unsafe; many had slowed or crossed the centre-line when they saw me trudging along the shoulder towards them, giving me a wide berth, sometimes raising a single finger in an acknowledgement that made me feel seen, as though I was human. For every one of the thousand cars I'd encountered, I'd tried to make eye contact and wave back, to acknowledge their care. Maybe I was getting a more accurate picture of the community, I thought. Of what most people are really like.

In the week I'd spent with Stefan I'd started to make a new friend, and we'd begun building our own shared language, humour and history, a process that the trail had intensified by sheer proximity. It was extra precious for being so rare to me these days. To have it whipped out from under my feet was devastating. Now I missed my friends, my life.

* * *

I wound round the coast to Urquharts Bay, then climbed over Te Whara Bream Head towards Ocean Beach on the steep Te Whara Track, which I was astonished to discover was more than 700 years old. Māori had settled here more than half a millennium ago, and the remains of their pā, terraces and middens, some still with fragments of moa bones and eggs, were still here among the grass and forest. I stopped each time a new view opened through the trees and rock, transfixed by the dark green cloak clinging to the rocky volcanic-plug outcrops. The Hen and Chickens Islands, the Poor Knights and Aotea Great Barrier Island were speckled on the vast blue canvas of the sea. There were kiwi in this forest, too. I sat down to eat some salt-and-vinegar peanuts and a kākā swooped down low over my head, landed in a tree and began whooping and whistling.

My left foot, and then my right ankle, had been sore since the extravaganza of ankle-rolling on Pirongia, and then I'd gone over on the left one properly on the muddy Hakarimata Walkway near Ngāruawāhia. I'd mostly been ignoring the injuries as usual, taking Voltaren 75 when I remembered. But now both had begun to hurt with every step, and the left ankle felt a little unstable.

I hadn't spent much time on body inspection; I'd been in my hiking pants during winter, with long, skin-tight compression socks, and the evenings were dark. But I was wearing shorts now, and when I took a misstep on the track and gasped in pain, I finally got around to looking at my ankles in the light.

'Shit,' I said. Both ankle bones were hidden by swelling. The left was worse than the right. Each step sent shooting pain up through the anklebone to the side of my calf, but not enough to stop. I placed my feet carefully.

I arrived at Ocean Beach in the afternoon and decided to stop. I'd been planning to keep going but I'd mucked around in the morning, started late, spent ages over lunch, and the climb had been steep. I checked the app and saw I could camp at a private campsite run by a couple named Rupert and Wendy. For $15 per person it had the incredible luxuries of drinking water, a long-drop, a large covered shelter, a bench, a wooden table and benches and, best of all, a gas-heated shower in a plywood-walled cubicle. There was wind and rain coming, and the shelter and shower would be welcome.

I pitched my tent and saw that one corner strap on the fly had torn off in the wild night near Waitomo. I jammed the tent peg straight through the fabric instead. Nothing was sacred anymore.

I was fussing in the shelter when Rupert arrived.

'You've caught me on the hop,' he said. 'The toilet's not quite in order yet.' But he said the shower was working, which was all I cared about; public toilets were only just down the driveway at the beach carpark. He showed me how to turn on the califont, then we chatted for a while about other hikers, the trail and its small joys – hot chips, the evening and dawn, a cold beer glistening with condensation. He left, and I went off to wash with a scrap of soap. When I came back, clean and warm in my down jacket, I found he'd left me a wet, cold Speight's on the table. I could have kissed him.

I took the beer and walked down to the beach to see it before the rain came. I found a sheltered spot in the dunes and sat on the cool, soft sand, hunching into my down jacket and drawing up my bare legs, wrapping my arms around my knees as I watched couples walking with dogs and surfers stretching their arms as they snapped on wetsuits. I noticed I'd got my first sandfly bite in months. Spring was here and I was nearly done with the trail.

I had 400km to go, which included a 25km road-walking re-route around a 5km section of private land that wouldn't open for another two weeks. And I couldn't be bothered. The relentless drive northbound had consumed me for nearly eight months, but since Stefan had left I'd lost the point of the whole thing. I was not only wracked by a kind of grief, but embarrassed about feeling so bereft and lonely. The kilometres on roads, the disjoint of flip-flopping the sections, and the sheer tangle of urbanity on the Hamilton to Auckland leg had sapped my verve. Now that I was in Northland, the tarmac and gravel was relentless, and there were day-long country-road detours for trail closures in kauri forest or where private landowners had revoked access. I found it easy to walk 35–40km on the road now, but my passage forward was limited by legal spots to camp, and it was still getting dark around 6p.m.

So I dawdled in the morning, blitzed through the day's kilometres without stopping, didn't carry enough food or bother to eat properly in the evening and, with easier access to 4G and power, stayed up late texting. I couldn't have more than three weeks left on trail, even accounting for bad weather and low-tide crossings and reroutes. But I could not be arsed. I was bored.

However, as I trudged on, that began to change. At the Treasure Island campground in Pataua South, I met the owner, Nita, who asked me where I was from, then exclaimed she had family in Nelson, including Archdeacon Andy Joseph, a prominent, gracious, and much-loved kaumātua. I was sad to hear he'd died recently, aged 96; and when I said goodbye, her hug felt like family. At Whananaki, I stayed with my friend Kirsty's family and they took me to their friend's 65th birthday party. I hadn't been in a gathering of people since the small Matariki family event I'd gone home for, and certainly not in a group of strangers. I didn't know what to do with myself. I didn't know how to talk, felt overwhelmed by the noise and had to keep retreating. I gushed over the feeling of my bare feet on the silky carpet, stared with naked lust at the piles of fresh food and desserts, studied people's faces, and spent ages in the bathroom, touching surfaces and looking at things, admiring how candlelight played on the reflective surfaces, sniffing deeply of the scented soap.

That night, snug in my soft bed and heated room, I couldn't sleep. The evening had been too overwhelming. My life had been grass, mud, cows, gravel, sun and rain for months. Dusty floors and wooden walls, corrugated iron and animal shit. The final weeks of trail really began to hit home, and I started to worry about reintegrating into my old life. How weird had I looked tonight? If a party overwhelmed me, what was the rest of the world going to do?

Who am I now?

* * *

I saw a teenage girl ahead on the country road, dawdling and scuffing the gravel with her dirty pink Crocs, the way country kids do. She had long, beautiful hair caught in a ponytail held by a scrunchie at the nape of her neck, and was peering into some kind of dusty leather sleeve, which looked like it had fallen off a boat or piece of farm equipment. Her blue work-pants were held up with a length of baling twine knotted around her waist.

'Are you walking the trail?' she said as I approached, and I said I was. 'I'll walk with you,' she said, and we ambled down the dusty gravel road for a while. Her name was Jess and she was fifteen. Presently, I said, 'What's that?' and pointed at the leather sleeve.

'Umm, it's something, and it's got an animal in it,' she said. 'Like a gecko or something? I picked it up and the gecko fell out. And I put it back on the ground and the gecko went right back in.' She held out the sleeve; I stopped to peer in and saw a flash of a white-striped brown skink head, hiding just beyond the light.

'Wow,' I said. 'What will you do with it?' She shrugged and we kept walking. She began to tell me about the trail ahead, pointed out her neighbours and told me about their animals, and about her school, family and friends.

After a couple of kilometres, a car drove up with her friend and her mum in it. The mum examined me and there was a quiet exchange in the front seat before Jess's friend, Lily, got out, in gumboots. They both inspected the little skink, and we all walked up the road together.

Lily's gumboot heels slapped and dragged on the gravel, in the way gumboots do. My little toes were beginning to rub and hurt from all the road-walking lately, and I was struggling to keep them protected; my shoes were always too narrow in the toe-box. I looked at her gumboots and could feel every scrape of sweaty rubber on raw, hot heels exposed under slipped-down socks. But she was walking fine.

'Are you walking by yourself?' Lily said. She shook out her bun and put it into a ponytail like Jess's, and the two plumes of long, glossy hair streaked down their backs as they walked a little ahead of me up the hill.

'Yup.'

'We see lots of walkers in the summer coming down here,' Jess said.

'You guys should set up a stall and sell stuff to them,' I said. 'Some days I'd pay a lot for a Coke.'

We got to Jess's driveway, and she pointed out the broken back window on her family's parked ute. 'Mum backed into a possum trap,' she said. 'It was on a tree.'

'My husband did exactly the same thing closing the boot door on the recycling bin.'

They showed me a white sheep skull in the back of the ute, then stopped to confer for a second. 'Can we get a photo with you?' Lily asked.

'Sure,' I said. 'Here, I'll take one too.' We smiled for selfies, and I farewelled them and walked a little way farther before sitting down on the side of the road in a patch of shade and taking off my shoes so my feet could dry a bit. My right ankle had been feeling better but the left one was still swollen and sore, and my little toes throbbed. I prodded their swollen edges, winced and took two paracetamol.

I dug into my pack and ate half a Crunchie, half a bacon sandwich, some chips and salsa, a can of Charlie's Feijoa Fizz, a Nippy's banana milk, a raspberry Coke and half an OSM bar. It occurred to me that Jess and Lily were only the third and fourth people I'd walked with in the entire North Island. There had only been my friend Noon, who'd joined me for a morning walk in Wellington, and Stefan.

I was just finishing my small feast when the girls drove up on a banged-up Honda Big Red quad bike. 'We came to find you,' Jess said. Lily was now keeping the skink in an orange plastic lunchbox.

'Hi again,' I said. 'I'm just having some lunch.' They got off the bike and hung about, kicking the gravel, inspecting the road gutters and ferns, communicating in half-smiles, murmurs and side-eyes, and greeting the neighbours that drove past, each of whom paused to inspect me with a smile that didn't quite reach their assessing, adult eyes.

The girls told me about the walks they'd done with their families. 'Do you have any kids?' Lily asked, as I packed up my rubbish and buckled my pack closed.

'Not myself,' I said. 'But my husband has two lovely kids, Alice and Nate. Alice is your age. She has hair like yours.' We discussed the type of bark and leaf housing the skink might prefer, and I smiled. 'Alice and Nate would do exactly the same thing as you. They'd find a skink and put it in a lunchbox to look at it and make it a house.' I hoisted my pack to go.

'We came to get you,' Jess revealed. 'Do you want a ride?'

I'd been offered dozens of rides in the past 2700km and I'd never accepted one. I'd justified taking a ride for 11km when the track was flooded near Pōkeno and I would have been forced to walk illegally on State Highway 1. But now I looked at their two bashful smiles and didn't hesitate.

'I would love that.' I buckled my pack around my waist and got on the back of the bike with Lily, balancing my poles across my lap. Jess put the bike in gear and we drove on.

'Just don't look at this,' she said, putting her hand over a large, faded sticker on the fuel tank. I could see a big red 'No' circle across the words UNDER 16 and the text: WARNING: OPERATING THIS ATV IF YOU ARE UNDER THE AGE OF 16 INCREASES YOUR CHANCE OF SEVERE INJURY OR DEATH. NEVER OPERATE THIS ATV IF YOU ARE UNDER AGE 16. I gripped the bars behind me. 'It doesn't have brakes,' Jess added.

'How do you brake, then?'

'We just don't,' she said. 'I just put it in first. Once I ran into my sister's leg. But she was OK. She didn't break it or anything. We'll take you to the top of the hill.'

I clung on as she drove with one hand, pointing out various curiosities: big trees, a neighbour's whimsy, more farm animals.

The road climbed and narrowed, and I watched the steep cliff-edge streaking past on the left, packed with ferns and trees, and bit back the adult words 'Aren't we a bit close to the edge?' and 'Hope we don't meet any crazy drivers.'

'There are a lot of crazy drivers around here,' Jess said. 'They go too fast.'

The trees began to meet above us and we drove through a tunnel of greenery. 'This is my mum's favourite part,' she said.

I felt the air moisten and cool under the trees, and closed my eyes to let the light dapple my face. We sped easily, cheating the gravity I struggled against every day, and the sensation of air passing over my face was intoxicating. It had been so long since I'd been on a bicycle, or a horse, or a motorbike, or sprinted free in the wind, or sat on the back of a trailer or ute, and felt anything like this.

Jess pulled over at the top of the hill, a few kilometres up the trail, and I got off the bike. 'Thank you so much,' I said. 'You really saved my sore feet a bit of walking.'

'You're welcome,' she said.

'Bye,' Lily said, and Jess executed a three-point turn on the narrow road and drove back down the hill.

I walked on, the late sun in my face. I'd thoroughly broken my EFI rule now, which I'd cherished so deeply for eight months that it had become a part of my identity. But I no longer cared. These girls, nearly 30 years my junior, had walked with me and then wanted to offer me the only gift they could. I was glad I hadn't hesitated in saying yes.

* * *

Dusk was nearing and I was still a few hours away from a campsite. It had been an enjoyable 32km country-road walk that day from Helena Bay, where I'd stayed in a trail angel's caravan, but I now had to tackle a winding rural road with very little shoulder, in the dark. For southbounders the route between Paihia and Waikare included a 10km kayak, but there was a 13km road-walk and ferry detour and I'd chosen this rather than mucking about with the research, cost, tides and hassle of a reverse kayak, which would lose me a day or two.

A white ute passed with the licence plate KA KITE, definitely the best one I'd seen on trail so far. Far better than the DMIN8R in Bluff. I paused on the side of the road to adjust my hi-vis pack cover, and was attaching the red and white bike lights I used when walking at night when a farmer checking triplet lambs stopped me.

'How far are you going today? It's a really windy road.'

I hesitated. 'I've still got a ways to go.'

'You don't want to be walking that in the dark. It's very dangerous,' he said. 'You've seen the way the locals drive around here?' I had, actually; I'd nearly been sideswiped earlier that morning. 'You've got people going round corners halfway across the centre-line,' he continued. 'Tell you what – I always see walkers and always offer them a ride on this road. Let me go up and check on the missus, then I'll drive you to Russell. You can catch a ferry across to Paihia in the morning.'

'Oh no, that's OK ...' I started to say, but then stopped. I'd accepted the ride from Jess and Lily. I realised I was OK now if someone's impulsive concern and kindness shattered my brittle dream of perfection. This man wanted to help, too. Anyway, the road-walk I was about to do was a detour, not part of the official trail. A land waka it would be.

Kim put my pack in the back of his ute and we drove up to the house, where we were greeted by his wife, Tina, who had one hand and arm bound in a bandage and splint following a fall. They sat me down at their farmhouse table and she cut bread off a loaf and made toast and added butter, then Kim cut some cheese and added that, too. The cheese about sent me into orbit; it was a locally made Montbéliarde from Mahoe Cheese, Kim said.

'You wouldn't like an egg on top? Would you like some jam?' Tina asked. But I was happy with the bread and cheese, which I ate carefully, as though it was a sacrament.

As we left, Tina handed me the rest of the loaf of bread, some apples from their tree and two precious boxes of MTR Chana Masala meals, widely known among trampers as gold-star hut tucker.

'Are you sure you don't want to stay the night?' she said, but I wanted to get on, so she said, 'If you need anything, just come back.' Kim said he'd give me some fish, and stopped to pull two hāpuku fillets out of his shed freezer, then drove me to the Russell Top 10 Holiday Park. When I saw the tightness of the roads I was glad I hadn't walked them in the dark. He dropped me off, waited to see that I could get a tent site via the after-hours intercom, wished me well, and drove away into the night.

I walked down to my tent site, a little overawed by this last hour of enveloping kindness, dropped my pack and began hauling out gear. There was one other person in the campground, a man sorting stuff in the back of his campervan. He called out, 'Are you walking the TA?'

The voice sounded familiar, and with a start I realised where I'd heard it before.

'Mike?' I called back.

'Yes?'

'Mike Lim?'

'Naomi?' I doubled over in astonished laughter, and went over to say hi. Mike was the Whangārei TA hiker I'd interviewed for *Wilderness* at Whangārei Heads four weeks earlier. He was somehow in Russell on the same night as me, testing his new ultralight gear on some walks before he hit Te Araroa later in the season.

'Do you want a beer?' he said, handing me a Stoke ale. We sat at a tiny picnic table and drank them, then another one each, as the night blackened. I marvelled aloud at the kindness I'd been shown recently.

'Everyone feels sorry for you,' Mike said with a chuckle. 'They're like: "You're doing what? By choice?"' He put his van water-jug on the table and attached a light to it, and it refracted blue and white through the fluid, a bright oasis in the dark. We talked about the trail, food and gear; he'd studied industrial design and made his own tramping kit, including several iterations of an ultralight pack, and as a personal trainer he'd recently started a company called Hiker Health that specialised in preparing people for tramping. I was a bit ashamed to reveal my terrible diet and near constant lack of protein, but he knew what this life was like.

'It's tough to get in enough grams of protein per kilo of bodyweight on trail,' he said.

Then rain began to spit, and it was time for bed. I had hesitated over Kim's gift of fish; I knew I wouldn't be able to defrost and cook it that night, and I'd be racing in the morning to catch the 7a.m. ferry. I didn't want it to spoil on the long, hot walk the next day. Mike had already eaten, but he had a full campervan kitchen set-up so I offered it to him for his dinner the next day. He was happy for the good protein, and so was I, to pass on Kim and Tina's kindness.

I was in my tent eating cashews, an OSM bar, an apple and the heel of bread that Tina had given me when an old uni flatmate who I hadn't seen for about fifteen years texted me to say she was in Paihia, just across the inlet. She'd seen my Instagram and wondered if I was nearby. Delighted, we arranged to meet at the wharf at 7.20a.m.

I went to sleep in my tent peaceful and happy, listening to rain spitting on the fly. I'd had another day of kindness and connection in Te Tai Tokerau, the lack of which had tortured me so much this year. I thought back across this week of serendipity and realised I was enjoying the trail again. I felt like I was sixteen, full of energy and able to walk forever. Nothing on trail was a big deal anymore; I adjusted to and absorbed it, like a container ship pushing through swells. I rarely felt in danger. I knew if bad weather hit I could walk my way out of it or find somewhere sheltered and pitch my tent.

I didn't worry about drowning in rivers; the luxury of being alone, I'd discovered during the higher-risk areas of the South Island, was being able to indulge in extreme caution. If rivers were dodgy I just waited until they went down. I no longer worried about being attacked. The only things I still sometimes thought about were falling, knocking myself out or bleeding uncontrollably, or losing my two sources of survival: my dry sleeping bag and my tent. Being cautious had helped me avoid these so far.

I also no longer worried about food. At the beginning of the trail, starting as a regular tramper, being hungry had seemed dangerous, like I would immediately collapse and die if I went a few days without food. But I had discovered thru-hiking was nothing like my regular two- to four-day tramps, where friends and I carefully planned each stop, each meal. Going hungry would have seemed like a foolhardy and dangerous miscalculation in that world. But now I had experienced unplanned waits in the wilderness and having to walk for a couple days without food, and I knew how I felt: faded, but focused and even at times energetic. My body just kept me going until I found food.

The biggest gift the trail had given me was my lack of fear about being in the wilderness, and that was thanks to my PLB. I knew now that if I set it off but got trapped somewhere for a week, or even two, I'd be fine as long as I had water. And as a woman, with higher body fat, I had more endurance and energy reserves than a man. Each gram of fat I was carrying would help me last weeks without eating, if I stayed warm and in one place. My body stored fat for the times it needed to be used, and I was now encountering those times in a way I never had before in the real world. I replaced those calories easily when I found food again.

I never felt physically tired anymore; only my toes were killing the buzz. Joy had flooded in, replacing the lassitude I'd been fighting for nearly a month as I struggled through the last of the Waikato, then navigated the stressful urban corridors of Hamilton and Auckland, and the return to Whangārei Heads, where I'd been briefly haunted by Stefan's ghost. I realised I had let him go now. I had just needed to find people again, and feel their warmth.

Maybe it was that, or maybe because it was spring in the north, but that night the salty, damp air of Russell felt more alive to me than anywhere else on trail. There was a low hum of insects, and I woke hungry at midnight and devoured half an OSM bar and a fistful of cashews before quickly brushing my teeth again and falling asleep listening to kiwi and ruru calling across the dark. The dawn chorus woke me at 5.55a.m. with a complex, deafening symphony, the birds taking turns, their songs fading and rising again. I unzipped my tent door and put my phone outside to record it, then lay back in my sleeping bag with my eyes closed and listened. I wanted to be able to hear this later: to send myself back to this moment when I felt lucky to be here, to have this sound swelling all around me, and feeling flush with pleasure to simply be alive to hear it.

CHAPTER 13

RUSSELL TO NINETY MILE BEACH

It was late afternoon by the time I arrived at Puketī Forest Hut, and I was limping again. My left ankle was still swollen and sending pain up my leg, and weeks of road-walking had pummelled my little toes so badly that I was hobbling. For the first time, I'd chosen to invoke my medical exemption on taking rides, catching one some of the way from Kerikeri to make my DOC hut booking that night instead of wasting both that $25 and more dollars on accommodation in town. My budget was well and truly blown by now.

I'd stopped at Countdown in Kerikeri and picked up my trail food, then stood there next to the trolleys, making my usual scene as I opened everything, threw away the cardboard boxes and plastic packets, consolidated it all and crammed it into my pack. I re-dressed my foot wounds with fresh plasters and also applied one to the hole in my last good ziplock bag. Now, at the hut, I peeled off the day's plasters and inspected my feet and toes. They were red, raw and peeling again, and there was a new, long blister on the ball of my foot. They weren't going to get better any time soon. I just had to get through these last 200km.

Puketī was my last hut on Te Araroa, and even though it was a bougie one with power-points and cold showers, I felt sentimental about writing my name in a DOC hut book for the final time. I flipped back through the pages and smiled as I saw the familiar scrawls of names I'd last seen in the hut book on Pirongia.

Two carloads of men turned up as night fell. They were track-cutters who were working during the day and staying at the hut in the evenings, and were responsible for the two cooked chicken carcasses in the mini-fridge. They turned on overhead fluorescent lights I hadn't yet noticed and began preparing a beautiful, elaborate meal as I chewed on a cold spinach and feta roll I'd picked up from the service station. Two of them cooked and another two picked up guitars.

Oh God, guitars in huts, I thought, but the men began to sing 'Redemption Song' and 'House of the Rising Sun' very gently and sweetly, if slightly off-key. When they switched to Cat Stevens's 'Father and Son', all five men joined in, which was both unexpected and beautiful. I lay there in my sleeping bag on the top bunk by the window and sang softly too.

I leaned over and cracked the window open so the breeze would blow in all night from the south, and thought about it wafting a country's worth of my sweat and skin cells back to me and into my lungs as I slept. I was beginning to feel some grief about the trail ending. Tomorrow I'd pass the 200km-to-go mark. Tomorrow I would begin walking the last week before I went home.

* * *

I was up with the trackcutters at 5.30a.m. The trail notes said this section, which included several kilometres of wading the Waipapa River and a side stream, would take eight hours, but I got through in six and reached the next campsite at midday. I checked my feet; the rivers had softened them and they weren't hurting, though the long foot-ball blister was filled with black grains of sand. The cold water had also helped my ankles, as well as relieving the occasional twinge I still got in my knee.

I wasn't ready to stop for the day; in fact, I felt I could run another 20km, and maybe keep going forever. I jogged down the road and as late afternoon approached I decided to simply keep going to see how far I could get. The trail had been boring lately, with too many roads. I'd already done two days in one – why not return to the masochism of the South Island, make life interesting, and try for three?

The pain of those first days in Southland was long gone. My body did what I wanted now, without drama. I felt great every morning. During this whole year I'd not been particularly driven about churning out the kilometres, unless I caught a vibe and decided to race something for the fun of it; I'd tended to let my schedule be dictated by my energy levels, the weather, work deadlines, friends' plans, trail sections or mere whims. But with the late sun tipping over the paddocks in Omahuta and 33km already covered that day, I decided to try to blitz the last 165km as fast as possible, and destroy myself as much as I could in the process. Just to see what happened. Just to see what I could do. Just to feel something again.

* * *

Around 7p.m., I stood in the dark on the side of State Highway 1, outside Mangamuka marae, looking up at Venus shining over the spire of the church. It was fully twilight, the sky fading to pale blue on the horizon, and the highway was empty. Headlights appeared and a car zoomed past, but when I glanced behind me I saw red lights appear 100m down the road as it stopped, turned and slowly drove back towards me. I stood alone on the side of the road in the near-dark.

This situation was always a little nerve-wracking, but so far I'd had nothing to fear. I turned to face the car as it drew level and got my phone ready to start recording so my family might at least know what had happened to me.

'Are you OK, love? Do you need a ride?'

It was a woman behind the wheel, and the glowing faces of small children peered out from behind her in the dark. I smiled at her.

'I'm fine, thank you.'

'Are you sure? A woman walking alone in the dark? I drove past you and I thought, "She probably needs a ride". Do you have somewhere to stay tonight?' I didn't want to tell her I planned to simply walk until I reached at least Kaitaia, 42km away, so I said yes, I did.

'Are you camping? That campsite up the road? That's good, love. OK, you take care.'

'Thank you so much for checking in,' I said.

'That's no problem, love,' she said. 'You're safe in Mangamuka. There are good people here.'

She drove off with a smile and a wave, and I continued down State Highway 1, turned left into Makene Road and walked uphill towards the stars, stopping for a while to sit with the night and eat peanut butter, jerky and an apricot OSM bar. The trail went through a farm, and at around 9p.m. I filled up my bottles at a small seepage and replaced the batteries in my headlamp. I followed the trail for a good half-hour, in the dark through paddocks and gorse and sticky mud that trapped my feet. The light from my headlamp caught possum after possum, clinging to tree trunks, their gaze trapped in my beam of light. Just before 11p.m., I entered Raetea Forest, one of the most notorious sections of the entire country, and my night took a turn to the surreal. If I'd wanted a challenge, I got it in Raetea.

* * *

The Raetea Forest is muddy regardless of the weather, slow, steep and waterless. The DOC estimate for the 19km track through the forest was nine or ten hours, but the trail notes said that was on the low side; it could take anywhere from twelve to fifteen. I hadn't had a decent mountain challenge since Pirongia, though, and I was keen to tackle it as quickly as possible.

I brushed through spiderwebs freshly hung across the path, feeling them drape and stick to my face, and stopped dead in astonishment when on the side of a small cutting ahead I saw not one giant carnivorous snail, but two of them, the bronze whorls of their shells glinting in my lamplight and their oily, muscular black bodies searching, searching like a tongue. As I shone my headlamp on one and approached to study it, it retreated into its shell. I was astonished. I'd walked plenty of times at night and the only trace of a giant snail I'd seen was a shattered, rat-gnawed shell. Now I'd encountered a dinosaur. I would see four more that night. I had rarely felt luckier to be out here alone in the dark.

For the next eleven hours I trudged through the mud, which was further pugged by cow and pig trotters, my feet sticking and sucking, climbing over fallen trees, occasionally losing a shoe and having to dig my hands into the cold clammy mud to retrieve it then shake it free of muck, reaching into the toe-box to scrape out the last of it with my fingertips, before jamming it back on my foot. I almost wished for rain; it might have made this clammy, clinging muck a little more liquid and easier to move through.

The forest was cool and quiet, and stars shone through the trees. I had watched the waxing gibbous moon progress over my head all night and at 1.30a.m. it was shining golden and low though nīkau fronds to the southwest. But the forest had begun to sap me. Loops of supplejack trapped me every few steps, branches tripped me and carved notches in my legs, stabbing into the soft skin of my thighs. As I struggled for minutes to progress a few metres, it dawned on me that I didn't belong here. No one did. The forest belonged to the birds. I wanted desperately to be free of it, and this clawing, clinging wet earth.

I stopped for a half-hour or so and lay back on my pack, deliriously watching the stars through the trees. I remembered I had a wheel of brie in my bag and dove in to retrieve it, tearing off the silver paper and eating the whole thing in a few bites, like a hamburger. I tried not to think about how filthy my nails and hands were; they'd been plunged into mud so many times now to retrieve stuck feet and shoes, and there was no water to wash them with. I wiped them on leaves and tree bark.

At 5a.m. I saw the glint of Kaitaia shining through the trees to the north, and when I reached Raetea Summit at 744m twenty minutes later, I felt the transparency of the universe pour over me, the wind blowing mist over my skin. I saw the beginnings of a pale blue dawn creeping up under the night. I heard the first birds begin to sing. I saw the huge, deep prints of a big stag; saw how his hooves had slipped and sunk deep into the mud, too. As the light rose around 7a.m., I got my first glimpse of Te Oneroaa-Tōhē, Ninety Mile Beach, through trees to my right, a strip of silver shining to the northeast.

I was nearly there. Nearly done.

When the forest finally released me just before 11a.m., I ran down Takahue Saddle Road in glee, then sat down at a corner for a while to inspect the damage to my legs and filter some dirty water from a puddle. An older man on a quad bike drove past and gave me a cheery wave, and I waved back. My socks were thick with mud; I scraped a line with a filthy fingernail, studying with interest the sedimentary layers of dried and drying dirt that covered my skin. My legs were destroyed. My thighs were chafed and the skin was covered in scratches, grazes, stab wounds from sharp branches, sunburn and patchy dry skin.

I was still feeling OK, and had planned to keep walking the 20km along easy flat roads to Kaitaia, which should have taken only a few more hours. But the stop in the hot sun had been a mistake; the warmth and lack of water had begun to sap my resolve. My feet and little toes now felt completely raw and every step on the hard road was agony. I stopped again down the road to get a wider-brimmed hat from my pack, but when my sleeping bag fell out and rolled away down the hill I could only watch it go. It settled in a ditch 20m away. I stared at it. My feet hurt so much I felt unable to get up to retrieve it.

I hung my head and realised I was done in. I checked the map. I had about 135km to go until Cape Reinga; I'd walked 65km since 6a.m. yesterday. I'd greeted the sun, run down forestry roads and kauri forest trails; waded through the river gorges, falling in and saturating myself; strode along more forestry roads, country roads and State Highway 1; watched night fall, then tackled the muddy hell of Raetea. I'd seen the last big town on the trail, Kaitaia, shining silver on the horizon, and greeted the dawn. I'd squeezed three trail days into 29 straight hours, but now I needed to rest before I kept going.

'Is that your sleeping bag?' The man in the quad bike had returned and rolled up next to me, smiling. When I nodded, he went down to get it, then brought it back to me. 'Do you need a ride?'

'You know what?' I said. 'I think I do.'

* * *

I recalled a Facebook post from a place called Krishna Sanctuary, offering $10 camping and meals by donation. I knew it was somewhere nearby, but had no phone reception to check the map or call ahead. But the quad-bike driver, John, knew the place and drove me to it. He carefully avoided ruts and humps in the road, pointed out the banana palms lining it, and told me about his gardening work on a local marae. He'd been up to the trailhead to check out the Raetea Track for an upcoming trip.

'It's bloody rough up there,' he said, then pulled into a driveway on the right. 'OK, here we are.'

I had to laugh. The sanctuary was just 100m down the road – I could have crawled there. I got off the bike and my pack was immediately taken out of my hands by a tall, slim man with a Hare Krishna shikha ponytail, who introduced himself as Abhay. I asked if they could take a Te Araroa walker. They had just had their first southbound couple through the night before, they said, and were ready for the season. I was welcome.

'What a wild adventure,' he said, when he heard about my night. 'Come with me.'

Their hiker facilities weren't quite ready, so his wife, Jaya, gave me a towel and a stainless steel bucket for my clothes, and pointed me to their own shower, showing me how to get the hot water just right. I shampooed my hair and scraped the mud off my legs with my fingernails, and she offered to wash my clothes. I put on my down jacket and wrapped the towel around me. Jaya gave me some of her home-blended hibiscus and jojoba oil for my skin, and I rubbed it into my face.

'I've put some essential oils in the machine with your clothes,' she said, almost as if she was sharing a secret, then she sat me down at their table and gave me a plate of sliced homegrown white guava, pink guava and banana, all of which I ate, silent with wonder. I had never had a homegrown banana before, and I chewed it thoughtfully. It was more like a bread or meat than a fruit.

Jaya showed me where to charge my phone and battery packs and where to hose off my shoes, poles and pack, and hang my clothes. She said lunch would be ready around 3.30p.m. and we'd all eat together; it was by donation. She showed me to the camping space and pointed out the washing line and a clean, white cabin with a deck they'd just built, where I could lay out my sleeping mat, which would cost $35, if I preferred. It was freshly painted and I wouldn't have to walk with a wet tent in the morning.

I rolled out my mat and inflated it, then hung my tent and gear to air as well. Tears filled my eyes when I saw the laden plate I was presented with for lunch, and Jaya carefully took me through each thing she'd prepared: lentils and rice with fresh homegrown avocado, curried homegrown taro, cauliflower pakora, chutney made from homegrown mint, guava and coriander, and a thick, sweet semolina pudding for dessert.

* * *

In the cabin I washed my remaining food packets in the sink, rinsing crumbs off my capsicum and muesli bar wrappers, and consolidated my trash to dispose of in Kaitaia; I didn't like leaving it with trail angels. I collected my clothes from the line and went to bed at 5p.m., slept badly, and woke at 5a.m. to pack up.

I left them an extra $20 for the meal and their kindness, and farewelled Jaya, who was returning from walking their dog. She pressed a banana, a golden tamarillo and a guava on me, and I walked through their gate feeling high, fresh, and jaunty. It was 33km along country roads and state highway to Ahipara, but I wanted to see how far I could get along Ninety Mile Beach beyond there as well. I hadn't slept much, but that was nothing new; I rarely got more than five hours a night and it no longer seemed to affect me much.

On the road I ate my capsicum and the fruit, marvelling at their dense, complex taste. After a few hours I felt a surge of disbelief, then excitement when I saw a southbounder approach. I'd met my first southbounder off-trail in the bathrooms at the Russell Top 10 Holiday Park, but this was the first time I'd encountered one on trail since Arthur's Pass. His name was Toto and he was French, and we had a short, giddy chat.

Just outside Kaitaia I met a woman who asked me if I was walking Te Araroa.

'I am,' I said. 'Just a hundred and sixteen kilometres to go.'

'Did you come through the Raetea forest?'

'Yup.'

'Did you know it was closed?'

I stopped and stared at her. 'What?'

'You actually walked through?'

'Who said it was closed?' But then I was suddenly overcome with hysterical laughter, and then she was too, and we giggled so much that I never caught her answer.

* * *

I strode towards the Kaitaia Subway in desperate need of a large sandwich. But down the main street I was waylaid by a man sitting on a park bench, who asked, 'Are you headed to the beach?' I stopped and leaned on my poles.

'Yup,' I said. 'I'm hoping to get there and walk some of it tonight.'

'Aw, you shouldn't walk in the dark out there,' he said. 'There's some bad people around out there.'

'Really?'

'Yup. I used to stay on the beach. There's good people but some people – be careful.' He asked me where I was from, and said he'd lived far down south for a bit, but was in Northland now to escape skinheads. I asked him what had happened.

'I gave them a hiding,' he said. 'But not in a bad way. In a way that wasn't my fault.'

I smiled. 'I'm sure they deserved it.'

'My niece was down there and she was going, "Uncle, you're quite famous!" Anyway, my name's William.'

He told me about his old home on Ninety Mile Beach, when he lived in his car and tent in the rocky dunes, and the good living to be had out there: the huge trevally and snapper he used to catch, the mussels he used to prise off the rocks, the pipi he'd dig his toes around in the sands, the pāua he'd collect in the rare moments when the sea was calm, once in a blue moon.

'But when it's still water like that, you won't catch a fish because they can see your line,' he said. 'That's how crystal clear it is.

'I used to amaze people. I'd get a trevally, a snapper. I'd come back and there's tourists there and I'd fillet half of it and slice it into sashimi and go "Try it". I did half a trevally and these

German people said it was the best raw fish they'd ever had. It's a beautiful life up there.'

William had met plenty of Te Araroa walkers in his time living on the beach, most of them in the first few days of their walk as they headed south, most of them stunned by the sheer sweep and scale of the sands.

'I met this guy from Poland and when he saw the whole beach he was like, "I just realised how small we are",' he said. 'Because that's all you can see. He goes, "Places like Poland, Denmark – it's just flat. Building, building". But when they come out here, they're just like, "Wow". Have you got sunblock?'

He told me to be careful on the narrow part of the beach near Waipapakauri, where the tide could sweep you away, and instructed me on where to get spring water, dyed brown with tannins but good.

'Just be careful,' he repeated as we parted. 'Some guys can be – creepy.'

'What should I do if they are?'

He paused, thoughtful. 'Just carry on walking, I guess,' he said at last. 'Just be like, "Hi! Sorry, I've got to move". Would you like my number in case?' I thought I would very much like the number of someone who'd given skinheads the bash. We swapped phones and put in each other's numbers, and I hugged him and left, smiling, in search of my sandwich.

I ate a foot-long teriyaki chicken sub and three cookies at Subway, then rather desultorily wandered the aisles of a small supermarket, trying to find anything I could stomach for the next few days. I eventually settled mostly on a stash of Primo flavoured milks and a few bottles of Up & Go Protein Energize, along with biscuits, jerky and muesli bars. I was so over finding food that I just didn't care anymore; I only had a few days left anyway. I picked up a plastic tub of gummy lollies, beautifully arranged like a 3D mosaic, a packet of Hokey Pokey Squiggles, a can of squirty chocolate mousse, a packet of chips and a few other things. I was far more interested in cold drinks and novelty at this point than actual nutrition.

I walked along the highway to Ahipara, but there was so little road shoulder that I had to spend long minutes standing in rubbishy ditches to let trucks and cars pass. My feet had begun to hurt like hell. I was soon feeling demoralised and sat for long minutes on my pack whenever I could, to escape the cars and the pain. But eventually I shook myself, took more paracetamol and kept hobbling.

When I got to Ahipara in the late afternoon I smelled fish'n'chips, and a little girl led me to Bidz Takeaways. It was a Friday, so I lined up inside with hordes of locals, then ate outside at a picnic table with two German southbounders who were having their first burgers since coming off the beach. We sat for a while chatting as night fell, and when the dark blanketed me I realised my resolve to walk Ninety Mile Beach in the dark had evaporated. I walked a couple of kilometres to the Ahipara Top 10 Holiday Park instead and set up my tent in the fading light, determined to get 62km down the beach tomorrow to Maunganui Bluff.

* * *

I woke up at midnight, starving, and tore into a bag of Delisio caramelised onion and balsamic vinegar chips while I checked all my weather apps. There was a polar blast coming, and I decided I didn't want my last days on Te Araroa to be struggling through the cold and wet. I'd stay an extra day here and hide in my tent.

But in the morning, I couldn't sit still. The sky didn't look too bad. Maybe I could at least get 15km up the beach, to the Ngapae Holiday Park, or 30km to Hukatere Lodge? I ate the rest of the chips as I packed up, determined to walk through anything. But when a heavy, cold rain began to lash the holiday park palms at 8a.m. I knew it was too cold and wet for me to be out there. I stayed another day instead, working a little and trying to dry my shoes for the next day's trek along the beach. Wet shoes and socks plus sand would destroy my feet further.

I drank some strawberry Primo and ate the packet of Squiggles for lunch and dinner, then decided to inspect my toes. When I peeled off the bandages, I gasped. Both little toes had black patches on them and I couldn't tell if it were mud or something dead. There was no toenail left on the left one. I bandaged them up and tried to get some sleep.

I woke in pain at 2a.m., my toes throbbing, and hobbled to the ablutions block, determined to debride them or wash them or whatever else I had to do so I could keep walking. In the shower block I heated up a needle in my lighter flame and poked at the black flesh on my left foot. The pain and nausea that shot through me was so strong I nearly passed out.

I sat down in the shower, wrenched my foot around and studied it through the steam, gently prodding it to reveal more red and black flesh, but I couldn't quite tell what was going on. It was just a misshapen mess. I washed it as best I could, swallowing back waves of nausea and dizziness at the pain, then smeared both of my little toes in Crystaderm and plasters. I did the same with the other red and raw patches on my feet. I also loosened the laces to give my toes more room and considered cutting open the sides of my shoes, but decided to leave that as a last resort: it would only let in more sand.

At 4.50a.m. I drank a banana Primo, a chocolate Up & Go Protein and a blackcurrant V, then swallowed two paracetamol and a Voltaren and set off for the beach in soft, sprinkling rain. I'd lost a day waiting out the weather and was still determined to finish this trail as fast as possible. I had only 102km to go now, and I knew I could walk that in two days. Stefan had walked the 81km from Ngapae Holiday Park to Cape Reinga in 21 hours, and I was privately keen to see if I could best him. To be conservative, I set a goal of getting 30km down the beach to Hukatere Lodge, just in case my feet caused me hell.

I got to the beach at dawn and walked the long, white sweep of sand, kilometres disappearing under my feet. My toes didn't hurt. I felt like I could walk forever. Fishermen beamed at me as I passed, inviting me to admire their catch.

As the sun rose higher I slathered on sunblock and kept walking. I met a string of southbounders, including Annie and Sylvan, two Nelsonians who I'd first met at Kiwi Hut near Te Anau in February. They had walked the South Island northbound last summer, and were now walking the North Island southbound. Although we'd only spent one night in each other's company and had barely exchanged a word, it was a joy to see them again.

By 1p.m. I'd walked 30km and arrived at my destination for the day, Hukatere Lodge. I smelled horses on the breeze, then saw them: a wild herd grazed the dunes in front of me, moving just ahead as I approached. I looked for the owner, planning to check in, but then realised I actually wanted to keep going. I thought about food and realised I'd forgotten to buy any more: the extra day in the holiday park at Ahipara had eaten up some of my supplies. I checked my food bag: beef jerky. A couple of cranberry OSM bars. A few sachets of Pic's peanut butter slugs. And the can of chocolate mousse.

In my regular life I'd shave my head before forgetting a meal, but this had happened so often on trail lately that I'd stopped noticing or worrying about it. I just simply did not care anymore. I had canvassed the same packaged stuff in the same supermarket aisles for so long that I couldn't be bothered with it. Way back at Mavora Lakes, near the start of the trail, I had found I could no longer face dehydrated food, an aversion so strong that I'd preferred to walk without eating for 36 hours until I could get to Queenstown. Although I kept persevering with them, I had barely been able to stomach dehy and freeze-dry ever since.

Aside from the hideous expense, there was a particular oily, rancid smell about a rehydrated meal that closed down my oesophagus. Nothing could induce me to finish a bag. I simply carried the meals, gas and my stove without eating them until I could find a decent tearoom and buy a pie, or an egg sandwich, or a chicken roll, or a mince savoury, and a Coke. When I did try to cook them, I shovelled down a few spoonfuls, then abandoned them, nauseous. Not even the hikers' favourite, the Real Meals Sri Lankan Curry, could tempt me.

Eventually I just went with what my body demanded. I stopped buying the meals and ate whatever I wanted whenever I could get it. I still covered the kilometres, though I knew it wasn't a good or smart way to do it from a nutritional point of view. But I couldn't fight my stomach. Only sandwiches, pies, cold drinks and fresh, hot meals tempted me to eat.

For most of the trail, I'd lived off cherry tomatoes, Vintage cheddar, Cheds or Vita-Weats, apples, mandarins, carrots, capsicums and OSM bars. Occasionally I bought packets of Farrah's wraps, spread them with cream cheese or avocado, and rolled them up with lettuce, cherry tomatoes and cheese. Getting enough protein was an ongoing problem; I couldn't face salami by this stage of the trail, either. I didn't even buy chocolate anymore; it was heavy, and also went uneaten in my pack, unless I made the mistake of buying a large block of Whittaker's Creamy Milk which, like a packet of lollies, I would eat in half a day and then suffer such a severely low mood that I had to avoid it altogether.

I squirted some chocolate mousse down my gullet and kept walking. I decided to aim for Maunganui Bluff, which was another 27km away, making it 62km for the day. I reckoned if I knuckled down I could get there by 8.30p.m.

As I walked away, the owner of the lodge came up to greet me. I explained I'd intended to stay but had decided to keep going.

'But where will you stay? There's no camping until Maunganui Bluff. You can't camp in the dunes,' she said. 'You can't make it to the bluff now, anyway. It's a day's walk away.' I smiled and said goodbye.

* * *

I'd had a tailwind that day; the wind had blown relentlessly against my back all the way down the beach, until it turned towards evening and began assaulting me from the west. I kept walking.

I watched heavy foam blow off the waves and avoided their pull; with my foot problems, getting wet shoes on this beach would end me. I dodged the sea and watched seabirds soaring up, dropping shellfish, swooping down to inspect them, then picking them up and dropping them once more, shocking the small molluscs into opening their shells for a second so a beak could peck inside.

Around 5p.m. I realised I hadn't sat down all day except once to crouch in the dunes and apply sunblock, so I stopped for a few minutes to sit behind a sandy hummock and chew peanut butter and beef jerky, inspecting the drifts of plastic rubbish surrounding me: tubs, caps, bottles. When darkness began to fall I felt my old surge of dusk anxiety, but told myself there was no one around, put on more music and continued on the dark sand, singing. The moon was hidden behind clouds. I'd been walking since 5a.m. and had covered 57km straight. I was feeling fine, and considered pushing on like Stefan and going through the night to Cape Reinga.

But at 8p.m. I felt an intense wave of fatigue fall over me, and I knew I'd have to stop. Maunganui Bluff was just a few kilometres away. The moon came out, which helped. But then, just a kilometre from the campsite, the tide came in and engulfed my feet in the dark, and I knew that there was no way my socks and shoes would dry overnight. Tomorrow I'd be in trouble.

I took a wrong turn into the dunes and wandered about in the dark for a while, but eventually found the campsite by the light of the moon and bunked down in the cooking shelter. But I hadn't counted on mosquitos; I couldn't even remember the last time I'd been bothered by insects. I woke up at midnight burning with itchiness, and pulled my tent fly over me, spending the rest of the night dropping in and out of sleep. The herd of wild horses galloped near once, waking me again. I heard them whinnying and snorting and the drumbeat of hooves outside the shelter and saw their shapes in the dark. In the morning, I woke at 5a.m., brushed sand off my shoes with the campsite broom, and followed their hoofprints back down to the beach to walk the last 42km to Cape Reinga.

But I had only gone 10km when I knew I was in trouble. My feet started burning as though I was walking on ground glass; the sand was so fine that I essentially was. I sat down to inspect my feet and found the old blister and skin under my toes was sore and reddening, and my heels were raw, too. My plan was to walk 33km to the cape before dark and hitch to a town, or somewhere I could legally camp, but my feet were in a bad way.

I decided to check out my little toes again. I prised off the plasters and peered at the left one. Walking in wet socks and shoes had softened it, and I looked closer, poking at it with my fingernail, then gingerly lifted what looked like a flesh trapdoor. The toenail was already long gone, but to my horror, the entire upper of my toe lifted up like it was on a hinge, revealing a dark red, raw chasm underneath. Half of the toe was hanging by a thread.

I dropped my foot and shrieked in horror. What the fuck?! What was *that*? I stared back down the beach, suddenly alert. I'd had an insect bite on my arm once, and had casually called Healthline when red streaks began to appear, fanning up towards my heart; I had some notion that was a bad thing. The nurse told me it was an extremely fucking bad thing, and to get off the phone and get the hell down to Urgent Care at once.

I knew sepsis could kill you in a day, and these toes had been open for days and exposed to all sorts of muck in the last few, including cow shit and God knows what else in the Waipapa River and Raetea Forest. Yesterday morning, the wounds had still been full of mud, and I'd only put the hydrogen peroxide cream on them for the first time the night before. Was that enough to prevent infection, with all this walking, sweat, dirt and filth?

I needed to get off this beach and get to town. Any town. I started getting out the last of the Crystaderm and plasters, taped my feet, and set off again at a run. But within five minutes, the wind began to blast me, and it began to rain, hard. And then it began to hail.

CHAPTER 14

NINETY MILE BEACH TO CAPE REINGA TE RERENGA WAIRUA

I woke three hours later, warm in my sleeping bag, sunlight dappling the green walls of my tent. I listened. It didn't sound like it was raining anymore, and the wind had died down.

I was snug in a protected cove in the dunes. I'd dashed here when the clouds opened and began thrashing me with cold, wet and gales, a deadly combination. I'd pitched my tent in a sandy depression, crossed my fingers that the water pooling outside didn't mean I'd camped in a dry riverbed that was about to flood, wiped up puddles of water from the tent floor with my T-shirt, inflated my sleeping mat, unrolled my sleeping bag, then lay down and fell asleep.

I checked my phone. It was 1.20p.m. My feet throbbed. I decided that although it was too late to make Cape Reinga and get a hitch to town today, I could at least get 20km up the beach to the Twilight Beach campsite, the last camp on the trail for northbounders.

But I had no water; I'd used the last of it to wash sand off my feet earlier that day, and there was no more until the campsite. I checked the topo map and saw a stream a couple of kilometres south. I would have to go back.

I made a sort of tape-slipper contraption to try to stop the sand friction on the hotspots, then broke camp and stumbled southwards to find the stream. My feet were killing me, but I put on my playlist and swallowed two paracetamol and turned my walk into a shuffling sort of run, which eased the pressure. I found the stream; it was fresh and tasted like forest. I screwed on my water filter, filled my bottles and then turned north again. The wind had changed again and was now blowing into my face. I jogged up the beach.

After an hour or so, a ute pulled up and asked if I wanted a ride. It had begun to rain again and I was changing out of my down jacket into my sodden raincoat. I hadn't bothered to put on a bra that morning so I stood there in my sheer, tight, black merino top and leggings as the driver chatted to me. The wind was so strong it was blowing my breasts around. I felt my cheeks flush and hunched over my pack a little.

'No thanks,' I called out.

'You sure?' he said. 'There's another weather bomb coming in about an hour.' This made me hesitate. I didn't want another night's delay, tenting in the dunes.

Fuck it, I thought. *Medical exemption.* I climbed up into the cab of his ute. The guy's name was Jason, and as we drove he offered to take me swimming at a secret spot in the dunes, but only if I didn't film it or take photos.

'I thought it was going to rain,' I said.

'Well, maybe,' he said, squinting over at me.

'Maybe,' I repeated. 'No thanks. I really need to get to Twilight Beach.' He gave me a bottle of water, apologised he didn't have a Coke, and drove fast down the hard, flat sands, opening another bottle of water and drinking it while he did so, letting the car steer itself. We must have gone 10–15km, but I told myself that erring on the side of caution with my toes was more important than skipping these kilometres.

A sheer wall of green rose before us as we approached the end of Ninety Mile Beach and the beginning of the Te Paki Coastal Track. The campsite was 3.5km away now, and I thanked Jason and got out to climb the wooden stairs to the top of the cliffs. I paused to watch him zoom off down the beach, then climbed the stairs until I was high over the dusty white sands, the white-capped waves. I stopped and turned for a last view. *I didn't walk all of you*, I thought, *but* ... I searched for optimism, acceptance, positivity. There was nothing. Nope, I wasn't ready yet to emotionally recover from taking this ride.

I put my head down instead and climbed the rest of the stairs, letting the beach fold back behind the hills, then splashed through cold, ankle-deep puddles flooding the track. On the cliffs the wind blew so severely that I feared it would pick me up and dash me on the rocks, so I braced against it with my poles as I had in the Waikato, put my head down and kept going. I reached Twilight Beach camp just as the rain began to lash down again, and sprinted for the little hexagonal wooden-and-concrete cooking shelter, which was open on all sides but at least had half-walls and a roof. Two SOBOs were there and had already pitched their tents: a young man called Tim, wearing pristine white Crocs, and his friend who was walking with him for a few days. They'd started the trail that morning and looked fresh and healthy, if a little wind-blown.

'Dear God,' I said, dropping my pack, sitting on the concrete floor under the cooking bench and huddling against the wooden walls, feeling a little shell-shocked from the constant blasting. I wondered what these two pink-cheeked SOBOs must think of me arriving like this: a feral, anarchic northbound trail rat, drowned, hungry, thirsty, hobbling on ruined feet, carrying a half-empty pack, with no food, stove or camp shoes. My selfies over the last few days had revealed deep blue circles under my eyes. Only the lower half of my face was tanned, from months of wearing an unsensible baseball cap that protected only my forehead. Dreadlocks were forming in my sun-bleached, ravaged hair, which hadn't been washed since ... well, I wasn't sure. I'd run out of shampoo.

271

I sat there on the cold concrete, occasionally swearing at the weather, scratching the bites on my arm and breast and drinking tea-coloured water from my bottle. I was not even fully dressed; I still had no bra on. And then I realised the sheer merino leggings I was wearing, which my jacket did not cover, were see-through too. I'd gone commando when I changed after the hail and had hung my shorts and both pairs of wet black merino underwear to dry on my pack. I was not in a fit state to be seen by new hikers.

I watched a tall, single blade of grass flick back and forth in the wind, rhythmic as a conductor's baton, then hauled myself up and went off to pitch my tent. I'd lost many tent pegs along the way so I broke apart stout sticks to drive into the wet ground instead, thinking Jason had certainly gotten an eyeful back there on the beach. No wonder he'd given me a ride.

* * *

Last day. I set out just after dawn the next morning to walk the 12km to Cape Reinga. My toes felt OK in their fresh set of bandages and strapping and loose shoelaces, and I was able to jog down the set of wooden stairs to the beach and stride along it, dodging waves tipped with thick creamy foam, watching the sunlight play on wind-whipped twisters of sand. A rainbow stretched across the horizon and the wind blew hard, driving spray and rain into my face, and I yelled in delight. *I love this*, I thought. *I love this energy. I love this power. I don't want this to end.*

I mounted the headland to wind my way towards the cape. And then I saw it. I squinted through the driving rain. The lighthouse, a tiny shadow on a cliff far in front. The end. It was just 7km away now.

The rain eased as I walked over golden sands and splashed across a river, surged through the incoming tide and climbed the hill. I staggered against the wind that coursed over the path and reached the crest, walking past the small, square, black-and-white Te Araroa trail sign, the ones I'd been following all this time. I caught a glimpse of the lighthouse and the bristling yellow sign at its base, and gasped and broke into a run. I jogged down the hill and down the long, red pathway, slowing when it straightened out and I saw the broad, paved circle rising full in front of me, the squat white concrete lighthouse and the slim, tatty metal pole to its left.

It was the sign of my fantasies, the sign I'd conjured hundreds of times in the past 265 days, out of the mud and loneliness and hunger and wet. It was nearly 11am, but there was no one else around as I walked past the lighthouse and up to the sign and found my arm stretching out in front of me, my fingers flexing and grasping the air, my breath beginning to come in fast, ragged gasps. But I was too stunned to actually cry. I clasped my hand over my mouth and grabbed the pole and tucked my arm around it, pushing the side of my cheek against a flat plane and hugging it against the wind, unable to stop circling, to stop moving. I walked around and around it, then stopped. I put my forehead against the freezing metal and thought: *Done. I'm done.*

I looked up at its sprouting, dirty-yellow signs covered in stickers, naming places far across the water, some of the boards missing like broken teeth. The signs pointed north to Vancouver, Los Angeles and the Tropic of Capricorn, but 'Equator' had been broken off. West was Sydney, but someone had broken off London, too. Tokyo was still there. The South Pole. And Bluff, 1452km south as the crow flies. But I'd walked more than 3039km to get here; the many reroutes and diversions didn't count as official trail kilometres.

I released the sign and dropped my pack, then went to the edge of the stone circle and looked down at Te Rerenga Wairua, the final point of land on this promontory. The actual northernmost point of New Zealand is 3km around the corner, at Hikurua de Surville Cliffs on North Cape. But this mighty convergence of weather, sea, spirits and sky was the leaping-off place in Te Ao Māori, where spirits passed from the physical world to the underworld. There was a tree down there named Te Aroha, an 800-year-old pōhutukawa, which a metal plaque told me had never been known to flower. Its wind-wrought roots formed the aka or ladder down which the spirits climbed, before travelling underwater to Manawatāwhi Three Kings Islands, where they climbed to the highest point before diving off and returning to Hawaiki.

The wind was so cold and strong I could barely stand up, so I retreated to the shelter of the arms of the squat, strong lighthouse, sitting on my pack for a few minutes in the calmest patch between its sturdy white concrete struts, gazing at the bright red stripe painted at its base. I stared out at the ruffled blue surfaces of the Tasman and Pacific oceans clashing into each other. *There is nowhere left to walk. This is the end of the line.* I leaned back against the cold concrete, cooling down too much, but not moving. The trail had released me at last, but I was not yet ready to leave.

Presently a German man walked down, pushing into the wind, and I asked him to take my photo with the sign. I had 1 per cent battery left in my phone. He took two awful ones but I was too cold to care.

It was 11a.m. There was nothing left to do and I needed to find somewhere to get warm and find food, so I started back up the trail the way I'd come, leaving the spirits, the lighthouse, the sign, and the tip of Aotearoa behind me at last.

* * *

I walked back up the path feeling something gentle tugging at me, and puzzled over it. It wasn't a strong emotion: it wasn't euphoria or joy or elation. It was something unfamiliar to me, quieter. As I walked I realised that it was contentment. Satisfaction. I'd simply done what I set out to do.

I was also smiling at the absurdity of my journey. The last eight-and-a-half months had deviated so wildly from my original plan that I had to laugh, thinking of that confident, clueless past self who'd serenely booked flights from Nelson to Kerikeri for 14 September 2023.

I'd originally intended to start at Cape Reinga on that day, and walk for five or six months until March, covering every inch of the trail and making lots of trail friends along the way. Instead, I'd started in Bluff in late December 2023 and made it here on 17 September 2024, making just about no trail friends at all. I'd walked north through all four seasons for eight months and twenty-three days, working on trail for much of the remaining summer, and on and off through autumn. I'd impatiently waited out nearly a month in total of illness and injury, and had spent the equivalent of another couple of weeks waiting for storms to pass. I'd also had a great time dallying with friends in Wānaka, Te Anau, Wellington, Auckland and Hamilton.

I had walked every inch of the trail from Bluff to Meremere, where flooding had forced me onto State Highway 1 and I realised I no longer gave enough of a shit about the original goal of EFI to walk illegally and face the police again. Instead I got in a car for an 11km ride to Pōkeno and kept going.

But, as I knew it would, that motorway lapse unleashed several others that would have been absolutely unthinkable in the 2400km prior. I felt OK about taking a few kilometres of rides now; they were offers of kindness when I needed them. Now I only felt full of the wonder and power of the last day, the joy of being blown about by the wind and foam and sand on the beach.

I walked through the arch to the toilet block, and took off my pack. I sat on it against the concrete wall and waited to hunt down a hitch. I took off my sandy, wet shoes and socks to dry my feet and toes. It was cold out here, and they began to numb. The remaining 1 per cent of my phone battery died.

A ute pulled up and dropped off a hiker, but drove away before I could approach. The hiker put on her pack and stopped for a minute to clip up her waist belt. She had poles stowed in her side pocket. I knew that look. I called out to her as she walked towards the arch.

'Are you just starting the TA?'

'Yes, I am,' she said, and came over. 'Are you?'

'I just finished,' I said. 'Just now.' And I couldn't help it. Tears sprung into my eyes.

'No way!' she shrieked. 'Congratulations!'

'You're really just starting? Right now?'

'Yes!' she said, then cocked her head as she took in my weatherbeaten face, stringy wet hair, rain-splotched down jacket, half-empty pack and bare feet. 'Have you had anything to eat?'

I must look completely deranged, I thought, then admitted I actually hadn't had anything for a couple of days. 'I kind of forgot about food at the end there.'

She unzipped the waistbelt of her pack and took out two mini Snickers. I protested, but she pressed and, actually, I really wanted them. I tore into them and accidentally dropped a shred of wrapper; she swooped down and picked it up before I could, tucking it into her pocket.

Her name was Claire and she was French. She had cropped, dark hair and beautifully manicured eyebrows, and was neat and clean in a fresh, dusky-pink Marmot jacket. She'd walked the first section of the trail northbound from Bluff to Otago last December, and was now starting from the north to join it up.

'I started in December, too,' I said. 'What date did you start?'

'Christmas Day,' she said, and I began to laugh. I'd started on Boxing Day. I'd been following her, just a day behind, but it had taken all this time to actually meet her – at the top of New Zealand when she'd happened to step out of a ute a half-hour after I'd finished the trail.

'You've been going this whole time? Through winter? What was it like?' she said.

'It was …' I hesitated. 'It was …'

What to say, about the cooling autumn and then those three months of frost? The fog, dark and cold? The nights in the mountains that stretched far longer than the days, the dripping moss and empty huts, the tent-site grass thick with wet, the year's wasted leaves strewn on campfire ashes cold in rings of stone? It had been horrible, sometimes. I had never been given a cute trail name; there had been no other hikers around to grant me one. But the pain and desolation on trail had always faded by the next day. It was the awe that remained.

'It was the best thing I've ever done in my entire life.'

* * *

Claire left me to walk towards Bluff, and I sat back down on my pack. But I was getting too cold. A woman emerged from the bathroom and I approached her with the awkward urgency of someone really beginning to need some help, asking if she was leaving and if I could please get a ride to a town. She looked hard at me and then down at my bare feet.

'It's cold! Where are your shoes?'

'Over there,' I said. 'Uh – I hurt my toes.'

She stared with horror at the raw, red shreds of flesh that my little toes had become, then called over her husband, who arrived with a look of concern and said, 'Are you injured?'

'Sort of,' I said.

'And you've fallen and ripped your pants, too,' the woman said. 'If you haven't found another ride when we come back we'll take you into town.'

They were Malaysian tourists and had been in New Zealand for two months. They would be heading back to Kaitaia that afternoon. I thanked them and sat down on my pack to wait, realising that my merino leggings now had a large, torn, fraying hole in the knee. When had that happened? I had no idea.

No one else left the carpark, but plenty of people began to arrive. A large luxury tour-bus pulled up and a crowd of well-dressed, calm and respectable Australian travellers stepped down one by one, pulled their jackets around them, exclaimed over the weather and walked through the arch and down to the lighthouse. Meanwhile, I was becoming increasingly wracked with both cold and pain. The freezing wind was searing the open flesh on both of my little toes, raw heels and raw soles; it was hurting so much that my mood plummeted and tears pricked my eyes.

The Malaysian couple had been gone for an hour. I was glad they were enjoying their adventure, but the wind kept blasting me. I swallowed two paracetamol and staggered over to the tour bus on bare feet to ask the bus driver if I could sit in the bus and wait while the tourists were gone. He took one look at me and told me to get in. I still had some beach-river water left but he handed me a fresh bottle of water and asked where my shoes were.

'Over there – I had to take them off,' I said, waving at my raw feet. He got up and started rummaging in the overhead cabinets. 'I think I have some slippers here somewhere that someone left on the bus. Ah – here. Put these on.' He handed me a pair of black fleece children's slippers I recognised as coming from The Warehouse, covered in golden stars and moons. They would probably fit a five-year-old, but I eased the tiny things over my toes and forefeet and sighed with relief as they enveloped my raw skin in warmth and stopped the cold air from biting.

'That feels so much better,' I said. 'Thank you.'

'It's cold today,' he said, and told me about a time he'd come to the cape when the wind was so strong it was flinging people around like skittles. 'One woman got blown to the ground,' he said. 'The wind picked her up like a flying nun and blew her right over. Do you need anything to eat?'

'No, no, I'm fine,' I said, but he said, 'When did you last eat?'

How bad did I look? I thought for a minute. 'I guess it was a while ago.' What had I actually eaten, and when? If today was Tuesday, and it was around 11.30a.m., then since the night of my fish'n'chips orgy on Friday I'd eaten only a packet of chips, a packet of Squiggles, a tub of lollies, a packet of beef jerky, a can of chocolate mousse, a couple of bottles of Up & Go Protein, a bottle of Primo banana milk, 30g of peanut butter and a serving of meal-replacement powder. In the entire two-and-a-half days and 102km of walking the beach I'd eaten only the chocolate mousse, the powder, the peanut butter and the jerky. As usual, I'd been so focused on getting onto the beach and then up it that I hadn't cared about eating, or nutrition either. But that wasn't the driver's problem.

To my horror, he opened his lunch bag, took out a pie, and started sawing it in half with a knife.

'You can have half my pie,' he said.

'No!'

'I don't need it – I have plenty of food here. It's mince and cheese,' he said. He took my hand and put the half pie into it, then sat back down in his seat to eat his half. I took a bite. It was still warm. And Jesus Christ, it was good. It was a proper bakery pie, with buttery, flaky pastry.

'Thank you,' I said, and tears filled my eyes again. 'What's your name?'

'Huey,' he said, and I nestled the pie in my lap and reached out and took his hand in both of mine and gently shook it.

'Thank you, Huey.'

'What's your name?'

'Naomi,' I said. 'Thank you so much.'

'You stay on the bus with me, Naomi. I'll take you to town.'

'Won't you get into trouble?'

'I'm the boss,' he chuckled. 'I'm seventy-three. I'm retiring in November.'

Despite more of my protests, he gave me the last quarter of his pie, and an apple. He also tried to give me some of his yoghurt and Nutri-Grain mix from home, taking my hand again and putting the container into it. But that I point-blank refused; he had to have something for lunch.

* * *

For the next four hours I rode the tour bus around Northland with the Australians, getting Huey's personal guided tour, which not only included waiata and stories from his friends, whānau and iwi but also revealed his dead-on comic timing.

We drove down Ninety Mile Beach and past Hukatere Lodge. I stayed firmly on the bus as the Australians got out to walk some of the blasted sands and boogie-board down the dunes, snatching haplessly at the air when the wind ripped the boards out of their hands and sent them sailing back behind the dunes. When we stopped for the tourists' late lunch break, Huey brought over a small cardboard tray of fish'n'chips, put it on my table, said, 'Here you go. Eat that,' and walked off.

I sat there and ate a piece of the hot, crisp fish, then realised I was learning another trail lesson. *You need to look after yourself properly*, I scolded myself, *or good people will be forced to sacrifice too much of themselves to help you out.*

But after Huey hustled his manuhiri onto the bus and began his next kōrero, I realised it was a little more complex than that. I was feeling the burn of shame at being helped, at feeling useless and not 'independent enough'. But giving when you had plenty was an easy, simple joy. I knew that; I'd given Lea food when she ran out and I had too much. I'd done it even on my first night in a hut on trail, when I'd made up some of my gourmet hot chocolate for two SOBOs who'd just finished the punishing Longwood Range.

Huey had more than enough lunch that day and was happy to share it with me. I needed to credit him that he wouldn't have given me what he couldn't spare. *You need to look after yourself, yes*, I thought. *But that is so you can put yourself in a position to help others, too.*

At around 4p.m. the bus arrived at Kā Uri, a Ngāti Kuri visitor, cultural and carving centre in Awanui, north of Kaitaia, where the Australians would be picked up by someone else. Huey told me to go inside and walk up the ancient kauri staircase, a circular set of steps carved inside a section of thousand-year-old kauri tree – the largest swamp kauri ever pulled from the earth and estimated to have fallen 45,000 years ago. My feet were bitter with pain and only half covered, but by now I would do anything for Huey.

I hobbled through the glass doors and found myself stepping up inside the tree on stairs sanded smooth, the deep bronze-golden wood enveloping me completely. I stood for a few moments absorbing the light and beauty of it, encased in this shell of a tree like an insect in amber, and felt a little surge back in time to when this tree was standing, felt the creak and smash of its fall.

When I emerged back into the blue-toned world, Huey told me to get back on the bus and wait for the next driver, Joe, who would take me on to Kaitaia. I stood to thank him and he clasped my hands in both of his for a moment, and then he was gone.

About ten minutes later, a beautiful ball of love and fury burst onto the bus.

'Oh, he's so *naughty*!' Joe shouted, frozen on the stairs, putting a hand to his chest and clasping the handrail for support as he looked at me, aghast. 'He just called me and told me he left a passenger on the bus! No, it's not your fault, love! Oh, he's *so* naughty!'

Joe started up the bus and told me he'd drop me at the cheapest backpackers' in town before he took the bus back to the depot. Was I getting the Intercity bus from Kaitaia in the morning?

'We run the Intercity as well! You can't walk there on those feet, so I'll get the driver to pick you up from here at nine thirty,' he said, dropping me at the Beachcomber Lodge. And then he was gone, too.

I hauled my pack to my room. Then, for the last time, I shook out my tent and hung it to dry. For the last time, I got into the shower and scrubbed sand and mud, food and sunblock, sweat and blood off my body, my shoes and my pack. I washed the dirt off my remaining tent pegs, hand-washed my clothes in the sink, washed my food bag and stuff sacks and my ziplock bags, and hung it all to dry on my length of rope, tied between the curtain rail and the table. I knew in the morning I'd have to finish everything off with a hairdryer ... for the last time.

My arm was itching, and when I looked at its underside in the mirror I was shocked to discover giant, raised, red-and-white mosquito-bite welts covering the underside of my arm and half my breast, from sleeping in the open cooking shelter at Maunganui Bluff in just my merino top. I counted them. Eighty-eight bites. I had no antihistamines left.

When my phone charged I rang Doug but I was so overwrought I could only hyperventilate down the phone. It was pointless to try to talk. He was disappointed that after following every step of mine on the tracker to Cape Reinga, I hadn't able to share the moment with him, and then I felt bad about that.

I got into bed and pulled up the stiff sheets and lay there, burning with itchiness. I itched and howled uncontrollably that night. The trail was over. I didn't know who I was if I had nowhere to set out for tomorrow morning, my pack on my back and the sun rising on my right, hidden behind cloud or glinting below a mountain range or scything through trees, shining into my face as I walked northbound until there was nowhere left to go.

In the morning my eyes were as swollen as my bites. I put on my children's slippers and hobbled 350m down Commercial Street to the BP and bought some jandals and some Savlon. The shop was out of plasters, and I was in too much pain to walk the 1.4km to the supermarket. Instead, I got an egg sandwich, a mini quiche, a yoghurt and a banana milk at the bakery and dressed my feet and toes with Savlon and cotton torn from tampons. I eased them back into the jandals, packed up and went to the front of the Beachcomber to wait for the bus. But half an hour before it was due to arrive, Joe came to get me in his car.

'I felt sorry for you sitting out there for another half an hour, and I went "Oh my gosh, I'm going to turn around and go back",' he exclaimed, hustling me into his car. He'd gone down to the bakery to buy pies for morning tea for his crew, who were spending the morning washing the buses, and had remembered me halfway.

'I said to them, "Do you feel like a pie for morning tea?" And they go, "Aw yes, please! Do you want some money?" And I said, "No, my treat. Yous can treat tomorrow!"'

'Lamingtons, maybe,' I said, and he sucked in a huge gasp.

'Oh! Oh, now don't talk about that!' he said. 'I'm terrible!' We spent the rest of the ride to the bus depot discussing the enormous, round, cream-filled lamingtons the size of whole cakes, that a bakery in town sold for $12. When we arrived, he said goodbye to me and distributed his pies, and the driver invited me to sit in the bus until it was time to go. I lounged in the warm quiet, marvelling at the last 24 hours, the love and help that everyone had shown a foolish, injured, lone hiker.

The bus rumbled awake and we drove out of Kaitaia. The couple across the aisle snuggled into each other. I watched the land flying past, the kilometres coming easy when not stitched together by foot. I pulled the hood of my down jacket over my eyes against the flashing sun and said another thank you and goodbye – to Northland, and to Te Araroa. I tried to farewell my trail self too, to leave that feral beast there at the lighthouse, safe at last; but tears came again when I thought about abandoning her. I let them wet my cheeks.

The last nine months had burned me away. Now I had to find out who was left behind.

CHAPTER 15

NELSON

In the days after I get home, I find myself sitting for long minutes, staring unfocused into space, trail memories swelling up in a jumble of sounds and colours. The stones I gathered on the beach in Bluff are on my desk now in a little dish, a cluster of tiny planets, along with the pink scallop shell I'd picked up with Stefan.

Throughout the South Island I had collected small talismans from each region and posted them home to Doug, and he's kept these as well: a peach-coloured sea-snail shell from the beach near Colac Bay, shiny inside and fluted like a trumpet; a piece of Otago quartz I'd picked up near the ridge before the lightning chased me to shelter; a sprig of yellow-green alpine plant from the Canterbury high country; a red, kite-shaped stone from a river in the Red Hills of Tasman.

'When I opened those, some of them were life-saving,' he says when he sees me handling them, a crack in his voice, then puts his headphones back on and leaves the room. I know his loneliness was worse than mine.

He has built me a walking track in the nearly nine months I've been away. He arranged with our neighbours, Sally and Aidan, to dig a 500m-long loop track on their property for us all to use, then spent weekends and winter nights clearing gorse and blackberry, felling trees, and installing a wooden bridge. It's a metre-wide, hand-dug track, properly benched and drained. Good surface. No mud. He has marked out another kilometre of track that winds into Sally and Aidan's forestry block. I walk along it in the mornings and evenings, the dog trotting in front. Doug named it Te Ara Iti.

I look through my photos and videos. I send my friend Michelle, the mother of my godson, a video of the wild horses that had woken me in the night at Maunganui Bluff, which had made me think of her, for no reason I could put my finger on. You couldn't see anything but you could hear the shrill, guttural whinnies in the dark pool of night beyond the phone's light.

'That sounds like souls in the wind,' she replies. 'Like the release of spirits in the air.'

* * *

'You're more self-centred now,' Doug says a week after I get back, when he realises I've zoned out while he is trying to have a serious relationship chat. 'More confident.'

'More obnoxious,' I say, and he doesn't disagree. I can feel it. And, to be honest, I'm not entirely sure that these are bad qualities for a woman to develop. A layer has fallen off me these past nine months as I stopped caring about anything except moving forward and avoiding injury and death. By now I've spent decades in relationships, distracted by anticipating the needs of others and focusing on helping them before even realising what I wanted or needed, let alone doing anything about it. Now I've had the experience of being on my own all year, doing whatever was necessary to keep myself physically and mentally safe enough to continuously move forward. A balance will return, unless I want to be alone forever. But I want to keep this new side of myself, the woman who takes a second to assess what's best for her before acting, or reacting.

'I didn't know who I'd get back when you returned,' he says. 'I didn't know if it'd be a woman who'd outgrown me, or a woman who'd realised her life was too entwined with mine to let go.'

'Who do you think you got?' I ask, but he hesitates. I can see he doesn't yet know, but doesn't want to say it.

I think about how he watched my GPS tracker every day from Bluff to Cape Reinga. Every ten minutes a new red dot would lodge on screen. He saw what time I'd started in the morning, where I stopped for lunch or a swim, and where I stayed at night. When I was stuck near Te Kūiti for three days without reception and my friend had started worrying and contacted Mum, which worried her in turn, he pulled up Google Earth and showed them the farm shed me and my tracker were stuck in. He'd arranged friends to come and meet me with beer and chips and rides. He saw me move through the night, cross-referenced the satellite tracker with the topo map and weather, and deduced where I'd end up from my pace and the terrain. He watched in agony as I climbed mountains in dodgy weather, and in jubilation and relief when I reached a hut before nightfall. Just a few days ago he'd seen me dash for the dunes when it hailed on Ninety Mile Beach, stay there a few hours, then trek across the sands and tide and arrive at the lighthouse the next morning. He hadn't mentioned this often; he knew I'd turn the thing off if I felt surveilled. But I'd known he was there, looking down on me like an angel.

And he wasn't the only one; Mum and Dad and my in-laws had also watched the red dot like a hawk, and so had some curious friends. Doug had also frequently shared updates on his absent wife with his work colleagues, none of whom I'd ever met. I'd never really been alone on trail, after all. My family and friends and even strangers had been urging me on from the sky.

I sit there watching his uncertainty, thinking that if I want to keep my partner after this, I'll need to rein in the selfishness that got me through trail and adjust once more to being one half of a whole, to consider someone else and put them first again. I pull myself out of my head and make an effort to focus on what he is saying, to nod and agree and promise in all the right places, and remind myself to keep doing that, to notice and answer the daily little bids for connection, affirmation and attention; the tiny pebbles that, bound together, will build a mountain.

Who am I now?

'I'm not sure either,' I say, and give him a hug. 'We'll work it out.'

'You have a silver streak now,' he says into my hair. 'I never noticed it before.'

'I'm losing my hair colour.' This realisation had only just slid home to me on trail. Some reflection in a holiday-park mirror over the winter had delivered the blow that the natural colour of each strand of my hair would gradually fade out and never return.

'Leave it,' he says. 'You're going to have beautiful white hair just like your Auntie Lyn.'

* * *

A week later, I am still unable to wear shoes. On my left foot, the remains of my little toe's nail bed – the toenail itself hasn't been there for months – is hard and yellow, cantilevered above the toe. On the right foot, half of my little toe skin, including the toenail, has sloughed off and turned into a dead, hard, yellow, crusty flap while the new skin develops underneath, but it's still hanging on. The new toe without its nail looks like a tiny red foetus.

The problem is that this thick carapace has become so hard and curled over that it's needling the pink remains of the nail bed and causing so much pain I can't wear shoes. I visit a pharmacist about the toes, and she says, 'Oh dear,' when I remove my socks.

She recommends Soov with pain-killing lidocaine and if that doesn't work, an anti-fungal as well. We peruse a selection of protective toe sleeves, bandages and plasters, but I've already tried them all. I know nothing is going to help the pain but time, along with not jamming my feet into shoes and walking through rivers, mud and sand for 12 hours a day.

This wouldn't really be a problem except the next day I am racing in the hills of Tasman in my first adventure race, a women-only running, mountain-biking, rafting and orienteering epic called the Spring Challenge. My teammates, Dale MacDonald and Kelly Smith, are two university friends who also happen to be a former international elite cyclist and a Winter Olympian skeleton racer, as well as experienced adventure-racers. In fact, in 2021 Dale joined long-time multisport powerhouses Susie Wood, Britta Martin and Eloise Fry and won the Spirited Women adventure race. Her quadriceps are, frankly, aspirational.

This is a little intimidating. I have not been on a bike for nine months. I had originally planned to be home to train quite a bit earlier than a week before the event, to be honest, but that can't be helped now. When we entered, I thought, 'I can definitely go for nine hours.'

'You realise that's about the time the winners will complete it in?' my friend Joanna had said. 'You could be going for up to fifteen hours or more.'

On the day of the race, we are up at 4.15a.m. for the 6a.m. start, gathered with dozens of other women in the dark, excitedly

293

chatting. There's a 500m sprint start to the 10km raft section, and I go and then keep going. I streak over the muddy farm track with the pack of women racing to the boats. I haven't run for years but I feel so light and fast I am shocked. I feel like I've had a full body transplant. *Who am I now?*

I love the event; I love being part of a team. Definitely the weakest link, but we're in it together, working together. I have never done this before but soon realise everyone has their role. In my first adventure race, or indeed first ever multisport event, my role, I realise, is to simply hang on. To look after my energy by cramming in food and drinking water; to look after my mood and theirs by staying positive and focused; to not do anything stupid to derail us; and to just go as hard as possible.

When we cross the finish line on the sands of Rabbit Island twelve hours later, I know Kelly and Dale weren't going nearly as hard as they could have, and I know that as experienced athletes and teammates they would have been quietly monitoring my breathing, mood, position and pace the whole way, adjusting constantly to ensure I could keep up and stay on the edge of maximum effort. But I felt good. I stayed with them, my energy didn't crash, I kept my mood up, and I felt good and strong just about the whole way. I didn't fuck up. I hung on. And I loved it.

'You did well,' Dale says as we mill about, meeting family, at the finish. 'There's no way I would have attempted that on no training. I wouldn't even have started.'

But it wasn't me who did that, I want to say. *It was the trail.* Dale and Kelly were proper, world-class athletes, with intelligent, research-backed approaches to training, fuel, competition and recovery. I had no experience of this past my high-school athletics team. But the trail had given me a kind of anarchic ferocity. I would never have had the confidence to tackle that event beforehand – nor the fitness.

Did I just accidentally find a new hobby? I wonder as we drop off our race numbers, trackers and timing chips. I am not completely destroyed; really, I realised, that was just twelve hours of continuous effort. On trail, I recalled, the longest I'd kept going without sleep or proper rest was 30 hours, wading and tramping 65km through rivers and mountains. And then, after sleep, I'd easily walked 33km the next day. And then, after the storm forced a rest day I didn't want, I'd walked another 62km in fourteen straight hours, sitting down just once for a few minutes to eat. No problem. Then another 25km the next day.

The day after the race, I was sore and tired in a way I hadn't been since the Tararua Ranges, and I was happy about it; I'd found a new, sharper edge of my fitness. I remembered staggering and crying, my hips and feet throbbing in pain after walking 39km on the flat from Ōhau to Twizel. After a day off, it had then taken me 24 hours to go 55km through the night from Twizel to Takapō, also on the flat. I'd exhausted myself so thoroughly that I'd had to take the following two days off.

I had evolved. This fitness had crept up so slowly I hadn't noticed. I was a different person from the one who'd let go of the pole in Bluff on the first day, the one who'd been tired after walking 8km. I'd been so destroyed after walking 28km on the beach to Riverton that I'd had to take two days off. The biggest shock I'd had on trail was finding that my body adapted willingly if I alternated days of huge effort with resting until I felt ready to go again.

Slowly, the efforts took less out of me, I covered more distance, and the rests got shorter. I had barely noticed it unless I happened to compare numbers and terrain. My body did it for me. I realised it had been weeks since I'd felt the hip and Achilles pain that had crippled me for months, making me hobble and stealing my sleep.

So how much harder can I go now? I wonder. *How much faster? How much longer? How much better can I be?*

I used to laugh with people who joked about all the clichéd personal-development stuff around going for a long walk. Was I finding myself on Te Araroa? Was the trail changing me? Was I seeking a new life? Having a mid-life crisis? I answered no to all of them. I just always wanted to try it, I said. See if I could do it.

I still would have said that when I got to the end of the South Island on 1 May. I didn't feel much different then. But after slogging through four-and-a-half months of relentless dark, solitude, injury and illness in the North Island, I had felt change begin to creep over me. Now, after spending two weeks at home in my old life, I could admit it: it *did* change me. How could it not have?

I set out to follow the line and once I did, the trail grabbed me by the wrist and hauled me from Bluff to Cape Reinga. It made me feral and I loved it. It sent me scrambling up mountains alone, boulder-hopping through storms alone, wading through rivers that threatened to sweep me off my feet and drown me, alone. It led me through sweat and snow and ice. It made me cry from loneliness and scream with joy. It ruined me, built me up and made me stronger. It made me less afraid, more pragmatic. More open. More friendly. Calmer. More grateful. More loving. More confident. And more curious about what I could do.

All I had to do was hang on.

EPILOGUE

It has been more than a year since I started Te Araroa, and I decide to go for a hike. I've been back from trail for four months, and the memories have faded so much that it seems like I read about them in a book.

The ankle ligaments I tore on Pirongia still hurt, but I pull out my pack anyway and pick the familiar items out of storage: sleeping bag, PLB, water filter, stuff sacks. I go straight into autopilot, my hands moving like a mechanic's: knife in the top, PLB in the right hip pocket, phone in the left.

I walk to Rocks Hut, the closest hut to Nelson, in the Richmond Ranges, listening to my TA playlist. That playlist had been my obsession and my lifeline when I was walking. I had forgotten. I'd added to it daily on trail; every song I happened across that spoke to me went on there, and listening to it became compulsive. I listened all day, and sometimes through my sleep. Every genre, every era, every mood. It helped me feel less alone.

Sometimes on trail I would have to stop and wrap my arms

around my gut at the power of a lyric or stretch of sound, my stride halted by the havoc they wreaked on my emotions. As I got fitter, the music became more essential. By the time I got to the North Island and the trail became less overwhelming, the walking easier, I started to crave more sensation: ice, crunching vegetables or chips, banana milk, fizzy drinks, music. I joked about it on Instagram: 'Just so I can feel something again'.

* * *

When *Northbound* was nearing publication, I had to answer some questions for publicity, and one of them was so simple yet so huge I was floored. I started typing a quick answer, then stopped and sat back a bit, unable to finish.

What did you get out of it in the end?

A life changed, I thought. Simple as that. In the last part of the trail, with the daily physical pain behind me and my once-cluttered life empty of people and distractions, I realised my brain had begun a new background task: chewing over my life history as I walked. It made me think of yoga, originally developed as a way to ease the body and allow undistracted meditation. Freeing the body's pains let the mind gallop. The easy walking of the North Island delivered me that.

One day near Waitomo I realised I had been subconsciously exploring painful past mistakes, arguments and relationships that had gone wrong, but that I was starting to feel, first, the total disappearance of the anger or hurt surrounding them, and second, the urge to fix them. I haven't studied philosophy or religion, but I knew there were concepts thousands of years old – not to mention modern neuroscience – which covered these simple human processes of coming to an understanding, but they were new to me. These errors, traumas and pains that had built up on my life like plaque faded into the background during my normal life. I never visited them. But out on trail, I sensed how they festered, nibbling at my identity, my confidence, my joy. They began to seep from my subterranean consciousness like liquefaction, and once I saw them, fixing them became vital. Walking along gravel roads and farm tracks, I began to send messages to people to apologise for past wrongs.

The intensity with which I experienced this ground-up rebuilding of my relationships was sometimes painful, irritating or mystifying to those I targeted, the people with whom I had stuff to sort out: friends, family, exes. Sometimes I didn't manage to gain much ground, or made the situation worse; it depended on how the other person wanted to receive the approach. I eventually realised I couldn't force it; my healing and resolution was my own problem to fix.

When I read about this sort of thing happening to others on long walks, I had assumed it was a conscious process, but I discovered on trail that it wasn't. I was always under the impression you had to think your way to a resolution, reason them out. Instead, I emerged into peace and conclusions without even noticing. It was only when an embarrassing or hurtful memory no longer caused a stab of pain or avoidance that I realised it was gone.

The music I had listened to, that I was listening to now on my walk up to Rocks Hut, had become part of this process. The songs had narrated those days of endless thinking, reminiscing and ruminating. Now, off-trail, a year older and forever changed, I found the songs were fresh again and I discovered new conversations happening within and between the tracks. Songs singing back to each other across time and distance. Loss, love, mistakes, misunderstandings, pain, joy, things left unvoiced, maybe forever. Songs that put me in new places. But I don't need them so much anymore. I'm able to walk in silence more easily now than I could on trail, because my life is full again with people, sights, sounds, foods.

When I'd been home for three months, I talked to my old journalism friend, photographer Rob Suisted, about what happens to your mind on a long walk. He said he had always found the mountains to be a place where he experienced a return of pure love, for himself and others; love that was otherwise corrupted by expectations and disappointments. 'In normal life you begin to build up skins over giving and receiving love,' he said. But when he went into the mountains as a young man working for DOC, he felt those skins falling away.

I got my astrological chart done when I was 29, in May 2011. It wasn't something I'd normally be into, but a colleague had turned out to be a closet astrologer. I was newly in love and my world had tilted towards mysticism, so I was ripe for a reading. I was amused and at times a little shocked by how uncannily the chart seemed to pinpoint me, though I believed at the same time I was merely subject to the same vanity and confirmation bias as everyone else who believed in horoscopes. I put it away and forgot about it.

But when I got home, I spent a month clearing out the house and I found it again: a thick, dog-eared set of papers tucked away in a tub of university materials, its staple rusty. I sat down cross-legged on the rug in my office to read it again, vanity and confirmation bias be damned. I smiled as I flicked through the pages. I had clearly not yet evolved to my highest self; some of the aspects of my personality that the astrologer had identified were still challenging me. I was still rash, impulsive, wilful and forthright. 'Act in haste, repent at leisure,' the astrologer had written. 'Once you get something in your sights, you will get there no matter what. Out of my way.' I smiled again. Te Araroa had proven that, if nothing else.

But one of the paragraphs jumped out at me now in a way it hadn't when I was 29. 'You are being challenged in this lifetime to let your joyful emotions be free,' the astrologer had written. 'You will be truly surprised at the transformation in your life if you love yourself and all others without condition. I suggest you make this your mantra.'

I was thunderstruck. *That* was what had happened to me on trail, what I was only just realising now, months later. It was an upwelling of new love and joy. They had arrived somewhere on trail and were already in place by the time I'd got home. I'd felt their stirrings as an absence of emotional pain, some of it so old it had fossilised inside me.

I wouldn't say I 'loved myself' now so much as I was simply allowing myself to be who I was, and people could take or leave it. If they were able to really see me, they'd see the whole, and the whole was fine as it was.

In the last part of the trail, joy and love had begun to come very easily; they simply poured out of me. I don't remember that happening before the TA. Before I started, and indeed for most of the way through, I still had undercurrents of hurt and anger. But I couldn't have told you where some of them had come from – just from living; from forgetting, from running from pain, from hurt, from never looking at it; from never letting my heart break and my body be wracked by bouts of sobbing, for weeks or months, until it cleared by itself.

I never gave it a chance to do so. There is not much time in life for that; you need to get on with things. But on trail, there was sometimes nothing else to do but cry and rage. Te Araroa gave me the time and space to force myself through pain and hurt and out the other side, and gave me a new ability to express joy and easy, uncomplicated, unconditional love. Their caveats, limits and demands had disappeared somewhere out there in the bush, in the sands and tides. My skins had fallen away.

How would I hang onto this feeling? That was my challenge now.

I pause on my way up to Rocks Hut and look across at the Richmond Ranges, which I'd struggled across so many months before. The sun is hot and prickles the sweat on my brow. The world has come nearly full circle since I started the trail. It is good to be back in the hills again.

ACKNOWLEDGEMENTS

Most of *Northbound* was written on trail through winter 2024, in dozens of North Island bush clearings, sand dunes, campgrounds, huts, hostels, couches, spare rooms, cafés and libraries. Thank you to those who hosted me while I wrote, and to everyone who eased the journey from Bluff to Cape Reinga.

For meals, beds, beers, couches, showers, rides, debriefs, messages, encouragement, offers of help, surprise visits and joining me on trail, thank you to my family and friends: the Arnolds, Kerrs, Brookses, and Jamesons, particularly Lynda Kerr and Michael Smurthwaite for hosting me. Thank you Charles Anderson, Lora Bailey, Lisa Black, Hazel Boot, Alice Bradley, Jessie Bray Sharpin and Matthew Wightman, Amy and Nick Burn, Richard Campion, Jonathan Carson, Jackie Clemmer and Forest Smith, Aimie Cronin, Simon and Caroline Curtis, Sarah Daniell, Tracey Dearlove, Martin de Ruyter, Mary de Ruyter, Nicole De Sac, Michelle Duff, Beck Eleven, Kate Evans, Isobel, Jack, Ali and Mark Ewing, Hannah and

Luke Faed, Joanna, Vaughn, Elliott, and Gully Filmer, Faith Firestone, Bette Flagler, Lauren Fletcher, Pete Foley, Samantha Gee, Kate Gudsell, Victoria Guild, Anna Jamieson, Sally Jamieson and Aidan Pykett, Kirsty Johnston, Stephen Finnegan, and Aoife Finnegan, Cristina and Lasse Holopainen, Megan Jones and Lance Teague, Mike Joy, Stacey Knott and Abe Dia of Alamir, Michelle Langstone, Arun Jeram and Sunny Langstone-Jeram, Kirsten McDougall, Kerry McNatty Sunderland, Andy Macdonald, Dale MacDonald, Britt Mann, Frances Marshall, Jamie Marthaler, Veronika Meduna and Andy Reisinger, Kylie, Richard, Max, Tommy and Cameron Middleton, May Miller-Dawkins, Bill Moore, Tracy Neal, Kate Newton, Connie May Nisbet, Brittany, Tim, Eloise, Addie, and Sylvia Norman, Clare North, Madeleine O'Connor, Skye Patterson-Kane, Anna Pearson and Joe Harrison, Anke Richter and Frank Kueppers, Tom Riley, Anna and Adam Roberts, Elissa Phillips and Sarah Stewart, Brad Taylor, Nicola Toki, Mike, Becky, Ben, and Emma Sargent, Noon Sirisamphan, Kelly Smith, Haidi, Dallas and Maisey Spence, Jim Tully, Sarah and Nic Turner, Kimberley West, Lawrence Wharerau, Rebekah White, Virginia Woolf, and Sarah Young. I am so thankful for you all.

Thank you to my trail friends, trail angels and the people I met along the way. You illuminated my journey and astounded me with simple kindnesses. Geoff Chapple and Miriam Beatson, trail founders: you are a force of nature and a delight. Margaret Gruys, Anna Liddell, Lance, Glenn and Vanessa Waddell, Denis

Stanton, Al and Stephanie Shearer, Nicky Walker and Fergus Wheeler, Alison and Andy of the Lake Coleridge Powerhouse Lodge, Peter Chandler, John Perry and Casey Huffstutler, Mike and Jackie Cosgrove, Brian Way and Paula De Goldi, Abby Thompson, Tim Smith and Eleanor, Mike and Jo Gallen, Fiona Burleigh and Anthony Behrens, Donna Tua, Shantel Ranginui, all of the members of the Jerusalem rongoā Māori wānanga, Sue Sands, James, Cynthia and Andrew Mackenzie, Stu Bennett, Mike Lim, Irene Middleton, Rob Firmin, and Marius Rademaker.

Thank you to the Te Araroa Trust, the Te Araroa Regional Trusts, the volunteers who believe in the mission and support the dreams of many.

Thank you to those who read and gave feedback on parts of this manuscript generously and enthusiastically: Michelle Duff, Kirsty Johnston, Charles Anderson and Kate Newton. Special thanks to Rebekah White, Jessie Bray-Sharpin and Bill Moore for reading and commenting so insightfully on the whole.

Thank you to the team at HarperCollins: Holly Hunter, for talking with me about new book concepts for years, shaping this idea and shepherding it through; Margaret Sinclair for picking up the reins; Shannon Kelly, Sarah Ell and Eva Chan for your sharp editing eyes.

Thank you to my regular publishers and editors and the team at Forest & Bird for your grace in allowing me flexibility or time away from contributions to walk the length of New Zealand.

Thank you RNZ for your early interest in this journey and for broadcasting interviews with me on Summer Report and Jim Mora Afternoons throughout 2024.

And thank you to the countless, impulsively kind people of Aotearoa, who will pick up a hitchhiker, offer food and coffee, water and beds, conversation and encouragement, and a smile. With such small gestures you made me feel part of humanity again.

Finally, a lifetime of thank yous, Douglas Brooks. You saw me off, watched me every step of the way, and welcomed me home at the end.